The New York Waterfront

The New York Waterfront

Evolution and Building Culture of the Port and Harbor

EDITED BY KEVIN BONE

Essays by

Mary Beth Betts
Eugenia Bone
Kevin Bone
Gina Pollara
Donald Squires
Michael Z. Wise
Wilbur Woods

Commissioned photographs
Stanley Greenberg

THE MONACELLI PRESS

First published in the United States of America in 1997 by
The Monacelli Press, Inc.
10 East 92nd Street, New York, New York 10128.

Library of Congress Cataloging-in-Publication Data
The New York waterfront : evolution and building cul-
ture of the port and harbor / edited by Kevin Bone ;
essays by Mary Beth Betts . . . [et al.] ; commissioned
photographs, Stanley Greenberg.
 p. cm.
Includes bibliographical references.
ISBN 1-885254-54-7
1. Waterfronts—New York (State)—New York—
History. 2. Waterfronts—New York (State)—New
York—Design and construction—History. 3. Harbors—
New York (State)—New York—History. 4. City
planning—New York (State)—New York—History.
I. Bone, Kevin.
HT168.N5N55   1997
307.1'416'097471—dc21   96-53253

Printed and bound in Hong Kong

Designer: Kim Shkapich
Copy Editors: Jen Bilik and Jennifer Lee

Cover
NORTH RIVER PIERS, MANHATTAN
Photographer unknown. Circa 1950.
Department of Marine and Aviation.
NYCMA.

Frontispiece
PIER A, HUDSON RIVER, MANHATTAN
J. Nordstrom, photographer. 1903.
NYHS.

ACKNOWLEDGMENTS

I must first acknowledge an individual I will never meet but who contributed immensely to this study, an individual whose legacy has allowed others to enjoy the unencumbered pursuit of art and invention. Peter Cooper established his union to support the free search for ideas, and it is from within his school that this project has come. This study began with Cooper Union's students; it came to include many individuals from its academic community. Professor Mary Beth Betts cocurated the exhibition and has provided a critical historic perspective throughout the project. Gina Pollara, an architecture graduate, worked heroically on the exhibition, and her endless enthusiasm for the material has contributed immensely to the project. Kim Shkapich, the director of the school archives, did much more than design this book: she was the bookmaker, and without her persistent commitment to excellence, this volume would not exist.

Dean John Hejduk of the Irwin S. Chanin School of Architecture says in his preface that he was only a distant observer of this work, but somehow his observations, support, and encouragement seemed to arrive just when most needed. John Jay Iselin, president of the Cooper Union, has been dedicated to maintaining and reinvigorating Cooper's commitment to New York City, and his support of the Essential City program is evidenced by this publication. Former chair of the board of trustees George A. Fox, himself a great builder of this city, also provided critical support.

Beverly Wilson was the project coordinator leading up to the exhibition and organized the remarkable public programs that accompanied it; Marilyn Hoffner and Camilla Brooks assisted us in the ever important work of fund-raising.

The Cooper community was aided by many able and inspired contributors who found merit in the work and a passion for the subject. Photographer Stanley Greenberg not only contributed his own remarkable photographs but worked extensively with the historic photographic materials used in the exhibition and book. Eugenia Bone, in addition to her contributions as a writer, assisted throughout the editing process and helped shape much of the text. Donald Squires brought to the project his marvelous work on the harbor geography and ecosystems, and Michael Z. Wise provided his journalistic skills in sorting out the Hudson River story and evaluating the status of current projects. Wilbur Woods participated in the public forums and assisted us in better understanding the contemporary city planning picture with regards to the waterfront. I would also like to thank Richard Tristman for his early reading and editorial guidance, and Riva Lava for her assistance on the first manuscript.

Many New York City municipal agencies and the dedicated people who work in them also contributed to this project. We offer particular thanks to the New York City Municipal Archives, its director, Kenneth Cobb, its principal archivist, Leonora Gidlund, and Rob Dishon, project archivist; special archives director Laura Rosen of the Triborough Bridge and Tunnel Authority; Jonathan Ridgeway and Michael Cetera of the New York City Department of Environmental Protection; Vivian Warfield and Deborah Bershad of the Art Commission of the City of New York; Elizabeth Goldstein, director, and John Bagley, P.E., of the New York State Office of Parks, Recreation, and Historic Preservation, New York City Region; Barbara Bartlett of the City of New York Department of City Planning; Steven Rizick from the Map File Division of the New York City Department of Parks and Recreation; Jonathan Kuhn from the New York City Parks photo archives; Ann Buttenwieser and Jonathan Winer from the New York City Office of Economic Development; Tom Fox, former director of the Hudson River Park Conservancy; Anthony Smith, deputy commissioner of the New York City Department of General Services; Robert Ronayne, director of the Route 9A Reconstruction Group, New York State Department of Transportation; and the Battery Park City Authority.

Additionally, the following people and organizations deserve special thanks: the New-York Historical Society; the Port Authority of New York and New Jersey; Davis, Brody & Associates, Architects; Queens West Development Corporation; Richard Dattner, architect; Chelsea Piers Management Inc.; Riverside South Planning Corporation; T.A.M.S. Consultants; Liselot van der Heijden; Robert Kousoulous, Bone/Levine Architects; Claire Beckhart; Nicholas Quennell; Peter Rothschild; and Henry Smith-Miller + Laurie Hawkinson.

Finally, Cooper Union also thanks those organizations that have generously supported these studies: the National Endowment for the Arts; the New York State Council on the Arts; the Port Authority of New York and New Jersey; Manhattan borough president Ruth W. Messinger; the Daniel and Joanna S. Rose Fund; the J. M. Kaplan Fund; the Dorothy Schiff Foundation; and the Green Fund.

—Kevin Bone

MASTERWORKS

John Jay Iselin

Any short list of attributes of great cities would include a category for masterbuilders. Since Dutch days, New York City has demonstrated a remarkable capacity for building soundly. Successive stages of the city's support system have propelled New York's surge to unqualified greatness.

But where are the bold plans for tomorrow's New York City?

With a few notable exceptions, the titans and the techniques of pioneering construction have largely been overlooked. Possibly the city's mercantile motivation has left too little room for contemplation. Whatever the reason, the quality and complexity of New York's massive infrastructure are but dimly comprehended by its concerned citizenry.

Shall there be another stage of masterworks and another surge forward by the greatest of cities?

Indisputably, New York's propensity for superb building has increasingly been matched by a proclivity for distressing neglect. Each administration has had its budgetary excuse for ignoring mandatory maintenance and improvement of the city's lifelines.

Happily, public awareness of New York City's oft-cited crumbling support system is a rising, countervailing factor.

To promote enhanced understanding of the city's proud building heritage, the Cooper Union established its Infrastructure Institute. This center for urban research aims to incorporate the expertise of its three professional schools—Art, Architecture, and Engineering—to advance sound city designs.

One of the early initiatives of the institute was to assemble the saga of New York City's formative waterfront. Since Dutch settlers shrewdly recognized that New Amsterdam could be a year-round trading center, the thriving port has shaped robust commerce and influenced vibrant culture. That astonishing record of building, however, has lately been endangered by the threatened abandonment of essential engineering documentation.

Two members of Cooper Union's Architecture faculty, Kevin Bone, architect, and Mary Beth Betts, historian, intervened to assemble an astonishing exhibition of masterbuilding along the waterfront. Professor Bone subsequently edited this illuminating volume of essays on the origins of New York City's port and harbor.

This enthralling account extends the annals of masterbuilding in the city. True to the traditions of building well, this scrupulous chronicle provides a sturdy foundation for the waterfront's enduring contributions to New York life.

THE PRINTED WHALE
(In Search Of)

John Hejduk

During the production of this book by its authors and participants, I have been a distant observer . . . perhaps in the safety of a harbor lighthouse with a telescope to view, then focus on, some kind of turbulence within an apparently calm sea. Due to some minor storms the picture became somewhat blurred, but one could see that a struggle was going on, a monumental one: there was some kind of outline of a ship, with figures running around; at times a face would come into view, somewhat gaunt and even haunted by the task undertaken. Last but not least, I think I saw the possible outline of a *printed whale.* In fact, the ship's crew was in search of the printed whale that was Manhattan in plan (fig. 2.7, p. 45). This whale was not white, but the color of black ink. Printed on its surface were the casualties of a number of generations. The netting of the whale—in this case, the enclosing of its outline by the construction of bulkheads following the shape of the island—was a military action against a natural landscape, initially led by a Civil War general who was determined to triumph. The whale was to be molded or cast into a tight corset; a slight compression was to take place. Interestingly enough, in the 1980s the condition reversed —that is, a good part of the Hudson River would be filled in or dumped upon. The whale was to absorb more girth and weight. The river artery was to be somewhat clogged. Returning to the general's time and thereafter, the Spuyten Duyvil umbilical cord to the Bronx had to be removed: a connecting small rock mountain was cut through (demolished), opening up the possibility of more bridging. . . . Equally, in other places where shoals interfered (Hell Gate area), they too were cleaned out and leveled.

The efficiency and pragmatism of the cutting and removal within waters and whirlpools overwhelms. It also reminds one of the Dutch, who when arriving in Manhattan, desired to cut canals through the island's southern tip, although the difficulty of cutting through granite rock—in their time—brought on a foreboding.

There is a plan in this book (fig. 2.23, p. 59) showing the southern tip of the island, which is saturated with extended piers. It looks as if whalers had thrown innumerable harpoons into the head of the printed whale. This also seems the case in other parts of the edges of the whale. Later the harpoon piers were broken—some disappeared altogether, and some remained half-sunken. However, a new net was beginning to be instituted upon the printed whale—that is, the grid, abstract at first, but later to be the passageways of the city streets.

Within the book's essays dredging is mentioned: the dredging of water beds. Since I am referring to the *writing* upon a city whale, the words *to dredge* still-stop one. Somehow, for me, the *dread* seems formidable, again no gentle undertaking. We fill in our rivers, then we dredge them.

Throughout the essays there seems to be some sadness or even a *lament* about the passing of certain city agencies or authorities, and in a way, I sympathize with that sense, due to the massive collection of monumental drawings of the highest quality that they produced. Yet . . . yet . . . the most compelling, haunting, devastating part of the book's visual material is the photographs of abandoned land, buildings, structures, and people. *They are haunting because they are real.* One is riveted by these distanced objects, lives, imagined stories, and one begins to realize that these are the deciphered messages upon the printed whale. They are also related to the earlier time, the time of the arrival of the immigrants, who worked and lived at the water's edge, *life's* edge. They lived real, difficult lives that matched the photos taken of them. They didn't arrive on luxury liners docked side by side next to the piers. They arrived on Ellis Island. I must confess I cannot work up enthusiasm for the young stockbrokers and traders leaving their new apartments on the new fill on the Hudson River, crossing bridges into the markets of Wall Street. One would think a better vision would be to flood the city's edges with marvelous affordable housing for the needy, the poor, and the homeless. The printed whale would then, could, should, spout a fountain of water in celebration.

All who have created and worked on this book have made a monumental contribution to the understanding of our city, and I celebrate them. Their work provoked my thoughts and other views.

They, we, all of us, are strapped in the bounding grid upon the printed whale. And we must know that at times the whale plunges down to the deepest depths, and when he rises, not all of us surface with him. Some are lost in the lower depths, and it is those with whom we should be concerned. In a way, this book does a sounding on this and other situations.

I believe that in the Cooper Union Foundation Building built by Peter Cooper in the nineteenth century there was a whale suspended between the third and fourth floors in an open well. I think it probably reminded Peter Cooper of people in need. His understanding of creative energy was that energy had to do with education and the spirit of humanity. Today whales are an endangered species.

The passion, commitment, and determination of Kevin Bone, architect, and Mary Beth Betts, historian —who led the extraordinary team of Gina Pollara, architect; Michael Z. Wise, writer; Wilbur Woods, architect and city urban planner; Eugenia Bone, writer; Donald Squires, marine biologist; Stanley Greenberg, photographer; and Kim Shkapich, maker of this book—have our deepest gratitude and thanks, for it is this kind of caring soul that will save our heritage, our environment, our nature, our cities.

Special thanks should be given to Beverly Wilson and Marilyn Hoffner of the Cooper Union for their unique support and caring.

The struggle I alluded to concerning turbulence in the water was due to the authors and maker of *The New York Waterfront: Evolution and Building Culture of the Port and Harbor,* who were engaged in saving the printed whale.

REFLECTIONS ON THE ESSENTIAL CITY

Kevin Bone

In the early spring of 1991, the Building Technology class from Cooper Union's School of Architecture studied the New York City building culture and the particular building problems posed by the New York maritime environment. Students explored issues relating to piers, seawalls, and the reshaping of Manhattan Island. Very little published material was found on the subject, and it became evident that we would need to tackle the sometimes resistant New York City government for sources.

One student discovered an archive of the former Department of Docks that was still accessible, casually housed in the Battery Maritime Terminal in Manhattan. Shortly thereafter, he brought an archival drawing to school—an original plan for upper Manhattan prepared by General George McClellan's Department of Docks, dated 1870.

It was exhilarating to see such a rare and beautiful drawing, and to learn that there were many more. Concern over the archive's preservation prompted members of the Cooper Union community to investigate both its present state and its official status as a repository of historical records. What we found was a crowded and disorganized mass of documents and drawings—many of high artistic accomplishment—which were poorly stored, minimally catalogued, and unprotected by any form of security. The deteriorated condition of the archive was compounded by the fact that the city was in the process of dissolving the agency that had created it, leaving the prospect of any future care for the invaluable collection in doubt. Staff members of city government and a small number of scholars were aware of its existence, but in general the collection was unknown. Most of its holdings had never been properly studied or conserved, and the materials had never been publicly displayed. We felt compelled to assist the city in the cataloguing and preservation of this important body of work.

It took a full year, and a good deal of persistence, to penetrate the bureaucracy surrounding the collection. Once that was accomplished, however, the agency that had inherited responsibility for the work agreed to transfer the entire collection to the New York City Municipal Archives, rendering work with the material more practical. While the Municipal Archives could stabilize and safeguard the documents, its limited budget and its own established cataloguing and conservation priorities prevented the newly transferred collection from being made readily available to the public. In an innovative move supported philosophically and financially by President John Jay Iselin and Dean John Hejduk of the Irwin S. Chanin School of Architecture, the Cooper Union offered to administer a collaboration with the Municipal Archives whereby student interns would organize and catalog this valuable resource. The New York City Department of Economic Development set aside additional funds for preservation work, and in the summer of 1992 the internship program began.

The goal of the program was to study the contents of the collection and to aid in its conservation and cataloguing. Cooper Union students, four to six at a time, spent two summers on this project. The Municipal Archives staff, in conjunction with professors from the Cooper Union, trained the interns and supervised their efforts. Early on, we recognized the importance of making this collection available to the public. In light of intensifying battles among developers, environmentalists, and community associations over the waterfront's future, we thought it timely and appropriate to provide the public with a more detailed picture of the evolution of the maritime waterfront, one that would review and analyze the changing New York shoreline within its historical context.

The Cooper Union set forth to produce an exhibition and accompanying symposium of panel discussions devoted to examining the past and future of the waterfront, as well as to publish a book on the subject. This project expressed the institution's ongoing commitment to the investigation of urban structure and municipal planning. With the generous support of the National Endowment for the Arts and the collaborative efforts of the academic and civic communities, the exhibition opened on January 21, 1994. After two years of additional research, which explored other germane waterfront-related topics, including environmental and political issues, *The New York Waterfront: Evolution and Building Culture of the Port and Harbor* was completed.

The archival drawings and photographs display a vigorous municipal commitment to high-quality architecture and engineering, and recall an age when basic, practical structures were treated with aesthetic consideration. In addition to selections from the archives of the Department of Docks, the book includes documents from various municipal agencies including the Robert Moses–era Triborough Bridge and Tunnel Authority, the Parks Department, the New-York Historical Society, the New York Economic Development Corporation, and the New York City Department of Environmental

Protection. Materials on contemporary waterfront projects, including the ongoing Hudson River debate, details of the defeated Westway project, plans for the approved Hudson River Park and associated highways, and an overview of recently enacted zoning provisions for the waterfront known as the Comprehensive Waterfront Plan are also presented. Contemporary photographs of current waterfront conditions by photographer Stanley Greenberg, originally prepared for the exhibition, are included among the works published.

This volume's intent is twofold: to offer a perspective on the history of waterfront building so that the lessons of the past can inform decisions about the future; and to inspire a quest for the kind of greatness in public works that has distinguished New York City in the past. It seeks to provide a forum in which to examine the city's historical commitment to its physical support systems, and to debate approaches for their renewal. The book provides a geography and history of our urban shoreline, examines the built products of our maritime industrial culture, and assembles a general view of the contemporary waterfront.

The New York Waterfront traces 250 years of divergent conceptions of the waterfront, from the Colonial Dutch structures to the Department of City Planning's comprehensive plan to ring Manhattan Island with an "emerald necklace" of parks and bicycle paths. These and other developments like Battery Park City, Riverbank State Park, the North River Pollution Control Plant, Waterside, and Queens West are detailed in the pages that follow.

Most of the drawings and photographs included in this volume (many of them published here for the first time) have been culled from thousands of survey maps, architectural and engineering drawings, photographic prints, and glass-plate negatives held in the Department of Docks' archives. They depict every imaginable facet of waterfront life and commerce and vividly preserve the history of municipal port development.

The importance of the Department of Docks archive lies partially in the enormous diversity of the construction methods it records. It is an encyclopedic record of the building technologies of the period, supplying detailed information on the preparation and research involved in the department's projects and their progress of construction. Among these documents are records of the internal debates between builders and engineers regarding specific techniques for a given task or site, which are a rare and wonderful find. They record a building culture indigenous to New York Harbor, which heralded the arrival of rational building systems, long-span trusses, and lightweight steel frames.

Conscious of the rich information to be gleaned from these records, *The New York Waterfront* uses, wherever possible, the actual account given in the Department of Docks annual reports. In some cases, archaic spelling and grammatic anomalies have been changed to accommodate the modern reader. From its 1870 inception to its 1991 dissolution, the department had several different names; for the sake of clarity, however, all references to the annual reports will use the abbreviation DoD. Reports were issued at the end of the fiscal year. During the nineteenth century the city's fiscal year ended on April 30, but by 1897 this was changed to correspond to the end of the calendar year, December 31.

Other drawings included in this volume document the tools and machinery required to contend with specific problems in maritime construction: floating derricks, drilling machines, and diving bell apparatus. Visionary proposals originally solicited by the Department of Docks are also included: a series of finger piers; replications of harbor works found in the European ports of Le Havre, Liverpool, and London; and a variety of other proposals from the utilitarian to the fantastic.

While the Department of Docks material looms large in this volume, the essays included are devoted to thorough discussions of many waterfront-related issues. Chapter 1, "The Beautiful Lake," examines the geography of the New York–New Jersey Estuary. It assesses future developments and appraises the environment's chances to recover its long-impaired ecological health. Improved water quality, combined with the demise of the commercially viable waterfront and an emerging political climate in favor of change, has placed New York City in a position to revitalize its watery edge. Chapter 2, "Masterplanning," provides a documentary history of the administration of the city's shore from the colonial period through our own century. The central figure in this history is the New York City Department of Docks, and the chapter surveys its evolution and philosophy. Chapter 3, "Horizontal City," offers an account of the architecture and technology that shaped the waterfront. Beginning with the earliest efforts of Dutch settlers, this chapter traces the evolution of a unique building culture through its days of glory in the late nineteenth and early twentieth centuries, to its disappearance with the collapse of the maritime city in the mid-twentieth century. Chapter 4, "Transforming the Edge," focuses on several particularly bold and decisive projects that illustrate the city's historic determination to rethink and reshape itself. Chapter 5, "Evolving Purposes," reviews the unsettled state of contemporary planning along

Manhattan's Hudson River waterfront and the painful civic struggle that has characterized efforts to reintegrate the waterfront into the life of the city. Chapter 6, "Modest Endeavors," examines the projects currently underway, which may bring about that evolution.

In any study of such a broad topic, omissions are inevitable. We chose to focus on subjects that are not well documented elsewhere; thus, we have not included discussion of Ellis Island, Liberty Island, or Roosevelt Island. The social and cultural life of the waterfront also receives only passing attention. It should be noted that we have tried to avoid duplicating the material presented in Ann Buttenwieser's *Manhattan Water-Bound*, an enormously valuable history of the waterfront. We owe a great debt to Buttenwieser and her seminal study of the waterfront, as well as to Carleton Greene's 1917 work *Wharves and Piers: Their Design, Construction and Equipment*, which, at the time, was the primary manual for designers and builders of the harbor. Greene assembled case studies and technical papers, many of which were drawn from the files of the New York City Department of Docks.

Stanley Greenberg's stark and poignant photographs evoke the melancholy beauty of the waterfront in its present derelict state. Greenberg not only offers views of the major modern sites—the Red Hook Water Pollution Control Plant, the Port Authority grain elevators, the Fresh Kills landfill, and the Brooklyn Navy Yard—but also captures the nameless, inhospitable tracts whose only landmarks are the rusting remains of a once vital commercial life.

After visiting New York City in the early 1940s, Le Corbusier, one of the most influential architects of the twentieth century, wrote:

> Along the avenue which skirts the river, the docks and ships form the teeth of a comb as far as you can see. The arrangement is clear, logical, perfect: nevertheless, it is hideous, badly done, and incongruous; the eye and the spirit are saddened. Ah! If the docks could be done over again!

In compiling *The New York Waterfront: Evolution and Building Culture of the Port and Harbor*, the authors hope to inspire a similar pursuit of integrity and greatness in the design of the urban fabric of the next millennium.

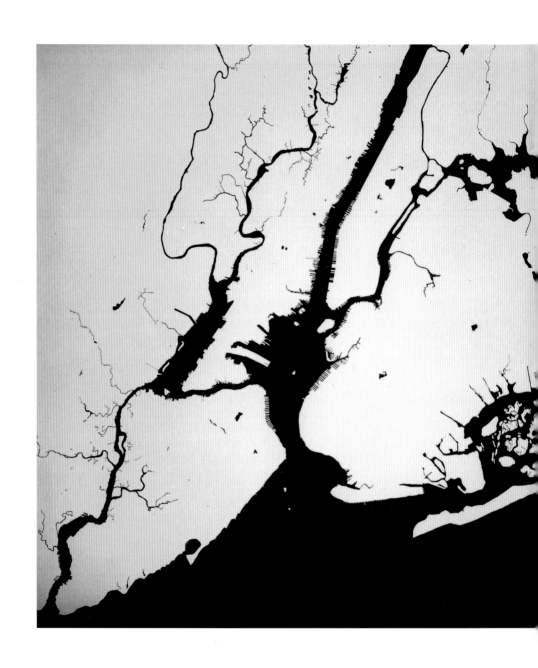

THE WATER FEATURES OF THE NEW YORK HARBOR AND ESTUARY SYSTEM
Map. Kevin Bone, Jose Figueroa, artists. 1994.

1

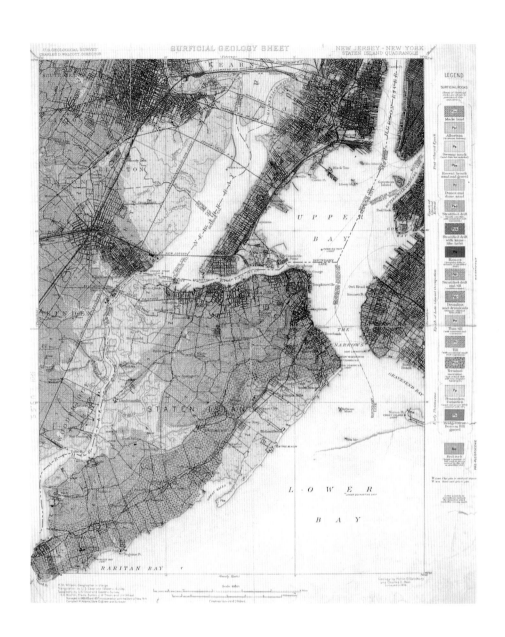

1.1
TOPOGRAPHY, STATE OF NEW YORK
Brooklyn quadrangles represented by state engineer and surveyor.
Surveyed 1888–89. 1908 edition.
New York City Department of Environmental Protection.

THE BEAUTIFUL LAKE
The Promise of the Natural Systems

Donald Squires and Kevin Bone

After visiting the mouths of the Chesapeake and Delaware Bays on his first voyage to the New World in 1524, Giovanni da Verrazano sailed north to New York Harbor, where he found a "pleasant situ-

ation among some little steep hills through which a river of great size, and deep at its mouth, forced its way to the sea."[1] Finding anchorage in the Narrows, Verrazano left his ship and traveled farther inland in a small boat. He emerged into a calm body of water surrounded by wooded hills and luxuriant shores, the

New York Bay, which he called the "Beautiful Lake." Henry Hudson, who first saw the bay in 1609, also marveled at the beauty of the region, with its dense, primeval forests and its verdant banks. Hudson and his crew eagerly began to gather the riches of the land, trading with the indigenous peoples for the furs of beaver and otter, and collecting samples of the local abundance to demonstrate to those back in England the exotic fertility of the New World.

The harbor that so delighted early explorers was in fact one of the vital environments of the eastern coast of the North American continent (figs. 1.1, 1.2). the "Beautiful Lake" was just one part of a vast complex of rivers, wetlands, and tidal estuaries. The confluence of the Hudson River, the Long Island Sound, the Great South and Jamaica Bays, and the waterways of the Hackensack Meadowlands yielded a unique natural system that has retained its greatness despite the drastic impositions of the modern industrial age.

The Boundaries of the Harbor

New York Harbor is the center of this system of waterways and constitutes an area of about 1,500 square miles with over 770

1.2
GEOLOGICAL SURFACE MAP
Staten Island quadrangle. Surveyed 1896. 1901 edition.
New York City Department of Environmental Protection.

1.3
NEW YORK CITY
Photomosaic. 1969.
From *Plan for New York City*, New York City Planning Commission.

miles of waterfront. New York Harbor itself is subdivided into the North River, the Upper Bay, and the Lower Bay (fig. 1.3). The North River is actually the southern end of the Hudson River, and may be defined as the stretch extending from the southern tip of Manhattan Island to the Piermont Marshes of the Tappan Zee, several miles north of New York City. Those marshes represent the northern extent of the marine-rooted aquatic vegetation of the New York–New Jersey Harbor Estuary, and the southern extent of freshwater-submerged aquatic vegetation in the Hudson River. The actual head of tide is about 140 miles north at the Federal Dam in Troy, New York. The Upper and Lower Bays of the Harbor are separated by the Narrows, a 0.3-mile strait between eastern Staten Island and western Brooklyn. New York Harbor empties into the New York Bight of the Atlantic Ocean. In addition to the harbor and its interconnecting waterways, the New York–New Jersey Harbor Estuary includes Raritan, Newark, and Jamaica Bays.

Raritan Bay, a large, shallow body enclosed by the recurved spit of Sandy Hook on the east and Staten Island on the north, is the estuary of the Raritan, Navesink, and Shrewsbury Rivers. The latter two conjoin and empty into Sandy Hook Bay. Newark Bay, immediately south of the Hackensack Meadowlands and west of the Bayonne Peninsula, is now largely an artificial body of water. Once a broad,

shallow embayment rimmed with tidal marsh, it is now the locus of commercial port activities for the greater metropolitan region.

Jamaica Bay, a complex of tidal mudflats and wetlands, was originally conceived as a wildlife refuge by Robert Moses in 1924. It was officially opened as such by the city of New York in 1954 and remains the centerpiece of the Gateway National Recreation Area. It is bordered on the east

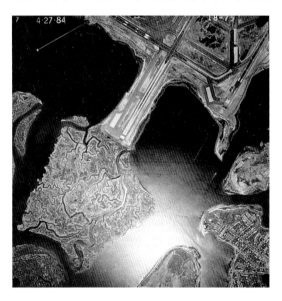

by John F. Kennedy International Airport (fig. 1.4) and on the north and west by sanitary landfills or urban housing built on landfill (fig. 1.5). To the south, the bay is separated from the New York Bight by Rockaway Spit.

Dominating this aquatic system is the Hudson River, which arises in the Adirondack Mountains about 315 miles

1.4
JAMAICA BAY, JO CO'S MARSH, AND RUNWAYS OF JOHN F. KENNEDY INTERNATIONAL AIRPORT
Allied Map Co., photographer. Department of City Planning. 1984.
New York City Department of Environmental Protection.

north of the Narrows and drains an area of 13,370 square miles. Entering the estuary through Newark Bay are the Hacken-

sack and Passaic Rivers. The Hackensack, about forty-five miles in length, arises in Rockland County, New York; flows south to the Oradell Reservoir in New Jersey; then passes through the Hackensack Meadowlands, a body comprising approximately fifty square miles of highly disturbed and altered marsh. The Passaic River arises south of Morristown, New Jersey, flowing about eighty miles to Newark Bay. The Shrewsbury and the Navesink Rivers, both approximately eight miles in length, are located south of Raritan Bay, but reach the bay through a common outlet west of Sandy Hook, New Jersey.

There are no true rivers on the eastern side of the New York–New Jersey

Harbor Estuary. The Harlem River is really a ship channel, significantly altered by marginal landfill and dredging, connecting the former Spuyten Duyvil Creek with the East River (fig. 1.6) at the northern end of Manhattan Island. The East River is actually a tidal strait connecting the Upper Bay with the Long Island Sound. Both the Arthur Kill (fig. 1.7) and the Kill van Kull (fig. 1.8), which separate Staten Island from the mainland, are also narrow tidal straits. Used as shipping channels, the two are perhaps the most trafficked waterways in the Port of New York.

Geological History

The rich hydrology and biology of the New York–New Jersey Harbor Estuary, as well as its excellence as a port, ultimately derive from its geological complexity (fig. 1.9). Rocky shores, enormous shallow marshes, and a network of tidal channels and islands are all present in a single locale. No other estuary on the East Coast possesses a comparable array of different shore habitats. While underlying bedrock provides the estuary's framework, its visible form is the terrane created by the

1.5
JAMAICA BAY LANDFILL
Skyviews, photographer. 1964.
Triborough Bridge and Tunnel Authority Special Archive.

glacial ice of the Pleistocene Epoch. That ice covered the entire area, blanketing it with moranic deposits including the terminal moraine stretching across the estuary from northern New Jersey to Long Island, New York.

Extending southward, the New England Province's metamorphic-rock prongs of hard igneous granite form the region's core. One prong forms Manhattan

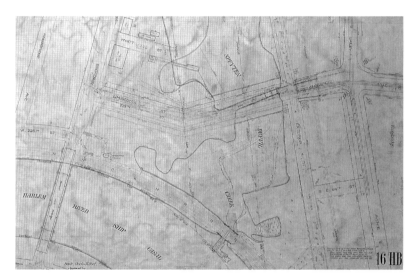

Island, the other the Hill and Valley Province of northeastern New Jersey. Stretching in a northeasterly direction between the two prongs is a continuation of the Piedmont Plateau Province, sometimes called the New Jersey Lowland. Soft Triassic sandstone and shale underlie the lowland. At its eastern margin, diabase basalt intrudes, forming the Palisades. As this sill dips southward, it forms Bergen Hill and

the spine of the Bayonne Peninsula. The diabase stretches down to Staten Island, where it is breached by the Arthur Kill. The seaward side of the Piedmont Plateau slopes rather sharply to the Coastal Plains Province. This boundary, the Fall Line, is marked by various rapids and waterfalls that constitute the head of navigation for the New Jersey rivers entering the estuary. More recently deposited Coastal Plain Province sediments fringe the harbor, extending to the margins of Newark Bay and the Hackensack Meadowlands, and are most conspicuous on Long Island.

The spine of Manhattan Island is made of Fordham schist, Manhattan gneiss, and Inwood marble. The first two are exposed all along the length of Manhattan Island, which rises in elevation irregularly and gradually from south to north. Inwood marble, a metamorphic dolomite, is very soft; thus its outcroppings along northern and northeastern Manhattan were easily eroded to form the channel of the Spuyten Duyvil Creek and Harlem River. Between lower midtown and the southern tip of the island, the bedrock dips to about one hundred feet below the surface, too deep

1.6
HARLEM RIVER SHIP CANAL AND SPUYTEN DUYVIL CREEK
Survey map. Department of Docks. Hilton, surveyor. 1906,
modified through 1914. NYCMA.

1.7
ARTHUR KILL, STATEN ISLAND
Stanley Greenberg, photographer. 1994.

1.8
KILL VAN KULL, STATEN ISLAND
Stanley Greenberg, photographer. 1993.

for the footings for support of skyscraper construction, thus creating visible effects on the Manhattan skyline. Until European settlement and subsequent landfill, the Battery was separated from the rest of Manhattan during spring high tides by tidal marsh and water.

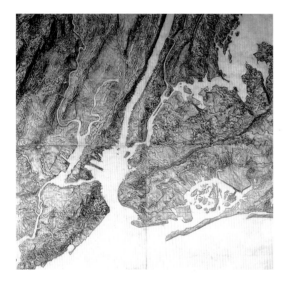

Pleistocene glacial ice shaped much of the estuary region, but the blanket of moraine—earth and stones carried and deposited by retreating glaciers—is more conspicuous. Important to the geologic history of the region are the deposits that formed in the huge, postglacial Passaic, Hackensack, Flushing, and Long Island "Lakes." A terminal moraine (marking the farthest extent of glacial ice), the Ronkonkoma Rise, stretched from northern New Jersey across Staten Island to Long Island and continued to Cape Cod.

Acting like a dam, it contained the accumulated glacial meltwaters to create lakes lined with thick deposits of varved sediment.

New York Harbor is a drowned estuary, the result of the postglacial rise in sea level. During the periods when glacial ice covered the region, sea levels were much lower, exposing the continental shelf. The proto–Hudson River flowed across that shelf, eroding the Hudson Shelf Canyon. As sea level was raised by the melting glaciers, this steep canyon filled with sediment, and salt water replaced fresh in the glacial lakes. Both the great Hackensack Meadowlands and Newark Bay, for example, are remnants of former Lake Hackensack. About five thousand years ago, the sea level stabilized to its present rise of about 1.5 millimeters per year. Tidal marshes were established in many of the shallow embayments. The westward movement of sediment along the south shore of Long Island, resulting from the impact of waves on the beaches, formed the Rockaway Peninsula that increasingly isolated Jamaica Bay from the ocean.

Situated mostly in the Piedmont Province with its low-lying Triassic lands, the New Jersey portion of the estuary was characterized in precolonial times by extensive tidal and freshwater marshes extending a considerable distance up each river. The lower Hackensack and Passaic Rivers emptied into the huge tidal, brack-

1.9
TOPOGRAPHY OF NEW YORK AND ENVIRONS
Model rubbing. Kevin Bone and Pia Moos, artists;
Lily Zand, modelmaker. 1994.

ish, and freshwater marsh of the meadow-lands and then into the tidal-marsh-rimmed waters of Newark Bay. West of Staten Island, the New Jersey shore of the Kill van Kull also consisted of extensive marsh. East of the Bayonne Peninsula were broad, shallow mudflats extending over a mile beyond the shore, terminating in a long series of oyster reefs that paralleled the coast. In contrast, the New York shore was primarily rocky or bluff; deeper water was found close to the shoreline, particularly on Manhattan's western shore. Tidal marshes were found especially along lower Manhattan and northern Brooklyn. The largest shore wetlands of the eastern mainland shore were probably those of the Hutchinson River system in the Bronx (figs. 1.10–1.17).

Harbor "Improvements"

The European colonists were quick to discover the geological attributes that made New York Harbor so hospitable, though such advantages did not deter them from making "improvements." The necessity to establish commerce with their home countries led the settlers to build docks and bulkheads extending into the harbor, behind which fill was poured—some of it household refuse, but most consisting of soil and rocks collected from the leveling of land and from basement excavations (fig. 1.18). With the development of the suction dredge in the late nineteenth cen-

tury, dredge spoil became the main landfill material. The traditions of European port development, emphasizing bulkhead wharves, resulted in the establishment of a sharp, steep built interface between land and water that replaced the natural shelving of beaches, wetlands, and rocky shores.

Manhattan was the first portion of the harbor to be developed, particularly along the East River, which was better protected from the winter ice floes. By 1800, most of the southern tip of Manhattan had been ringed with bulkhead and landfill, in keeping with public policy, adding about 729 acres of new land (fig. 1.19). As the city spread northward, fresh and tidal marshes were filled to make space for the growing number of piers, wharves, and other commercial shoreline facilities. The large marshy areas north of Corlears Hook on the East River, and at 14th Street on the North River, reputed to bisect Manhattan at highest tide, were filled. The continuous extension of land into the East River was halted, or at least severely regulated, by the Federal Rivers and Harbors Act of 1888, which established the United States Army Corps of Engineers as the agency responsible for setting lines beyond which piers, wharves, and landfill could not reach.

Brooklyn's waterfront proceeded more slowly, but by the early nineteenth century extensive modification had taken place as the shore adjacent to the high bluffs of northern Brooklyn was pushed

1.10 top
SHORE PARKWAY, FORT HAMILTON, AND VERRAZANO BRIDGE
Allied Map Co., photographer. Department of City Planning. 1984.
New York City Department of Environmental Protection.

1.11 top
HELL GATE, EAST RIVER, HARLEM RIVER WITH MILL ROCK
Allied Map Co., photographer. Department of City Planning. 1984.
New York City Department of Environmental Protection.

1.12
JAMAICA BAY, STONY CREEK MARSH, YELLOW BAR AND RULERS BAR
HASSOCKS
Allied Map Co., photographer. Department of City Planning. 1984.
New York City Department of Environmental Protection.

1.13
EAST RIVER AT WILLIAMSBURG BRIDGE WITH EAST RIVER PARK,
MANHATTAN
Allied Map Co., photographer. Department of City Planning. 1984.
New York City Department of Environmental Protection.

1.14 top
HARLEM RIVER SHIP CANAL AND HUDSON RIVER WATERFRONT
Allied Map Co., photographer. Department of City Planning. 1984.
New York City Department of Environmental Protection.

1.15 top
BROAD CHANNEL IN JAMAICA BAY AND ROCKAWAY PARK
Allied Map Co., photographer. Department of City Planning. 1984.
New York City Department of Environmental Protection.

1.16
HUDSON RIVER PIERS, FROM PIER 59 TO PIER 99
Allied Map Co., photographer. Department of City Planning. 1984.
New York City Department of Environmental Protection.

1.17
EAST RIVER AND BROOKLYN NAVY YARD
Allied Map Co., photographer. Department of City Planning. 1984.
New York City Department of Environmental Protection.

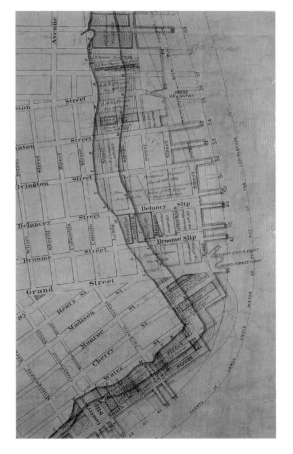

1.18
WEST SIDE IMPROVEMENT, LANDFILL OPERATION FROM 69TH STREET
Alajos Schuszler, photographer. 1935.
New York City Parks Photo Archive.

1.19
MAP SHOWING THE HIGH- AND LOW-WATER MARKS AND ORIGINAL CITY GRANTS
Plan. Department of Docks. General Charles K. Graham, engineer in chief; John Meehan, assistant engineer; David T. Keiller, compiler and draftsperson. 1873. NYCMA.

outward into the East River to form new land. The shoreline from the Brooklyn Bridge south to Bay Ridge was the first to develop, anchored by three major constructions: the Atlantic Basin, begun in 1841; the Erie Basin, begun in 1864; and the Brooklyn Navy Yard in Wallabout Bay, begun in 1867. Extensive marsh complexes were obliterated and Red Hook Island was connected to the mainland. The New Jersey coast evolved as a port even later, due discouragingly to extensive tidal marshes and broad mudflats. When development did begin, however, its magnitude was enormous. The ports on the New Jersey shore of the harbor eventually proved more accommodating than those on the New York side for modern, larger ships and changing shipping technology.

Alterations for port and related activities were not without significant ecological impact. The steepening of the land-water interface via shoreline armoring and attendant dredging wrought extensive change in nearshore habitats. Landfill installed to create space for facilities destroyed marshlands and mudflats. Channel dredging, either for navigation or for spoil, progressively narrowed and deepened waterways and bays, affecting not only habitat but also water circulation.

Today the estuary is surrounded by some of the most dense human populations in the United States. However, that density has been achieved only within the last 150 years. The estuary's present flora and fauna, however, developed within a climate and hydrology which had been stable for at least 1,500 years. It is important to note that the abruptness of human impact has made it impossible for the bios of the estuary to adapt.

Tidal marsh, mudflats, and other nearshore habitats have been lost in more recent times to housing, retail, and office construction, most of which has occurred since World War II. Between 1953 and 1973 alone, the New York shore of the estuary lost over 5,000 acres of tidal wetlands while the New Jersey shore lost nearly 12,000 acres, a consequence of climatic change resulting from glacial retreat —over one-fifth of the estuary's *total* tidal-marsh losses (figs. 1.20–1.22). The magnitude of that depletion, as well as similar destruction elsewhere in the nation, inspired the enactment of protective legislation in the early 1970s. Since then, the rate of loss has been slowed if not stopped (fig. 1.23).

The Future of New York Harbor

At the end of the twentieth century, the New York–New Jersey Harbor Estuary has experienced major changes to its shoreline, and major losses of habitat for nearshore animals and plantlife, both aquatic and terrestrial (fig. 1.24). In New York Harbor, about 47,000 acres of tidal marsh have disappeared. In New Jersey, 29,000 acres of tidelands between Raritan

Bay and the George Washington Bridge have been filled, as well as a staggering 293,000 acres of underwater terrain—mostly the shallow mudflats and oyster reefs of the western shore of the North River. On the New York side, 9,000 acres of new land have been created. Only

In another thousand years, the Hudson will still drain the waters of the upstate mountains into New York Bay, and ocean currents will still bring nutrients to some form of thriving life. In some areas, nature has already taken swift advantage of our slowing maritime activity: as dredging

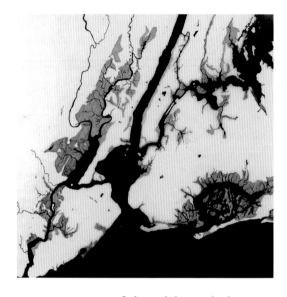

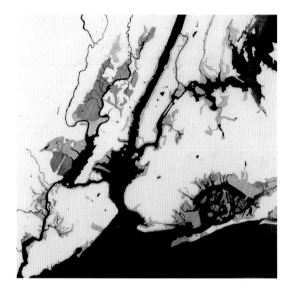

twenty percent of the tidal marsh that was once the core of the estuary remains today.

For the immediate future, it is difficult not to be pessimistic about the possibility of recovering much of the "Beautiful Lake." The human population of the estuary may continue to grow in numbers, drawing upon and sometimes abusing the finite resources of both water and land. But, for all of civilization's abilities to distort and damage the natural order, it is reasonable to believe nature possesses a resiliency that we have not yet impaired.

operations in the harbor have been cut back, river silts have once again begun to accumulate, and along the banks of shipping channels marsh grass has begun to form wetlands. The River Project, a study group of marine scientists, reports that the unused slips of the lower Hudson are gradually reverting to wetlands. As sediment accumulates in the Harlem River it is returning to its preindustrial state as a tidal estuary. Comparable examples of such regeneration can be found throughout the harbor (fig. 1.25).

1.20
MARSHLANDS AND MADE LANDS IN THE NEW YORK–NEW JERSEY HARBOR ESTUARY IN 1900
Dark hatched areas indicate marshlands, light hatched areas indicate filled-in marshlands. Kevin Bone, Kevin Kavanagh, after Donald Squires. Marine Sciences Institute. 1992.

1.21
MARSHLANDS AND MADE LANDS IN THE NEW YORK–NEW JERSEY HARBOR ESTUARY IN 1968
Kevin Bone, Kevin Kavanagh, after Donald Squires. Marine Sciences Institute. 1992.

The massive industrial transformation of the waterfront in the nineteenth and early twentieth centuries was the result of a widely shared vision of New York as a city of the world, a commercial port of unprecedented breadth. It was a great accomplishment for human beings.

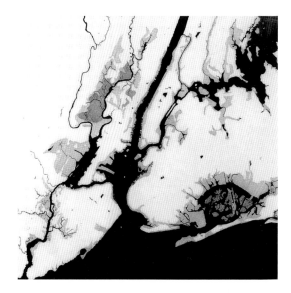

Now an equally shared environmental consciousness offers an opportunity to reclaim the "Beautiful Lake" on which the port was based.

Recent global changes in maritime commerce and in the technologies of ship construction and cargo handling have resulted in a diminished role for the Port of New York–New Jersey in the nation's commerce. Today we are at a decisive point: should the port facilities be restored in the hopes of reinvigorating commercial and industrial use of the harbor, or should we

pursue a course that seeks to make the harbor into a useful natural resource suitable for a wide variety of civic purposes, like recreation?

If port restoration is the chosen path, ecological improvements could still be possible with wise and sensitive development. If revitalization of the natural harbor is the chosen path, economic benefits are still a possibility through increased land values and a more livable city. Both assessments are, however, totally dependent upon a public awareness and efforts to prevent further abuse as well as the cooperation of public and private developers to work to restore the harbor's ecological functions.

NOTES

1.   Leonard, p. 11.

1.22
MARSHLANDS AND MADE LANDS IN THE NEW YORK–NEW JERSEY
HARBOR ESTUARY IN 1989
Kevin Bone, Kevin Kavanagh, after Donald Squires.
Marine Sciences Institute. 1992.

1.23
FRESH KILLS LANDFILL, STATEN ISLAND
Stanley Greenberg, photographer. 1993.

1.24 top
CHELSEA, STATEN ISLAND
Stanley Greenberg, photographer. 1993.

1.25
LONG ISLAND RAILROAD BARGE FLOAT TERMINAL, HUNTERS POINT, QUEENS
Stanley Greenberg, photographer. 1994 .

OYSTER MARKETS, PIER 32, EAST RIVER, MANHATTAN
Photographer unknown. Circa 1910. NYCMA.

2

2.1
PIER 6 (LATER PIER 5), EAST RIVER, MANHATTAN
Photographer unknown. Circa 1900. Published by A. F. Nesbitt. NYHS.

MASTERPLANNING
Municipal Support of Maritime Transport and Commerce 1870–1930s

Mary Beth Betts

> It is very easy and natural to enthuse with the proponents of speed highways, esplanades and bridges, but in this there is grave danger of losing sight of the fact that the North River and East River waterfronts below 34th Street have given New York City the world preeminence it enjoys today.
>
> —John McKenzie,
> COMMISSIONER OF DOCKS, 1931

These words marked the end of an era for the New York City waterfront. In the late nineteenth and early twentieth centuries the waterfront had been a district of bustling wharves, piers, and ferry terminals, its streets teeming with traffic and lined with waiting cargo. The vast quantity of goods that passed through the port fueled the city's economy, making Manhattan the dominant American seaport and metropolis before the Civil War, and one of the world's major international ports by 1900 (figs. 2.1, 2.2).

During the late nineteenth century, the waterfront—consisting of the banks of the East River, the Harlem River, and the North (or lower Hudson) River—came under the jurisdiction of a single city agency, the New York City Department of Docks. While the creation of "Greater New York" in 1898 enlarged city boundaries to include Brooklyn, Queens, and Staten Island, most waterfront construction and shipping would continue to be concentrated in Manhattan. During the 1930s, the waterfront began gradually losing its maritime livelihood with its corresponding physical character, devolving into a fragmented terrain of highways, bridges, esplanades, and parks under the disparate control of several city agencies.

The Department of Docks was established in 1870 to formulate a master plan for the waterfront and to oversee its systematic development. Newspapers such as the *New York Times* hoped for a scheme that would rival the greatest European harbors, with monumental stone and iron piers to replace the New York City waterfront of 1870 which, as the *Times* reported, consisted of "mean, rot-

2.2
HARLEM RIVER AND VICINITY
J. Nordstrom, photographer. 1903. NYHS.

ten and dilapidated wooden wharves"[1] (fig. 2.3). The subsequently adopted plan was less ambitious, at least in its architectural features, but it significantly altered New York Harbor and succeeded in creating an overall approach to the waterfront that would continue to guide construction for the next fifty years.

In addition to devising and overseeing this enduring master plan, the New York City Department of Docks actively supervised the greatest public-works projects of the period, employing over a thousand workers, and enlisted the most advanced engineering technologies to create the vast built fabric of Manhattan's riverwalls and piers. Yet the department's incredible impact on the city is not immediately visible to the late-twentieth-century eye. From 1870 to 1930 the Department of Docks largely accomplished its vision of the waterfront as a great corps of piers supporting the commerce of New York, but all that has long since vanished with the abandonment of the master plan and the demolition of much of its built legacy. The successes and failures of the department as it studied, formulated, and implemented the overall master plan and important individual projects provide a case study for understanding a seldom explored but historically significant part of the urban environment, as well as the impact of city government on the built features of New York. The succession of engineers in chief, and later commissioners of docks, provides a rare model of a long-term plan that survived (despite subtle shifts of emphasis) the personal visions and concerns of its different stewards. Over a century later, this accomplishment seems remarkable in view of the difficulties our current planners face. Today, architects, engineers, planners, and politicians must achieve consensus among New York City's different communities to design a plan that can survive shifts in political power and aesthetics. The successes, compromises, and failures of the Department of Docks allow us to analyze the benefits and costs of implementing a long-range plan in the 1990s.

2.3
UNIDENTIFIED PIER INTERIOR
Photographer unknown. Circa 1910. NYCMA.

The department's legacy includes the radical transformation of the waterfront's geography. Massive landfills and the miles of riverwall that gird them are responsible for what we accept today as the natural contour of Manhattan, which

is thirty percent larger than the island the original Dutch settlers knew.

We can study the department in such detail because of the copious records it kept of its work in the form of meticulous maps, drawings, photographs, and memoranda. The department recognized the historical importance of this multitude of documents and its value in insuring the continued implementation of the plan. In the 1872 annual report, General George McClellan, engineer in chief, remarked on the amount of time his colleagues had devoted to recording and sifting data as well as rendering maps and drawings.[2] The engineering staff had spent the year examining seventy competing master plans, various solutions to the problem of constructing the riverwall, and more than 130 different proposals for piers. The department saved rejected designs as reference materials for the insight they might provide in establishing the harbor's future (fig. 2.4). The documents were of value not only to the department and the city but also to maritime engineers; the definitive textbook on post–World War I harborfront construction, Carleton Greene's 1917 *Wharves and Piers: Their Design, Construction and Equipment,* made extensive use of the department's photographs, drawings, and statistics. In the forty-eighth annual report, published in 1919, Commissioner of Docks Murray Hulbert understood the importance of the waterfront maps, noting that "the city has encroached at nearly every point on the original high-water line,"[3] such that the old maps preserved crucial but now obscure information (fig. 2.5).

Founding of the Department of Docks

Municipal jurisdiction over the waterfront dates to 1686, when British colonial authorities transferred all decisions concerning

2.4
DESIGN OF PIER
Section, details. Andrew Scott, designer. Circa 1850. NYCMA.

unencumbered land, including that under water, to city officials. Through the early nineteenth century, the sporadic and infrequent attempts to plan waterfront development usually originated in the legislative branch of city government, initially the Common Council and later the Board

of Aldermen. Through 1800, the Common Council also made most of the administrative decisions concerning the waterfront's use.

By the end of the first decade of the nineteenth century, New York City had become the most populous municipality in the United States and the most prosperous. Its port, the largest in the country, substantially contributed to this growth and prosperity (fig. 2.6). The nineteenth-century waterfront teemed with activity. Private individuals and businesses developed and used most of the waterfront

area, while its administration was divided among a variety of city departments in an increasingly complicated and confusing manner. The commissioners of the Sinking Fund, the predecessor to the Board of Estimate and the agency that approved the city's long-term financial commitments, controlled access to underwater land by issuing grants or leases to specific properties, while the Common Council, and later the Board of Aldermen, approved any landfill or construction of wharves and piers. Repairs to pier and wharf structures, as well as dredging of underwater property, were the jurisdiction of the street commissioner. The city's comptroller collected rents for underwater land and structures built on that land. This profusion of agencies made it difficult, if not impossible, to plan and administer the waterfront consistently.

The Department of Docks was established in an 1870 legislative act that also created the city's Department of Public Parks, Department of Public Works, and Department of Buildings. The need to regulate and plan the physical fabric of the booming metropolis had by now been recognized.

2.5
NORTH RIVER, MORRIS STREET TO CORTLANDT STREET, MANHATTAN
Survey map. Department of Docks. Circa 1895, modified through 1927.
NYCMA.

During the nineteenth century more than one short-term commission had recommended solutions to the waterfront chaos. In 1834, after seven years of negotiations which resulted in a treaty between New York and New Jersey, a bi-state commission succeeded in defining the bound-

ary between New Jersey and New York in the Hudson River and New York Bay. In 1855, a New York State commission for the preservation of the harbor made recommendations for the establishment of pier- and bulkhead lines which New York adopted, though New Jersey did not. The New Jersey legislature objected to the commission's findings, which blatantly favored New York City piers despite a western shift in river currents that created more favorable conditions for docking on the New Jersey shore. Prominent private

citizens also offered advice. Peter Cooper, manufacturer, inventor, and philanthropist, urged the city to build stone piers in order both to provide employment and to enhance the aesthetic importance of "our great commercial metropolis."[4] In 1857, the Board of Aldermen actively intervened in waterfront construction for the first time; after that date, no pier could be built without city permission.

By 1870, the derelict condition of the piers was widely regarded as a public hazard; the *New York Times* roundly condemned them as "rotten structures, the abode of rats and the hiding places of river-thieves . . . it is at great risk that a person can walk on them in broad daylight."[5] Both commercial and civic interests were calling for the port's wholesale renovation.

City officials and critics in the press agreed that the newly formed Department of Docks should implement a master plan for the entire waterfront. There was a general consensus that such a design should meet needs cultural as well as commercial. As New York was a city of worldwide financial significance, so should its cosmopolitan amenities compete on an international scale. The *New York Times* hoped

2.6
EAST RIVER PIERS, MANHATTAN
Photographer unknown. Circa 1900. NYCMA.

that the master plan would include aesthetic features suitably monumental such that "our citizens can enjoy the pleasure of a promenade along the broad iron or stone quays of our rejuvenated waterfront."[6]

The establishment of an agency so broadly empowered as to regulate all facets of the waterfront was unprecedented in the history of municipalities. As cited in the 1919 annual report, the Department of Docks was the "first sincere attempt at municipal ownership and administration of port utilities in America, for it had as its object the girdling of the waterfront of the old city of New York with new wharves and piers to be ultimately owned by the municipality, thus terminating all private ownership along the waterfront."[7] Though this civic consolidation would hold, in 1888 the federal Rivers and Harbors Act would give the United States Army Corps of Engineers jurisdiction over all activity on the country's navigable waters. The army alone had the power to determine bulk- and pierhead lines for harbors throughout the United States. While this act promised to alleviate certain local problems, such as disputes over the boundary lines between New York and New Jersey, it also eliminated an important component of the Department of Docks' authority to plan the waterfront by limiting its jurisdiction to control pier length. It should be noted that many other texts have dated the Rivers and Harbors Act to 1879, probably due to

confusion arising from the fact that all congressional appropriations of money for waterway improvements or legislation concerning waterfront jurisdiction were called "Rivers and Harbors" Acts. DOD annual reports and survey maps showing pier- and bulkhead lines indicate, however, that the congressional act giving the Corps of Engineers jurisdiction over all navigable American waters dates to 1888 (fig. 2.7). All of the department's subsequent activity should be understood as qualified by this broad federal legislation.

George Brinton McClellan was appointed the department's first engineer in chief, a decision that brought the new agency considerable publicity and signaled the priority the city placed on the waterfront's development. McClellan was a figure of national renown. He had been general in chief of the United States Army for two years during the Civil War, and in 1864 he was the Democratic presidential candidate. McClellan also had extensive experience as an engineer. After graduating from West Point in 1846, he designed fortifications and surveyed rivers and railroad routes. He became chief engineer of the Illinois Central Railroad in 1857, and president of the Ohio and Mississippi Railroad in 1860. Prior to his Department of Docks appointment, he had worked on developing a new type of steam-powered warship. McClellan's eminence and experience, however, were expensive; in 1872, his Department of Docks salary was a

2.7 top
**PIERHEAD AND BULKHEAD LINES FOR THE WATERFRONTS OF PART
OF NEW YORK CITY, AND FOR THE ADJACENT NEW JERSEY SHORE**
Map. C. G. Auerbach, compiler and draftsperson. March 1901.
NYCMA.

2.8
SANITARY AND TOPOGRAPHICAL MAP OF NEW YORK CITY
Prepared for the Council of Hygiene and Public Health of the Citizens
Association under the direction of Egbert L. Viele. Circa 1865.
Triborough Bridge and Tunnel Authority.

substantial $20,000. Two years later his successor, Charles K. Graham, would be paid only $5,500.

The Call For Plans

Having mandated the development of a master plan for the entire Manhattan waterfront, the city and its new department opened the planning process to the public, announcing a series of five public hearings to which it "invited all persons interested in inaugurating, in the harbor of New York, a proper system of wharves and piers, or who have special plans for the improvement of the waterfront." Participants were expected to recognize the scope of the department's ambitions: nothing less than a "new system of wharves, piers, docks, basins, and slips, which should accommodate the present commerce of the city and harbor, and should provide for the future expansion thereof, and for the facilitation of the transportation of freight along the waterfront, so as to render the whole waterfront of the city available to the commerce of the port."[8] In inviting public participation, the city acknowledged the importance of the waterfront plan.

Evincing widespread public interest, over seventy diverse plans for the waterfront were submitted to the Department of Docks by individuals and organizations. Proposals came from engineers, city and military officials, private warehouse and pier-construction companies, and cast-iron specialists. Among the participants was Egbert Viele, an engineer with wide experience in public works who had contributed to the planning and construction of Central Park, the layout and development of the Upper West Side, and the establishment of sanitation districts throughout the city (fig. 2.8).

Many of the plans included a city-wide system of piers. Ship captain James C. Nichols suggested a modest scheme that called for a stone bulkhead with simple pier platforms of undesignated material to extend over the water (fig. 2.9). Some of the other proposals were more elaborate, stipulating stone or iron structures. William H. Emmons, an engineer and city surveyor, worked with Franklin Kissam to propose solid stone piers with warehouses, a formula echoed in a slightly different configuration by naval engineer Ralph Aston (fig. 2.10). The Emmons-Kissam scheme envisioned piers connected to an elevated rail line with freightcars running along piershed roofs (fig. 2.11). In cooperation with John Burrows Hyde and John Heuvelman, the New York Pier and Warehouse Company submitted a design for an elaborate cast-iron warehouse to be placed on an iron pier, with the warehouse buildings elevated above the pier's deck atop a grid of open columns (fig. 2.12). Civil engineer Richard Gilpin's proposal called for triangular piers, a design recognizing that the inland side of a pier deck tended to become congested and therefore required a large deck area. Gilpin's design would also have eased the docking of vessels. Other contributors, including Captain James C. Luce and Onsville E. Prey, proposed a more traditional, European-style waterfront made up of a series of wet basins or docks. (figs. 2.13–2.17).

Few schemes addressed the city's stipulation that any plan should include facilities for the transportation of freight, beyond indicating that the inland sides of the piers should front on broad streets. In one public hearing, a man identified as H. C. Gardiner proposed the installation of railroad tracks along the riverfront street to provide "easy transportation out of the city . . . [and] do away with the necessity of the vast tenement houses."9

Many contributors addressed the need for the piers to incorporate a system of sanitation. Gilpin's triangular piers utilized waterways by which the tides and river currents would carry away debris. He devised a sewer leading out to the bulkhead line in order to dump sewage into the river current so that it would be carried away rather than stagnating at shore (fig. 2.18).

In some cases, proposals exceeded the mandated scope of the master plan. Aston submitted two designs. In one he proposed a system of simple, uniform warehouses across the street from the piers. The other scheme divided the waterfront into zones for different industries, such as coal, grain, and lumber, and their correspondent activities, along regularly placed ferry slips. He proposed square parks along the water's edge at given intervals, offering one of the few visions to link commerce and recreation (fig. 2.19).

A radical proposal by Samuel B. Nowlan called for a granite seawall, a system of floating docks, and the creation of a canal from Flushing Bay through the mouth of the Harlem River, crossing the Harlem Plains to the Hudson River. This plan involved the installation of a complex system of locks to control the East River tide, effectively creating a wet basin that encompassed two rivers (fig. 2.20).

The Department of Docks considered these proposals seriously. The transcripts of the five public hearings were published by the city, and the department kept all written material and drawings as part of its official records, studying them for any concepts that would be helpful in formulating a master plan. These proposals formed the nucleus of what would become a diverse archive.

Despite reviews and debates, the Department of Docks ultimately dismissed the suggestions contained in the proposals in favor of its own plan, though not without acknowledging their value in gaining public support for the overall project: "Many of them contain very excellent ideas, [though] the best of these . . . are not novel, and are such as should suggest

2.9 top
DESIGN FOR PIERS
Perspective. James C. Nichols, designer. 1870. NYCMA.

2.10
DESIGN OF DOCKS AND WAREHOUSES
Perspective. Ralph Aston, designer and delineator. 1870. NYCMA.

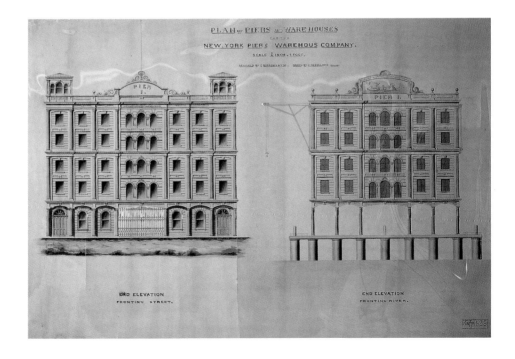

2.11 top
SYSTEM OF PIERS
Isometric. William H. Emmons, engineer and city surveyor;
Franklin Kissam, draftsperson. 1870. NYCMA.

2.12
PIERS AND WAREHOUSES FOR THE NEW YORK PIER AND WAREHOUSE
COMPANY, PIER 1
Street and river elevations. John Burrows Hyde, designer;
John Heuvelman, architect and delineator. 1870. NYCMA.

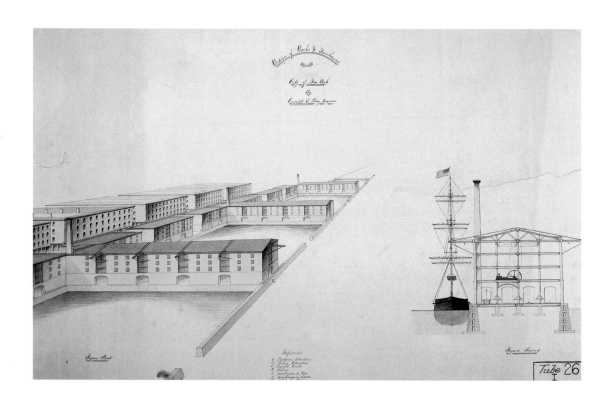

2.13
DESIGN OF DOCKS AND WAREHOUSES FOR THE CITY OF NEW YORK
Perspective and section. Onsville E. Prey, engineer and delineator. 1870.
NYCMA.

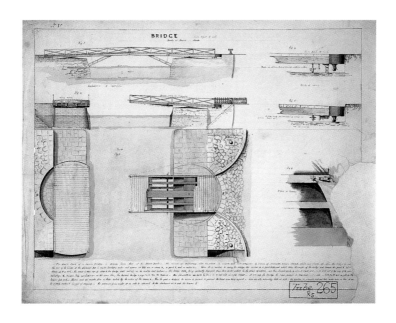

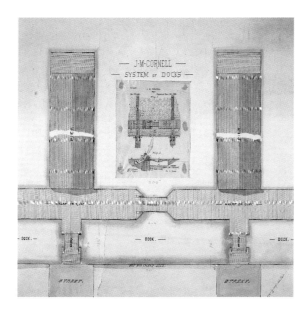

2.14 top
SWIVEL BRIDGE DOCKS AT LE HAVRE
Elevation, plan, details. Andrew Scott, draftsperson. Circa 1850. NYCMA.

2.15
SYSTEM OF DOCKS
Plan, section, details. J. M. Cornell, designer. Circa 1888. NYCMA.

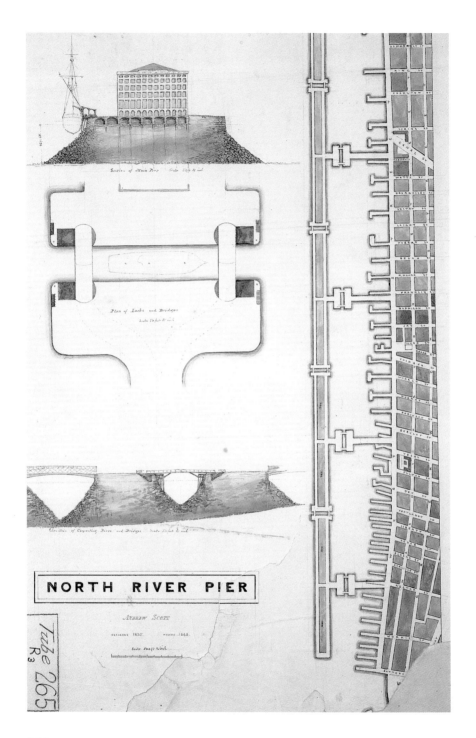

2.16
NORTH RIVER PIER
Plan, section, elevation. Andrew Scott, designer. Designed 1835, drawn 1849.
NYCMA.

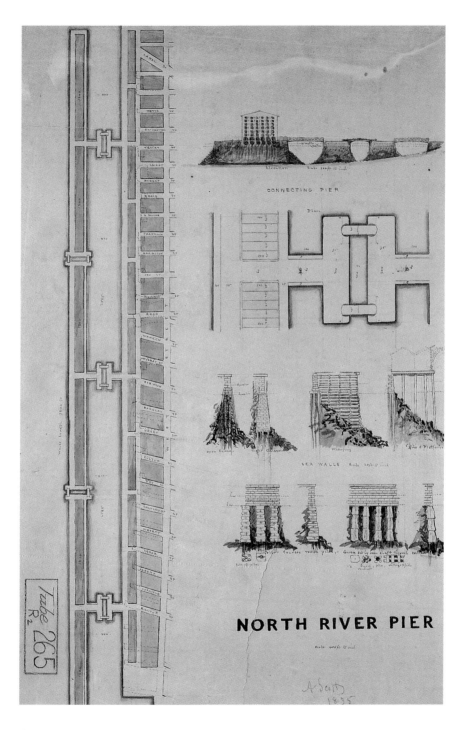

2.17
NORTH RIVER PIER
Plan, elevation, details. Andrew Scott, designer. Designed 1835, drawn 1851.
NYCMA.

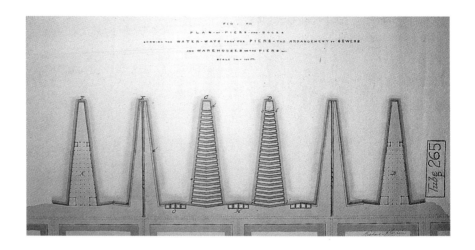

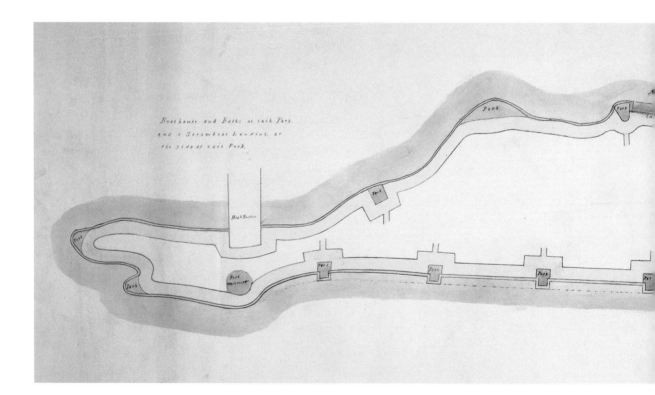

2.18 top
**PLAN OF PIERS AND DOCKS SHOWING THE WATERWAYS THRO' THE PIERS
—THE ARRANGEMENT OF SEWERS AND WAREHOUSES ON THE PIERS**
Plan. Richard A. Gilpin, civil engineer. 1870. NYCMA.

2.19
WATERFRONT IMPROVEMENT OF NEW YORK CITY
Plan. Ralph Aston, designer. 1870. NYCMA.

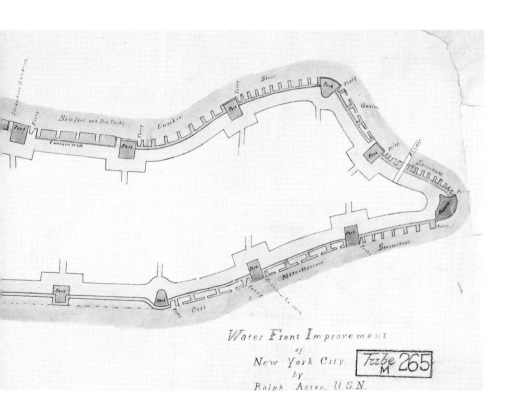

*Water Front Improvement
of
New York City,
by
Ralph Aston, U.S.N.*

themselves to any competent engineer charged with the direction of such work. Their chief value, then, and that no slight

one, consists in the additional weight they give to the conclusions reached by the Commissioners."[10]

McClellan's Master Plan

The alternative to the many outside proposals was a plan devised by General McClellan himself, which the department, and ultimately the city, accepted. McClellan called for the creation of landfill along the edge of Manhattan upon which to lay out sufficiently wide river-streets, and proposed a masonry riverwall to encircle the island with wood piers at given intervals. McClellan's plan addressed several issues raised during the establishment of the

department and throughout the public hearings. While he expressed knowledge of, and admiration for, the docks of Liverpool and London, and respected the distinguished engineering of John Rennie and Thomas Telford, McClellan believed that the vast physical differences between those cities and Manhattan made their system of enclosed wetdocks inappropriate and overly expensive for New York. Instead, his plan brought "into play all the extraordinary natural advantages of the port" while still affording "every facility for the cheap and rapid handling of vessels and their cargoes."[11]

To add weight to his own already impressive credentials, McClellan consulted with two formidable engineers: General Andrew Atkinson Humphreys, chief of the United States Army Corps of Engineers, who advised him on the placement of the riverwalls and pierhead lines; and General Quincy Adams Gillmore, also of the Corps of Engineers, who advised him on the design and materials of the bulkheads.

The department's first year was spent refining the master plan. In his first annual report, McClellan emphasized the intensive time and labor his office had devoted to the "thorough examination of almost every conceivable method of con-

2.20
PLAN FOR CONSTRUCTING A MAGNIFICENT FLOATING DOCK FROM MANHATTAN TO LAWRENCE POINT, QUEENS
Plan. Samuel B. Nowlan, designer. 1870. NYCMA.

structing the riverwall and the piers," adding that these studies enabled him to assert that "general sections have been reached, which give the best sectional area, together with the best disposition of material, that is compatible with a proper margin of stability for such an exceedingly important construction. . . . Estimates and investigations connected with some 130 different plans of piers have been made, and it is believed that no form of foundation and superstructure has escaped attention and examination"[12] (figs. 2.21, 2.22). After this year of exhaustive research, the department was at last ready to begin work on the actual plan.

Surveys and Mapping

Before any construction could begin, surveys were needed. Those would be conducted by the surveying-and-mapping section, a small but essential component of the department. From its inception, the section would concentrate on establishing accurate maps of the waterfront; providing baselines for the construction of the bulkhead and piers; and overseeing hydrographic research, the study of water conditions and behavior in the harbor. The section's ambition was to assure that "no injury should be done to the harbor, while increasing the commercial capacity of the waterfront to the utmost"[13] (fig. 2.23).

The first waterfront maps to be executed by the department's draftsmen were painstaking efforts based on earlier cartography by federal and local surveyors as well as on the department's own investigations. One of the most impressive of these achievements is a sixteen-foot map of upper Manhattan, compiled in part from United States Coast Survey maps that showed existing natural features as well as proposed piers and bulkhead.

In addition to large-scale maps, the section produced a series of smaller plats showing four- to five-block sections of the waterfront, as described by McClellan in the first annual report: "The new bulkhead and pierhead lines have been laid down on each map, together with a continuous belt of soundings, forty feet in width, on these lines, from Eleventh Street, North River, to Corlears Hook on the East River."[14] These highly detailed maps numbered six hundred and were in constant use, revised as buildings were constructed or demolished and as pier- and bulkhead-lines changed, and they continue to provide meticulous documentation of the waterfront's evolution (fig. 2.24).

The surveying section also conducted extensive preparation for the construction of the bulkhead. According to the third annual report, "Surveying parties have been engaged in completing the cordon of bench mark levels around the city and island for reference in establishing the datum lines for the construction of the pier and bulkhead at any point . . . [and] in executing the measurements of ordinates

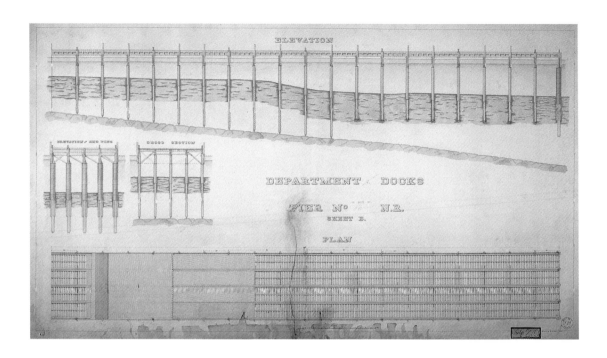

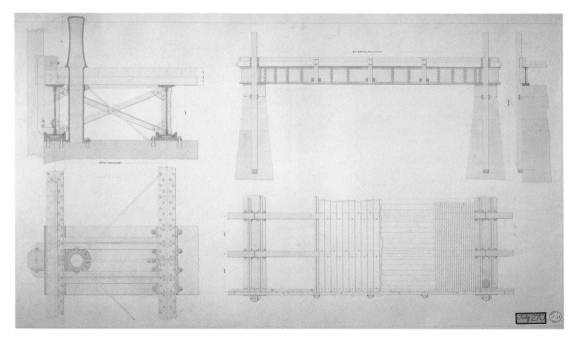

2.21 top
PIER 83, NORTH RIVER, MANHATTAN
Elevations, section, plan. Department of Docks. G. Soldan, draftsperson.
1871. NYCMA.

2.22
DESIGN FOR A PIER
Elevation, plan, details. Department of Docks. A. F. Voegelec, draftsperson.
1870. NYCMA.

2.23
MAP SHOWING HIGH- AND LOW-WATER MARKS AND ORIGINAL CITY GRANTS OF UNDERWATER LAND MADE TO VARIOUS PARTIES,
1686–1873, BATTERY TO 51ST STREET, HUDSON AND EAST RIVERS; ALSO PIER- AND BULKHEAD LINES ESTABLISHED 1750–1873
Plan. Department of Docks. General Charles K. Graham, engineer in chief; John Meehan, assistant engineer; David T. Keiller,
compiler and draftsperson. 1873. NYCMA.

which were required to determine the position of the new pier and bulkhead lines."[15] This type of work is usually not difficult, but the annual report discussed unique frustrations:

> As, step by step, the work of constructing the stone bulkhead advances, lines and levels are constantly requisite, and from the want of stability of any of the old wooden piers, or, in fact, of any wooden structure, the lines established have to be frequently checked. Owing to the crowded condition of the thoroughfares bordering the river, what otherwise would be a very simple matter, often became a very long, tiresome operation; so tedious that many of the principal lines, together with a survey of West Street, between Barrow and Canal Streets, have been accomplished entirely by Sunday work and the increased accuracy and rapidity obtained has justified the innovation.[16]

The department was so busy with these efforts that it had to call in "private parties . . . to make a number of minor surveys . . . in which the department maps were not sufficiently explicit."[17]

By 1878, the department had surveyed 13,700 feet of the waterfront on sections of the Hudson, East, and Harlem Rivers. The maps arising from these surveys were continuously updated to show existing structures and their positions relative to the bulkhead line. By 1884, the surveying force had expanded to twenty-three people, including the surveyor and assistant surveyor, levelers, rodmen, hydrographers, chainmen, sounders, boatmen, and inspectors of dumping dredged material.

The group's responsibilities included verifying baselines and bench marks in conjunction with the construction of the bulkhead and piers, and then giving lines and levels as work progressed (fig. 2.25). They measured and calculated quantities of materials for the bulkhead sections and established lines and levels for contract work on general repairs. They continually studied the waterfront, taking rod soundings to establish mud depths in the rivers and disk soundings to establish the water depths. They monitored the automatic tide gauges, and they supervised all dredging as well as the dumping of dredged material. They repeated such efforts when called for by special construction and dredging projects.

These duties swelled the survey division to forty-two employees in 1893, and seven topographical draftsman were added in 1899 to keep the prolific supply of maps flowing. By 1900, the surveying force had done extensive work in the Bronx, Queens, Brooklyn, and Staten Island. The annual report noted that 194 miles of waterfront in these boroughs had been surveyed, with baselines—the known length between two points, which allowed surveyors to establish other measurements—established for 41.6 miles and transit or secondary baselines for a 243-mile run. By 1908, the annual report announced the first stages of a "complete survey of the waterfront of the boroughs of Bronx, Brooklyn, Queens, and Richmond [Staten Island]."[18]

2.24
EAST RIVER, EAST 29TH STREET TO EAST 36TH STREET, MANHATTAN
Survey map. Department of Docks. Charles W. Staniford, surveyor.
Circa 1895. NYCMA.

By the 1920s, however, the survey section began to seek ways to maximize the waterfront's commercial potential. The section was given a new title in 1921, the Division of Surveys and Dredging. The division was no longer dedicated to averting injury to the harbor, but now provided its services solely to public and private dredging operations. Dredging could remove the silt that accumulated around piers or could radically alter the harbor environment by eliminating natural fea-

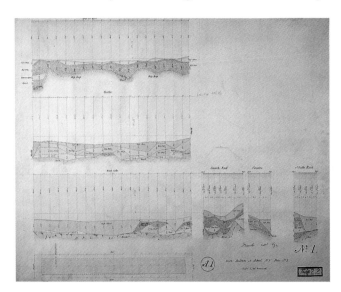

tures such as reefs or shoals. The new duties of the division during the 1920s included supervising repairs, construction, and dredging by private parties, as well as making rod and disk soundings in connection with dredging. The division continued, of course, to record the transformations of the waterfront; in 1922 alone, it

produced 1,064 surveys, which represented forty-five miles of coastline, and prepared 733 pages of field notes.

Hydrographic Survey

The recording and reconfiguration of New York Harbor's underwater topography and tides also fell under the jurisdiction of the survey section of the Department of Docks. It found that previous endeavors, especially the harbor commissioners' maps, adequately depicted the general hydrography of the harbor, at least in regard to overall soundings of water depths. But in order to get a better understanding of the harbor, the department had to contrive new instruments and initiate new kinds of investigation. The annual report of 1871, for instance, acclaims the "lines of soundings . . . on both the North and East Rivers" for their "great importance in studying the action of the tides."[19] The tides were further studied by thirteen newly established stations around the harbor that measured tidal levels. By 1900, the division had established twenty-one automatic tide gauges, and though that number would fall to fifteen by 1921, the gauges remained an important part of hydrographic research.

An even more critical hydrographic activity during the early years of the

2.25
RIVER BOTTOM AT ABUT 1, PIER 1, MANHATTAN
Plan, sections. J. Newton, assistant engineer. Circa 1880. NYCMA.

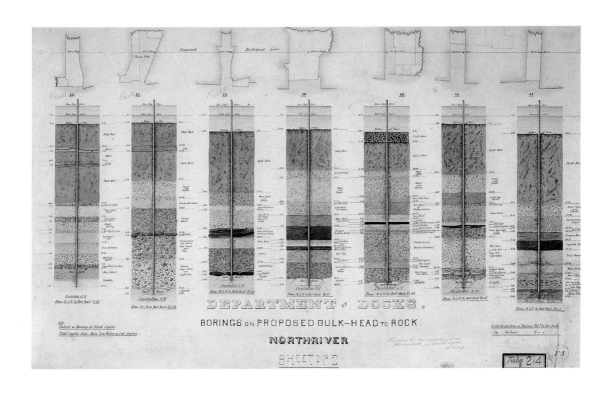

2.26
BORINGS OF PROPOSED BULKHEAD TO ROCK, NORTH RIVER, MANHATTAN
Sections. Department of Docks. S. W. Hoag Jr., assistant engineer. 1871–73.
NYCMA.

department was test boring, a procedure in which a tube was forced through the river bottom to draw up a cylindrical sample of the mud, sand, and rocks that formed the riverbed. McClellan viewed this work to be as important as any entrusted to his office. "Some six hundred borings," he wrote in the 1871 annual report, "have been executed, some with the hand rod, some with the machine called the 'Woodcock,' and the remainder with a regular artesian-well boring machine. These boring operations are laborious and expensive, but the data which are absolutely necessary before any work in the way of construction can be thought of, can only be obtained by these means"[20] (fig. 2.26).

By 1871, the hydrographic division had also established a dredging force equipped with "two Osgood dredges, two tugs, and six mud scows … they have been continuously employed in maintaining the requisite depth of water in old slips and in dredging to the proper depth alongside of new piers."[21] The department's overall approach to dredging during the initial years was conservative and kept close to shore, concerned primarily with maintaining the necessary depths for ships to approach the piers. The department did not dredge with the goal of radically reshaping the waterfront's underwater topography until the late 1880s, and then only on a limited basis. But with the gradual shift of the department's focus toward enhancing the city's commercial interests, dredging became both more intrusive and more extensive, reaching deeper and farther into the harbor. By the first decades of this century, dredging had spread throughout the harbor to include the widening of channels and the removal of reefs. The 1919 annual report listed several aggressive dredging projects:

> Widening 40-foot channel opposite anchorage grounds in Upper Bay. Removing Craven Shoal to depth of 30 feet. Deepening channel between Staten Island and Hoffman and Swinburne Islands to 16 feet, and 200 feet wide, extending from Belt Buoy 13A to Hoffman and Swinburne Islands a length of about 12,500 feet. The deepening of Red Hook Channel to 40 feet at mean low-water for its entire width of 1,200 feet. Maintenance of New York Harbor by removing any shoals which may obstruct the entrance channels.[22]

In Jamaica Bay, dredging that took place from 1913 to 1915 created a channel from Barren Island to Mill Basin that was 500 feet wide and 18 feet deep. By 1919, the entrance to the channel had been widened to 1,500 feet, extending 1,000 feet into the bay.

By the 1920s, the primary function of the division's hydrographic work was to open increasing areas of the waterfront to commerce. Operations like rod and disk sounding, once exclusive to research, were now enlisted in the service of dredging projects. While commerce always had a role in the department's plans, it now became its predominant concern, a one-dimensional emphasis that opened the way for overdevelopment of the waterfront and serious harm to the natural environment.

The Early Projects: Pier 1 and Pier A

Pier 1, located by Battery Park, was the newly established Department of Docks' first major project. Planning for the pier began during the summer of 1871 with actual construction commencing in 1872. While McClellan had decreed that the majority of piers would be constructed from wood, Pier 1 was to be "constructed of granite and concrete, the floor being sustained by arches resting on concrete supports. This pier will be permanent, obviating the inconvenience and expense of repairs"[23] (fig. 2.27).

Construction of the masonry pier was expensive and slow. As the sixth annual report explained, "[Over] eight months 124 feet were added to the length of the pier; five arches, with the subpiers upon which they rest, were completed, and two crib foundations laid . . . making the work accomplished during the season [before winter weather halted progress] equivalent to one-third the entire pier."[24] The pier was completed in 1877, three years later than expected, and even then its intended length had been cut back 50 feet for safer alignment with existing piers and to complete the project as soon as possible. This construction proved so costly that the department resolved not to build another pier of the same material. In the early 1970s, Pier 1 was submerged in the landfill of Battery Park City.

Plans for constructing the department's other significant project, Pier A, which still exists, date to 1884 (fig. 2.28). Designed by the engineer in chief, George Sears Greene Jr., the structure included a technically innovative fireproof building to house both the Department of Docks and the maritime division of the police department. This pier, 45 feet wide and 285 feet long, "springs from the corner of the bulkhead or riverwall south of New Pier 1, North River . . . [and] consists of 8 subpiers outside of the wall, supporting a deck, or floor, of iron girders with concrete arches between them."[25]

While the department initially projected completion of the pier for 1885, a contractor's late delivery of granite pushed the completion back to 1886. By 1900, the increased demand for office space forced by the incorporation of Greater New York necessitated the enlargement of the pier.

The Riverwalls

The main component of McClellan's 1871 plan to improve the New York City waterfront was the construction of a monumental and continuous masonry bulkhead. McClellan initially proposed that the wall extend twenty-eight and one-half miles from the Battery to 61st Street along the Hudson River, and from the Battery to

51st Street along the East River. He argued that this scheme would "provide ample wharf facilities for the present commerce of the city" which could be "further extended as ... increasing commerce requires accommodation."[26]

McClellan believed the department should focus on the downtown waterfront

below Grand Street on the east side and below 11th Street on the west side, where the majority of New York City's commerce was located. McClellan proposed a concrete, or *béton*, block bulkhead, with massive blocks to be formed in molds and manufactured in the open air at a special fabrication site (fig. 2.29). The blocks would vary in size according to each location's needs. After the blocks hardened, a floating derrick would lower them underwater to be placed on a bed of piles.

Construction began in the Battery. Because the department had not yet completed preparations to manufacture the béton blocks, it used granite for this portion of the wall. The wall was not built contiguously from the Battery up the Hudson; instead, separate sections were constructed at the same time, an approach necessitated by the riverbed's irregularities. Portions of the riverbed, particularly near Morton Street, had deposits of soft mud so deep that bedrock could not be located. The department had to survey this area and devise new systems of construction before it could begin building that portion of the bulkhead. Owners of waterfront property who refused the city's offer to purchase their land at any price further complicated the process with lengthy legal battles.

By 1874, there was evidently some dissatisfaction with the slow pace of the bulkhead-wall construction. The department had completed 84 feet of wall north of Pier 1 and the Christopher Street section was in an advanced stage of completion. McClellan's successor, engineer in chief Charles K. Graham, proposed a new system of construction that he believed would prove faster and more economical:

2.27
PIER 1, NORTH RIVER, MANHATTAN
Photographer unknown. Circa 1905. NYCMA.

using concrete en masse, a process in which concrete was poured into a wet caisson resting on a foundation of piles and then left to harden underwater into a solid mass. With this method, Graham estimated it would take two years to complete the

11,400 linear feet of bulkhead from the Battery to Hammond Street, but flaws in the Canal Street section, constructed under his supervision, led the department to abandon his approach.

The next engineer in chief, George Sears Greene Jr., appointed on July 16, 1875, recommended that an independent commission of respected engineers be appointed to investigate the design and construction of the built sections of the wall and, if necessary, recommend repairs and preferred methods of construction. The mayor appointed Generals John Newton and Quincy A. Gillmore of the United States Army, and William A. Worthen, a noted engineer. They con-

cluded that faulty workmanship, rather than Graham's system of construction, had caused the defects in the Canal Street segment. Graham, in prior reports, had hinted at his own dissatisfaction with the private contractors on whom he was forced to rely. In 1876, Greene reintroduced McClellan's block system with some slight modifications. These methods handsomely served the construction of almost all twenty miles of Manhattan's bulkhead. By 1880, the department was able to simultaneously recommence work on several sections of the wall from West 11th Street to the Battery (fig. 2.30).

In 1882, slight misalignments of the wall caused "some of our citizens, whose judgement command attention" once more to question its design, although, as the department pointed out, the recent construction was "substantially the same in every particular as that erected by the department during the past six years."[27] The department asked the same independent committee of engineers that had reviewed Graham's en masse construction —Newton, Gillmore, and Worthen—to examine the controversial wall. Their admiration for Greene's design was enthusiastically stated in their report:

2.28
BUILDING FOR PIER A, MANHATTAN
Elevations. Department of Docks. Circa 1884. NYCMA.

2.29
CONCRETE BULKHEAD CONSTRUCTION
Photographer and location unknown. Circa 1900. NYCMA.

This wall, taken as a whole, is the result of practical growth from the first inception of the work. It combines in a suitable measure the necessary elements of strength, endurance, and stability: it is ample in its dimensions, has a liberal factor of safety, is not difficult of construction, and appears thus far to have been well and faithfully built.[28]

The commission's words actually provide a very fair summary of the qualities

Greene's administration sought, and usually attained, in all of its work. In 1885, the city finally succeeded in acquiring several stretches of waterfront property between Chambers and Canal Streets, enabling the completion of a continuous bulkhead in that area.

McClellan had initially proposed that the East River be developed up to 51st Street, but work had only been approved to Grand Street. In 1883, the department

proposed to revise the plan to include the area above Grand to 34th Street in order to revive the "commercial interests of that portion of the city" and to provide "increased facilities and ample accommodations . . . to the regular steamboat lines and transportation companies running between this city and eastern ports, and as inducements to re-move [the burden] from the overcrowded piers on the North River."[29]

The department had regarded the area along the East River from 34th to 86th Streets as unsuitable for commercial piers because of the swiftness of the current, the narrow width of the channel, and the depth and rocky bottom of the river. In 1884, however, the department proposed to develop the waterfront above 86th Street along the East River to Third Avenue on the Harlem River by building a bulkhead, 125-foot-wide "marginal" street (a street demarcating the edge of town) and forty piers. The Sinking Fund withheld its approval of the East River development until 1889, though it approved the Harlem River plan in the year it was proposed (fig. 2.31). Despite such plans to develop the East and Harlem Rivers, most bulkhead-wall construction occurred on the Hudson River. By 1894, the department had

2.30
RIVERWALL UNDER CONSTRUCTION AT EAST 37TH STREET, MANHATTAN
Photographer unknown. Circa 1905. NYCMA.

completed a total of 2.9 miles of wall. An enlarged construction force accelerated progress, and the 1902 annual report was able to state that 30,454 linear feet of wall—almost 6 miles—had been completed.

Changing commercial- and land-use requirements created a constant demand for segments of the wall in new locations, a seemingly endless need for construction. In 1903, a proposal to develop the Claremont section, between West 129th and 134th Streets, anticipated "both the enlargement of the commercial facilities at this locality and also the building of an improved ferry terminal at the foot of Manhattan Avenue."[30]

The 1906 annual report predicted that "the improvement of the waterfront of Manhattan Island," begun in 1870, would "with the completion of plans now underway . . . be practically completed." The completion of the riverwall did not mean that Manhattan was fully encircled in masonry. Instead, the report stated, "Of the 39.90 miles of waterfront, 24.68 miles are owned by the city, 15.22 by private parties, 7.01 miles of the portion owned by the city are re-served for park purposes, 35,539.85 linear feet or 6.75 miles of bulkhead or riverwall have been constructed in Manhattan and 2,755 feet in Brooklyn or a trifle over one half mile."[31]

Subsequent annual reports reveal that the department continued constructing the riverwall beyond the date it had anticipated completion. By the 1920s, most of the work had shifted to the East River, although as segments of the Hudson River became available to the city, construction continued on that waterfront as well. The 1916 annual report summed up the department's massive achievement:

> The Department of Docks and Ferries has completed in all a total of 61,162 feet of bulkhead, including 8,887 linear feet of retaining structure at Rikers Island. There have been built by other city departments 31,940 linear feet of wall and by private parties 11,925 feet, making a total of 105,027 linear feet.[32]

The Department of Docks had achieved its original goal just as World War I and

2.31
EAST RIVER PIERS, MANHATTAN
Photographer unknown. 1903. NYCMA.

attendant federal involvement in the port brought municipal construction to a halt. Begun by veterans of the Civil War, the department's great project was completed in time to make New York City a principal port of embarkation for troops and equipment on their way to Europe.

The Chelsea Piers

The original plan for the Hudson River waterfront only proposed four piers between West 19th and 22nd Streets, with no piers between Perry and West 19th Streets. In 1880, Engineer in Chief George Greene submitted a new plan for the development of this southern area: widening West Street to 250 feet by removing the existing bulkhead wall, buildings, and existing piers; and constructing a new riverwall and twenty-one piers. Greene believed that this development would promote commerce and raise the department's revenues. His proposal also addressed the need to relieve the ship and cargo congestion below West 10th Street, as the existing piers would not be able to accommodate longer steamships.

Because Greene's plan for the new Chelsea development included changing the existing bulk- and pierhead lines, he needed approvals from the state assembly as well as the United States Department of War, which were not granted until 1889. Although piers would eventually be constructed between Perry and Little West 12th Streets, by 1889 Greene modified the scheme to reduce the number of piers to nine and focus on the area between Little West 12th and West 22nd Streets. In order to achieve the desired pier lengths, Greene innovatively excavated into Manhattan Island and placed the new bulkhead wall inshore from the previous one rather than

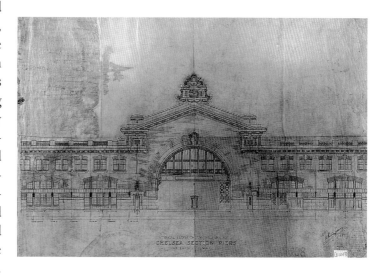

building the piers farther out into the river.

The department commenced building the Chelsea piers in 1902 and completed them in 1910. The piers were designed by the department's own engineers, with elevations by the architectural firm of Warren and Wetmore. The most modern structural and mechanical innovations

2.32
TYPICAL ELEVATION FOR PIERS 54 AND 56, CHELSEA SECTION
Warren and Wetmore, architects; G. M., draftsperson. 1907.
NYCMA.

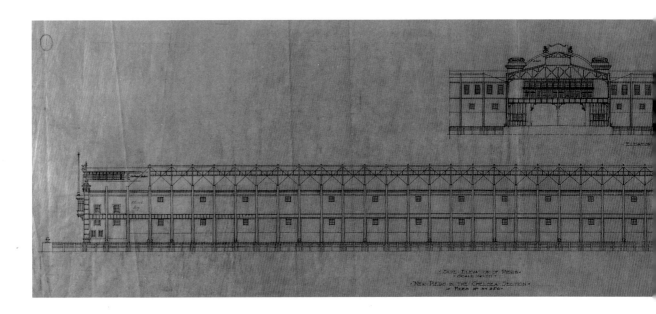

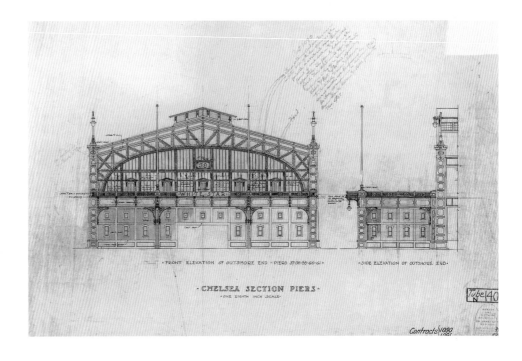

2.33 top
NEW PIERS IN THE CHELSEA SECTION, PIERS 54 AND 56
Side elevation of piers, elevation of bulkhead and section through piers.
Warren and Wetmore, architects; E. L., draftsperson; approved by
G. E. H. 1907. NYCMA.

2.34
CHELSEA SECTION PIERS 57, 58, 59, 60, 61
Elevation and section of outshore end. Warren and Wetmore, architects;
J. E. C. and G. M., draftspersons; approved by G. E. H. 1907. NYCMA.

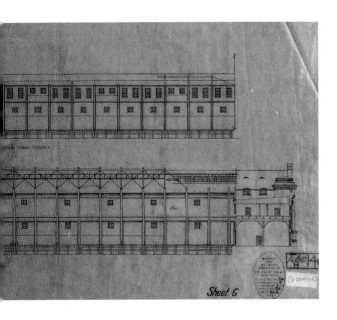

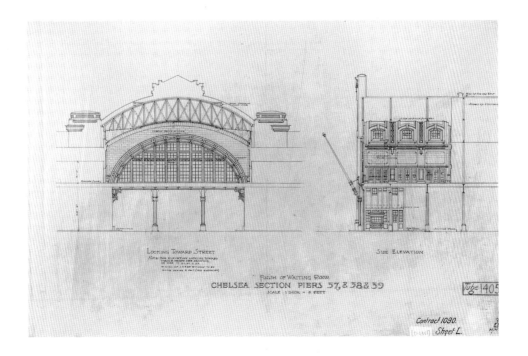

2.35
FINISH OF WAITING ROOM, CHELSEA SECTION PIERS 57, 58, 59
Interior elevations. Warren and Wetmore, architects. 1907.
NYCMA.

were combined with ornamental piershed facades, which the 1908 annual report called "more elaborate from an architectural point of view than any other built in the city of New York"[33] (figs. 2.32–2.35).

The Philosophy of the Department of Docks from 1873 to 1931

The 1873 resignation of McClellan, the department's inaugural engineer in chief, brought about a marked but short-lived shift in emphasis within the department. To replace McClellan, the board hired another Civil War general with a strong background in engineering, Charles K. Graham. Before the war, Graham had served as the construction engineer for the Brooklyn Navy Yard, from 1857 to 1861. He returned to New York City after the war and opened a private engineering practice with clients including the Beach Pneumatic Transit Company as well as the Board of Public Works and Commissioners of Public Parks, for which he oversaw surveys and improvements.

The annual reports from Graham's two-year tenure reveal a broader vision of planning and policy than waterfront engineering demanded. In the department's fourth annual report, Graham called attention to the plan's proposed widening of riverfront streets, evoking the themes of urban amenity that had been prominent in the department's founding arguments. Not only could West Street be "made the

most commodious thoroughfare in the city," Graham maintained, but there would remain enough space at the bulkhead line "for the construction of a viaduct railway for freight and passenger quick transit, combined with a system of warehouses . . . connecting not only with the dock and piers but with the entire system of railway lines converging to this port."[34]

Nor did Graham shy away from addressing controversial issues of public policy. During and after his tenure, the department was engaged in a series of legal battles with owners of waterfront property who did not want to sell their land. In 1874, Graham bluntly complained that the "existence of individual rights [has] stood in the way of the general good" while keeping up hope for a "system of mutual adjustments and cooperation."[35]

He was even more scathing in the fifth annual report. Graham believed that 1873 revisions to the city charter canceling the department's power to change the maximum length that piers and bulkheads could extend into the river would result in the suspension of all master plan Harlem River development.[36] While in a polemical mood, he also took the opportunity to castigate the New Jersey state legislature for failing to adopt the same pier lines along the Hudson River as those defined by the New York legislature, and questioned whether New Jersey had given any thought to "maintaining the capacity of the Hudson River as a tidal reservoir, and thereby keeping the channels at Sandy Hook the same, or whether the more narrow policy of looking after local interest merely prevailed."[37]

The controversy generated by the slow progress of waterfront improvements and Graham's introduction of the béton en masse technique of riverwall construction resulted in severe criticism from the press and the mayor. On June 9, 1875, Graham resigned. Whether his decision was due to the changes in the Department of Docks or the controversy over bulkhead construction is unknown. Despite his stormy tenure as engineer in chief, however, Graham continued to be a major figure in the development of New York Harbor, serving as surveyor of the port from 1878 to 1883 and as naval officer of the port from 1883 to 1885.

George Sears Greene Jr., the department's third engineer in chief, was appointed at the recommendation of a board of citizens. Greene was decidedly different from his predecessors: he was not a Civil War hero; at thirty-eight, he was relatively young; and he was not, according to the *New York Times,* an active politician.[38] He did, however, arrive at the department with a firmly established reputation as an engineer. He had studied at Harvard but did not graduate and eventually apprenticed himself to his father, working on the Croton Aqueduct, various railroads in Cuba, and mines near Lake Superior. He won a reputation as a skillful surveyor, improving the design of existing instruments and inventing new ones that would become industry standards, during his surveys of portions of Westchester County and Long Island. Greene would serve as engineer in chief at the Department of Docks for twenty-two years. While department literature frequently credits McClellan as the guiding spirit of its plans and ethos, Greene was actually more responsible for developing and implementing these plans and for articulating the department's philosophy.

Further, Greene introduced many technical advances and enhanced the department's reputation among harbor and waterfront engineers. He invented a method for constructing piles in mud conditions where bedrock could not be reached that was based on the principle of "skin resistance," the friction caused by the movement of a pile through underwater soil, and was renowned for his use of cement in underwater construction. Carleton Greene's textbook on waterfront construction liberally acknowledges that, under Greene and his predecessors, the Department of Docks had become the leading authority on the science of waterfront construction.

Greene had initially supported outside contracting for waterfront work, but by 1881 the department had started to assemble a construction force of its own. In 1885, it directly hired large numbers of laborers and dock builders, placing the execution of the master plan firmly within the department's purview. The number of department employees swelled during the 1890s and early 1900s, fluctuating between six hundred and twelve hundred.

Greene retired in 1897, but his next two successors, John A. Bensel and Charles Staniford, had both worked in the department under Greene's administration and shared his commitment to technical innovation and to maximizing the harbor's commercial potential. Like Greene, both had extensive experience in surveying. Bensel had graduated from New Jersey's Stevens Institute of Technology, and subsequently worked as a rodman for the New York Aqueduct and the Pennsylvania Railroad, where he was promoted to assistant engineer on construction projects. At the Department of Docks, Bensel had been put in charge of construction on the North River, a main focus of departmental activities from 1889 to 1895. Rising through the ranks, Bensel served as engineer in chief from 1898 to 1905 and then as commissioner of the department until 1907. Bensel's appointment as commissioner in 1906 was accompanied by the elimination of two other commissioner positions, making him the sole head of the department.

The 1898 consolidation of Greater New York brought two significant new responsibilities to the department: the municipal ferries and their terminals, and the recreational piers. But these additional charges did not affect the workload of the engineering staff, as most of the design and construction for these structures was contracted to private firms, with the department retaining powers of review and approval.

By 1910, a new approach to the waterfront was emerging. Commissioner Calvin Tomkins wanted to replace individual docks with larger "terminals" for rail and marine use based on the success of the recently completed tunnel under the Hudson River to the Pennsylvania Railroad Station in New York City. Tomkins championed a national rather than regional conception of the port. He believed that the construction of modern locks in the Erie Canal, the opening of the Panama Canal, and the proposed intercoastal canal connecting Baltimore to Fall River and Boston, Massachusetts, through New York Harbor would swell the volume of commerce flowing through New York City, creating the need for expansive, modern port facilities.

The 1912 annual report announced that the engineering staff had created detailed plans for an elevated distribution railroad between Cortlandt Street and the West 60th Street rail yards, and in 1915 the department reported that the staff had created two large-scale terminal plans. Most of these ambitious projects intending to modernize the port were not built, and the city began reducing the size and jurisdiction of the department. In 1918, the department transferred some of its major responsibilities to other agencies: the ferry bureau was transferred to the Department of Plants and Structures, while the responsibility for the care and maintenance of marginal streets was given to the presidents of the respective boroughs.

After World War I, the department again began to press for the modernization of port facilities. The 1919 annual report recommended zoning the waterfront for new piers with a coherent design policy that would include marginal streets with concrete-and-steel warehouses of five to six stories as well as a waterfront promenade connecting Battery and Riverside Parks. That year, after the retirement of Engineer in Chief Charles Staniford, the gap between the McClellan-Greene vision of the port and that of the current administration grew wider. Staniford was replaced by Traugott F. Keller, a West Point graduate who had worked in the department for more than sixteen years.

By 1920, the department had begun to plan and implement significant new projects, including a new ferry terminal in Stapleton on Staten Island that was designed with track connections to piers and warehouses. The department became increasingly receptive to the idea of culti-

vating the outer boroughs' waterfronts, ultimately proposing an extensive development of Flushing Bay, Queens, which would include the construction of a 12,000-foot quay wall with a platform for railroad tracks and revolving cranes. In the forty-ninth annual report, the commissioner also mentioned Jamaica Bay and Staten Island as potential sites for similar development. The waterfront would require more than modern facilities: not only did the department call for a "new plan for longer, wider piers with wider intervening slips . . . rail facilities and supporting warehouses . . . proper mechanical appliances and labor-aiding devices,"[39] but it also emphasized the need to substitute impeding legal mechanisms in the city charter with modern provisions more amenable to modern visions (fig. 2.36).

The vision of modernization and waterfront development in the outer boroughs continued to dominate the department's planning for the next decade, and though several projects to develop portions of the waterfronts in Brooklyn, Queens, and Staten Island were implemented, most of its other plans remained unbuilt. Concurrently, the department began to turn over large tracts of the waterfront to other agencies for noncommercial use. The huge scale of the transatlantic piers between 48th and 56th Streets had by now left large portions of the Hudson River waterfront inaccessible to trade. In 1924, the Department of Docks facilitated the enlargement of Riverside Park by constructing a seawall, foreshadowing the Department of Parks' domination of the waterfront during Robert Moses' twenty-six years as commissioner. By 1931, Department of Docks commissioner John McKenzie noted that much of the Manhattan waterfront had been taken out of commercial availability:

> In connection with the reconstruction of Riverside Park and the West Side Improvement Plan, the Department of Docks surrendered to the Department of Parks two piers at West 79th Street, and four piers at West 96th Street. New hospitals and apartment houses have accounted for much of the upper East River waterfront; and the intensive activities of the docks department itself along the North River will drive much traffic to seek accommodations elsewhere. It therefore seems desirable that surveys and studies be made of the east shore of the Bronx and Flushing Bay.[40]

Coming to the end of two decades of ambitious planning, the department had certainly created vast changes in New York Harbor, but by the early 1930s it had implemented only a small portion of its scheme to develop a citywide system of shipping terminals linked to warehouses

with rail connections. Increasingly, the waterfront was being turned over to real-estate interests and recreational uses (fig. 2.37). While the city and the department continued to plan for commercial development through the 1960s, by 1931 the era of traffic-clogged streets piled high

with freight had ended, and bold, resourceful innovations—once the hallmark of the Department of Docks—were relegated to history (fig. 2.38).

Aftermath: The Dissolution of the Department

In 1921, a compact between New Jersey and New York created the bi-state agency known as the Port of New York Authority. Initially a planning agency with no administrative powers over physical facilities, the Port Authority was established to ease

2.36
PROPOSED INITIAL PIER DEVELOPMENT, JAMAICA BAY
Department of Docks. 1919.
City of New York.

friction between the states over the port and to improve regional transportation. In 1925, the agency was authorized to build bridges and take over the construction of the Holland Tunnel. At first, this potential rival posed no threat to the Department of Docks; in fact, the department would

shortly expand its own jurisdiction over the port, assuming responsibility for city airports in 1929 and resuming control of city ferries in 1938.

The department changed its name to the Department of Marine and Aviation in 1942 to reflect these new responsibilities. The heavy use of port facilities during World War II revealed the obsolescence of the waterfront's physical structures

as well as the city's weakened financial and administrative abilities to care for its port properties. By the late 1940s, the Port Authority began to appropriate the department's powers.

In 1946, New York City mayor William O'Dwyer transferred the administration of city airports from the Department of Docks to the Port Authority, and in 1948 he proposed the Port Authority take charge of most New York City waterfront properties. This idea was rejected, and the city continued to resist attempts to transfer waterfront jurisdiction to the Port Authority for the next two decades.

Despite some successful construction projects, numerous waterfront plans, and a name change in 1969 to the Department of Ports and Terminals, it was clear that the department lacked the vision and resources to manage the waterfront. By the 1970s, the Port Authority generated and administered most major pier and terminal construction projects, although the Department of Ports and Terminals reviewed all plans for waterfront construction. The department again changed its name, to the Department of Ports, International Trade and Commerce in 1986, with the mission of stimulating development of the port, promoting the city as a commercial center, collecting rent for waterfront properties, and reviewing all plans for new construction.

In 1989, the department's name was again modified, to the Department of

2.37
PROPOSED DEVELOPMENT OF RED HOOK SHOAL
Department of Docks. 1920.
City of New York.

Ports and Trade. The decline in shipping on New York City's commercial waterfront and the increasing irrelevance of the department in the development and implementation of waterfront plans made it superfluous to a city government looking for ways to cut costs and reduce bureaucracy, and the department was quietly dissolved in 1991. Some of its promotional functions were transferred to the Department of Business Services, while its remaining waterfront duties were assigned to the Port Authority. The closing of the department, after 120 years of existence, was not even reported in the *New York Times*.

Despite its eventual closing and its lack of a visible physical legacy, the Department of Docks shaped the New York City waterfront in ways that still effect the contemporary environment. The ability to conceive and implement a long-term plan is frequently ascribed to individual vision and will. Yet, the Department of Docks offers an alternative model, that of a series of individuals implementing a plan over several decades.

The commitment to the plan was due to its promotion of the waterfront's commercial potential. The quantity of stereographs and postcards depicting New York City's cargo-laden piers and waterfront streets suggests that the public shared this belief in maximizing the economic viability of this area. When commercial shipping in Manhattan collapsed, the plan was doomed to fail.

NOTES

1. "Our Wharves and Piers," *New York Times,* 22 April 1870.
2. DOD, 30 April 1872, pp. 47–49.
3. DOD, 31 December 1919, p. 35.
4. "Our City Wharves," *New York Times,* 2 June 1870.
5. "Our Wharves and Piers," *New York Times,* 22 April 1870.
6. Ibid.
7. DOD, 31 December 1919, p. 5.
8. DOD, 30 April 1871, pp. 10–11.
9. "Our City Wharves."
10. DOD, 30 April 1871, p. 13.
11. Ibid., p. 36.
12. Ibid., pp. 48–9.
13. Ibid., p. 47.
14. Ibid., p. 48.
15. DOD, 30 April 1876, pp. 101–2.
16. Ibid., p. 59.
17. Ibid., p. 60.
18. DOD, 31 December 1908, p. 257.
19. DOD, 30 April 1871, p. 48.
20. DOD, 30 April 1872, p. 48.
21. Ibid., p. 59.
22. DOD, 31 December 1919, p. 40.
23. DOD, 30 April 1873, p. 100.
24. DOD, 30 April 1876, p. 47.
25. DOD, 30 April 1885, pp. 111–12.
26. DOD, 30 April 1871, p. 14.
27. DOD, 30 April 1882, p. 13.
28. Ibid., p. 42.
29. DOD, 30 April 1883, p. 16.
30. DOD, 31 December 1903, p. 184.
31. DOD, 31 December 1906, pp. 3, 5.
32. DOD, 31 December 1916, p. 11.
33. DOD, 31 December 1908, p. 244.
34. DOD, 30 April 1874, p. 34.
35. Ibid., pp. 33–34.
36. DOD, 30 April 1875, p. 70.
37. Ibid., p. 74.
38. "The New Engineer in Chief of the Dock Department," *New York Times,* 17 July 1875.
39. DOD, 31 December 1920, p. 3.
40. DOD, 31 December 1931, p. 12.

2.38
LOWER MANHATTAN
Photographer unknown. Circa 1920. NYCMA.

VERSA BOOM, 14TH STREET, NORTH RIVER, MANHATTAN
Photographer unknown. Circa 1910. NYCMA.

3

3.1
LOWER NEW YORK SHOWING EAST RIVER AND BROOKLYN BRIDGE
J. S. Johnston, photographer. 1894. NYHS.

HORIZONTAL CITY
Architecture and Construction in the Port of New York

Kevin Bone

With its vast system of rivers, streams, and marshlands, the great harbor of New York has been the foundation of economic and social life in the region since the arrival of the first European traders in the early seventeenth century (fig. 3.1). In the 350 years since Dutch settlers initiated small, local modifications to the New Amsterdam waterfront of lower Manhattan, the maritime and transportation industries have evolved rapidly (fig. 3.2). During the nineteenth century, New Yorkers subjected their land- and seascape to radical alteration, creating an evolving infrastructure of docks, earthworks, and support facilities. By the mid-nineteenth century, the city was maintaining civil engineering commitments on a mammoth scale and supporting them with research into new design and construction techniques (fig. 3.3). The sheer quantity and pace of building, combined with advancing technologies, created a resourceful building culture unique to New York Harbor.

The initial challenge that would dominate municipal planning for a full century was clear: to construct deep-water anchorages adequate to the needs of the expanding seagoing cargo and passenger transport industries. The construction frenzy that transformed New York City from harbor town to maritime metropolis began as the Industrial Revolution was propagating new ways to realize large structures, and New York Harbor served as a laboratory for emerging methods and materials (figs. 3.4–3.8). Until the mid-nineteenth century, many maritime building methods had not

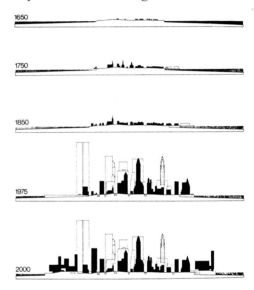

changed significantly since antiquity. Techniques first described by the Roman architect and engineer Marcus Vitruvius in the first century B.C.E. were still employed for constructing seawalls. But by the 1880s, with the development of lightweight, long-span steel structures— products of the modern industrial revolution in building—rapid and profound changes in technology and design occurred

3.2
WALL STREET DEVELOPMENT FROM 1650 TO THE YEAR 2000
Mayor's Office of Lower Manhattan Development, Department of City Planning, Battery Park City Authority. Wallace, McHarg, Roberts and Todd; Whittlesey, Conklin and Rossant; Alan M. Voorhees and Associates. 1966–73.

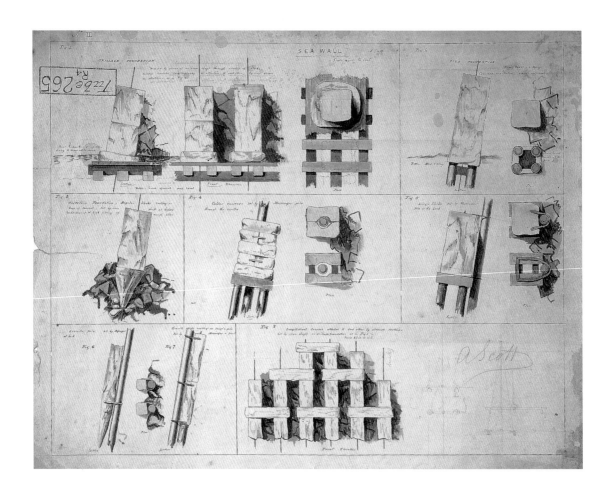

3.3
SEAWALL
Details. Andrew Scott, draftsman. Circa 1870. NYCMA.

3.4
MACHINE FOR LOADING COAL
Photographer and location unknown. Circa 1910. NYCMA.

3.5–3.8
MACHINES FOR LOADING, HOISTING, AND LATERAL MOVEMENT OF MATERIALS
Photographers and locations unknown. Circa 1910. NYCMA.

in every area of nautical architecture and waterfront construction. Without these advances the great transformation of New York Harbor would have been unimaginable. Yet the New York waterfront never became a monument to innovation for its own sake, and some of the most far-reaching decisions concerning its reconstruction were accomplished with proven techniques and materials.

The First Constructions

Through the eighteenth century and the American Revolution, early European settlers and traders used the protected deep waters of the lower East River and the lower North River (the Hudson) for anchorage. They moored their ships away from shore and shuttled goods and crew to land in smaller craft such as scows, rowboats, and canoes. In the 1630s, within ten years of establishing the first settlements on Manhattan Island, the Dutch began to erect small platforms and seawalls. In 1647, the year Peter Stuyvesant arrived and began his tenure as New Amsterdam's director, a dock was built at Schreyers Point (now Pearl and Broad Streets). Although its method of construction is not recorded, the dock was probably a simple wooden platform extending into the water from the timber sheet-pile retaining structures that were installed piecemeal along a short stretch of the lower East River. This structure was referred to as the Little Dock.

In 1654, the stabilized bank of the East River, known then as the Waal, was severely undermined by erosion, endangering the structure of City Hall, and the need for stable shore conditions was acknowledged as a civic necessity. The burgomasters, or civic leaders, called for proper protection of the area with further sheet piles. In the early-nineteenth-century *Iconography of Manhattan Island: 1498–1909*, I. N. Phelps Stokes described the solution:

> Sibout Claessen, on November 9, 1654, petitioned the city court for relief from intolerable conditions along the shore of the East River (now Pearl Street), and the court ordered his immediate neighbors to plank up their waterfront with sheet-piling … so that further loss be prevented by the high water. The city now requires the residents along the East River to line the bank with boards, in compliance with the earlier order, or the work will be done by the city at their expense.[1]

The burgomasters soon recognized the need for ordinances and basic codes to establish uniform guidelines for construction quality in civic structures. In 1657, for example, a citizen of New Amsterdam petitioned the city for permission to construct a *beschoeing*, or sheet-pile embankment of stone, at the water's edge along his lot on the East River. His neighbors had sheeted with timber pursuant to 1654 and 1656 orders, and the request to employ a less seaworthy method resulted in instructions to employ timber according to the general edict.

To create wooden sheet-pile seawalls, construction logs were driven side by side into the mud river- or sea-floor and anchored together with heavy horizontal wood planking secured to the outboard face of the piles. These fenders were attached with long wooden spikes called "treenails," and were filled in from behind with rubbish, cinder, and earth. This technique of shoreline control allowed the Dutch to extend the edge of the island farther into the rivers.

Sheet piles were made of local timbers harvested from virgin forests, which contained ample stock and variety to accommodate the region's building needs. Logs of dense, strong woods such as American white oak were first debarked to discourage decay and reduce skin friction, then sharpened into a driving point at one end, and shaped at the head to fit the pile cap. These fitted logs were driven into the mud floor with a heavy drop-hammer made of log or stone; the hammer of the driver was hoisted twenty feet up within a wood-frame gantry and then dropped upon the head of the pile. The frameworks and rigging for these primitive driving devices were made by local shipwrights skilled in heavy timber construction and the mechanics of lifting using rope, block, and tackle. The actual work of hammer hoisting and pile driving was done manually or with animal power, a slow and laborious task.

Though additional sheet piling was added along the East River, no real port construction would succeed Stuyvesant's dock for ten years, when, in 1659, the first pier of substance was opened. Measuring approximately twenty by one hundred feet, the wooden pile-and-plank platform structure stood at the base of Moore Street near Pearl. Known as the Wijnbruch, or Winebridge, it was extended in 1660. By 1661, an ordinance setting fees for its use had been established.

Early Stone and Earthworks

In order to facilitate port activities, fundamental transformations to the natural harbor would be realized by dredging channels into shallow waters, mud flats, and oyster reefs. In 1664, a group of citizens sought to cut a channel along the shore of Red Hook to allow more direct access to the mills of Gowanus. Prior to this connection, ships had to pass beyond the west end of the Bay Ridge Flats tidal marshlands and turn up a natural channel to the Gowanus Bay. The course of the new built channel would slice directly across Bay Ridge Flats at the tip of Red Hook. Dredging was done from floating derricks using heavy timber standing-rigs and block-and-tackle-assisted shovels. The water depths achieved using these techniques probably did not exceed ten feet.

In the early winter of 1676, the mayor and aldermen began discussing plans for the construction of the town's first stone dock. A basin was laid out around the existing Coenties Slip and the dock was in service by November of that year. Its structure, composed of two stone embankments that projected into the East River, was a combination of riprap (loose stone) girded with wooden sheet piling to keep the stone in position and provide a vertical face for the dock. One thousand loads of riprap, each containing approximately one hundred cubic feet of stone, were placed in the East River. The work was done by local residents who were divided, military fashion, into companies. As described in a document of April 15, 1676, craftsmen were critical to the dock's construction:

> The carpenters report to the provincial council concerning the frame of timber, or mole necessary to be erected in the Harbor . . . this report states in part [that] Adolph, the carpenter, and a great many of them being present . . . do unanimously agree and give their opinion that the groundsills beneath and plates above will be most proper.
>
> That at each end of a groundsill one beam to go athwart; that every ten feet a stud and a beam will be necessary, the beams to be laid at ordinary highwater mark and every other beam to be underbraced. To be filled with wood and stone, the wood all undermost and the stone uppermost.[2]

Called the Great Dock, this construction was monumental by the standards of the time. As a protected basin it served as the city's primary dockage until 1750 (fig. 3.9), and would be enlarged and modified several times.

The central-planning process that created the Great Dock stimulated associated projects on adjoining lands. The section of riverwall and marginal street between the Winebridge and the Great Dock was rebuilt using stone and wood, and property owners in the district were expected to conform to the town's requirements as described in an edict of December 5, 1691:

> The common council orders that buyers of land between the bridge and the dock (between the present Moore Street and Whitehall Slip), who are obliged to make the street (the present Water Street) under the direction of the surveyors, shall do so in the following manner: They shall build a good and substantial stone wall, three-and-a-half-foot broad at the bottom "to batter one foot inward on the outside." They shall protect it from the rubbing of boats by driving spoiles or stockadoes every five feet, and these shall be seven inches in diameter, bound together at the top plate. When finished this wall shall be kept in good repair by the owners of the lots fronting the street or wharf, who, nevertheless, are not to claim any property or interest in the street or wharf, which, instead, is to remain to the use of the city. The owners of this land, to fill up their respective lots, are obliged to use the dock mud twenty feet into the dock before their own houses.[3]

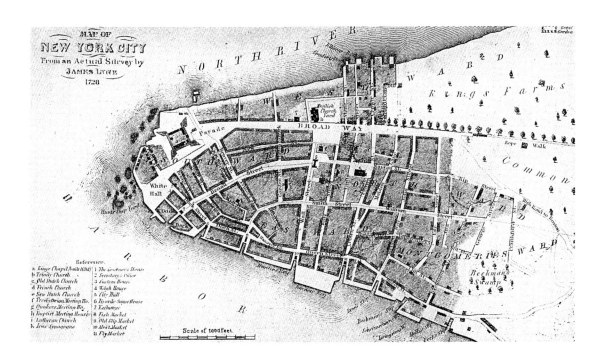

3.9
NEW YORK CITY AND NEW YORK HARBOR BEFORE THE AMERICAN REVOLUTION
The Great Dock is at the foot of Broad Street, adjacent to Whitehall.
Survey map. James Lyne, cartographer. 1728.
From John William Leonard, *History of the City of New York 1609–1909*, 1910.

Ongoing dredging was also required to remove the silt that would accumulate in the still waters of the basins. In 1720, the Great Dock basin required centralized dredging, and sixty scow-loads of mud were removed; that mud was used for filling lowlands.

The forces of nature constantly destroyed the frail handmade structures of prerevolutionary times. Subsequent rebuilding efforts assisted the advancement of construction methods and also offered the opportunity to expand dockage to accommodate larger ships and expanding waterfront activities. In particular, the great storm of July 29, 1723, demolished most of the city's dock facilities and vessels, and the consequent high tides destroyed many onshore structures. Much of the Great Dock was washed away. The task of reconstruction on this critical facility began immediately.

Ordinances were passed in 1727 that allowed the East River piers to project as much as two hundred feet from the seawall into the East River, and in 1730, a timber pierhead measuring forty feet long by twenty feet wide by twelve feet high was added to the rebuilt Great Dock. Larger ships and increased activity required more docking space, so in 1731 additions were made to extend the dock one hundred feet further into the East River.

Other significant maritime structures of colonial Manhattan included the Albany Pier—most likely a timber structure —built on the west side of Coenties Slip in 1750, and the Corporation Dock, a stone assembly built in the North River near the original Castle Clinton between 1771 and 1775.

All these early piers and walls employed, in various combinations, a few basic building methods: piles, plank platforms, timber sheet piling, and stone embankments. Both the Great Dock and the Corporation Dock consisted of solid, filled embankments with some timber appurtenances. These methods did not require sophisticated equipment or tools and could be built exclusively from local materials by small groups of reasonably skilled workers. The American Revolution, however, stopped all construction and maintenance of harbor structures, and by the war's end, the maritime needs of the new nation were putting heavy demands on its battered port facilities.

Cribworks

After the American Revolution, the construction of piers and wharves accelerated, and the first of several major construction booms began. Solid, filled pier bases and breakwaters were used in the Brooklyn constructions at Atlantic Basin, Erie Basin, and the Gowanus Bay. Two events dramatically increased shipping traffic and the need for piers and wharves: steamships arrived in New York Harbor in 1807, and the Erie Canal went into service in 1825. By 1853, there were 112 piers on the Harbor; 57 of them were in the East River and 55 were in the North River, some of them extending six hundred feet.

Early in this building boom came the implementation of cribworks, giant wood-frame boxlike receptacles that, when filled with loose stone, sink to the river-

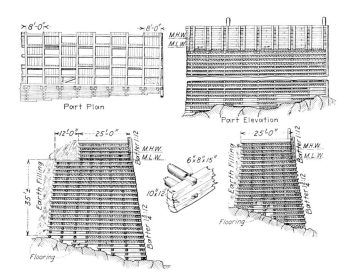

bottom and provide a base for maritime constructions (fig. 3.10). This subaqueous foundation technique permitted the construction of larger, sturdier docks where pile-supported piers and retaining walls could not be built, such as areas with hard beds in which driving piles would be impossible. They offered further stability against swift currents and impact with vessels and ice floes. Crib construction required large, coordinated labor forces as

well as sizable derricks and rigs. By 1800, the population of the city was such that workers were plentiful, and the community had the economic power and will to fund larger equipment (fig. 3.11).

In their most primitive form, cribs consist of logs that are notched or halved with axes and then dovetailed and fitted together with treenails, wrought-iron spikes, or bolts to form compartmentalized wooden boxes. Crib walls constructed from undressed timbers tended to rack and distort, so more durable and stable cribworks were made by using sawed timbers with accurately fitted joints (fig. 3.12). The harbor floor where the crib was to be situated would be dredged, clearing mud and loose debris to the bedrock or hardpan substratum. The resulting depths were then measured by divers or with rods or weighted ropes to establish plot points for a gridded topographical profile so that the crib bottom could be laid out to conform to the shape of the harbor floor. Constructed on scows anchored over the crib site, the boxlike assemblies incorporated several cells or compartments with solid floors and partially open side walls of interlocking planks. This timber frame was then filled with stones, each as large

3.10
CRIB WALL OF ROUND LOGS, MANHATTAN
From Carleton Greene, *Wharves and Piers*, 1917.

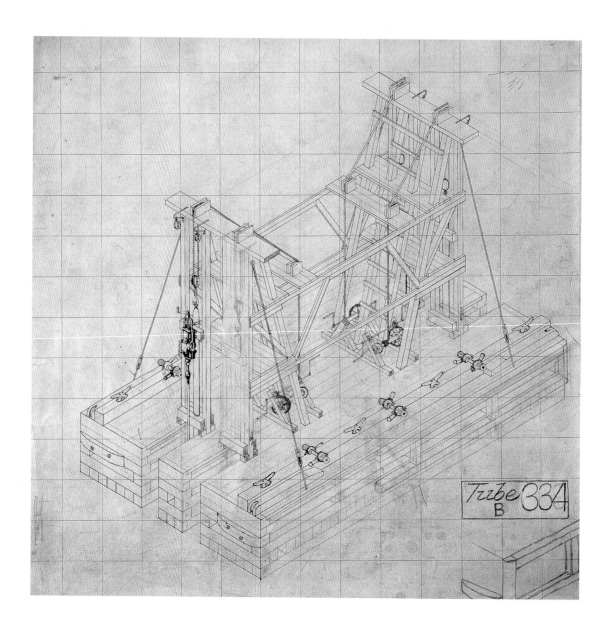

3.11
DRILLING MACHINE USED IN SUBMARINE EXCAVATION OF ROCK
Isometric. Designer unknown. Circa 1893. NYCMA.

as could be handled by one man, and their accumulating weight would sink the structure. The level of the crib was carefully monitored and the weight of each cell constantly adjusted to keep the assembly true. Stiffness and stability was increased by filling some or all of the pockets with concrete (fig 3.13). To prevent slippage on steeply sloping sites, divers would pin the crib to the bottom with large iron dowels

set into holes drilled in the substratum. After the structure was secured into position, construction would continue above the water.

Despite this significant advance in dock building, the massive and stable cribworks shared the fundamental problem of all wood-based marine constructions: wooden elements not constantly submerged were subject to decay and required major

reconstruction above the low-water mark every ten to fifteen years (figs. 3.14, 3.15).

Block and Bridge Piers

During the past summer it was decided by the Board of Commissioners that the new Pier 1, the commencement of the new system on the North River, should be constructed of granite and concrete, the floor being sustained by arches resting on concrete supports. This pier will be permanent, obviating the inconvenience and expense of repairs.

—DEPARTMENT OF DOCKS, 1873

The vast majority of pier constructions before the Civil War had been timber platforms on wood piles or, in some cases, on embankments of stone-filled cribworks. Prone to decay and fire, the New York piers and their sheds fell periodically into serious disrepair, and many citizens regarded the waterfront environment as squalid, disgraceful, and unsuitable for the international port and destination New York City was becoming. By 1870, New Yorkers were developing a distinctly cosmopolitan attitude, and thanks in great part to the technological innovations of the period, it was no longer an imaginative indulgence to envision the kind of public works that would put New York City on a par with the great European centers.

In this climate of idealism, the new Department of Docks wanted the first

3.12
CRIB WALL OF SAWED LUMBER WITH UPPER PORTION OF CONCRETE, BARGE CANAL TERMINAL, OSWEGO, NEW YORK
From Carleton Greene, *Wharves and Piers*, 1917.

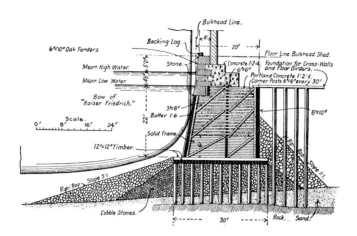

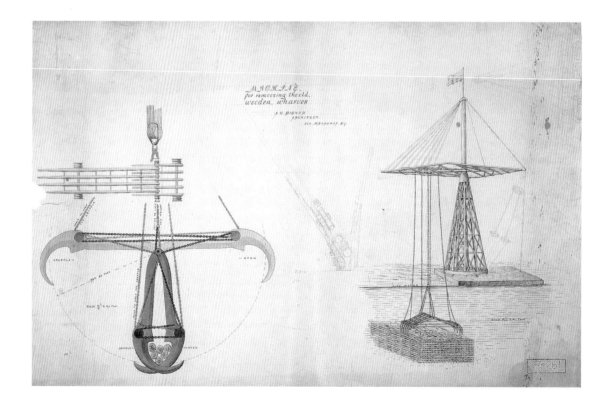

3.13 top
CRIB WALL WITH CONCRETE FILLING, NORTH GERMAN LLOYD CO.,
HOBOKEN, NEW JERSEY
Section. From Carleton Greene, *Wharves and Piers*, 1917.

3.14
MACHINE FOR REMOVING THE OLD WOODEN WHARVES
Detail, perspective. A. D. Bishop, architect. Circa 1880.
NYCMA.

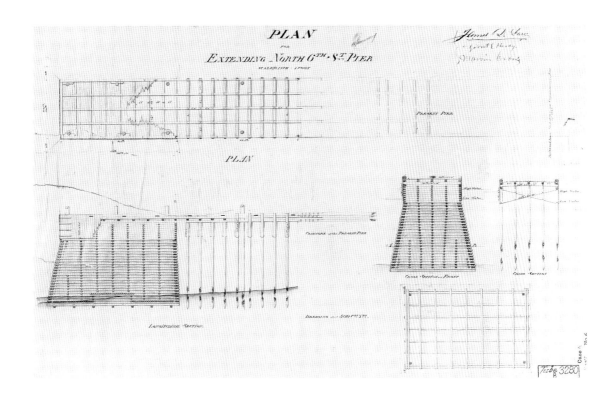

3.15
PLAN FOR EXTENDING NORTH 6TH STREET PIER, MANHATTAN
Plans, sections. Brooklyn Department of City Works. Circa 1890.
NYCMA.

piers built under its jurisdiction to be permanent symbols of New York's commitment to the finest port facilities. To fulfill this vision, the department designed and executed the only two masonry block-and-bridge piers in New York Harbor. Both located on the western margin of the Battery, Pier 1 and its sister structure, Pier A, were monumental structures, masonry bridges resting on stone-and-concrete blocking atop concrete beds. Begun in 1872 and completed in 1875, Pier 1 was 450 feet long by 80 feet wide and was formed of eighteen semicircular stone arches bearing on concrete cross-walls (figs. 3.16, 3.17). The cross-walls were assembled from large concrete units that were precast in the open air, floated into position, and set by derricks and divers. These blocks rested upon a concrete foundation that had been cast in place, fully submerged, in wooden forms lowered with weights to the river's bottom. This method had been primarily devised by General George Brinton McClellan, the first engineer in chief of the Department of Docks, and was used where water depth varied from twenty-five to fifty feet. Vertical guide piles were set at the plotted corners of the base to direct the form into its correct position. The form had a perimeter detail that allowed for movable planking to conform to the irregular contours of the river floor (figs. 3.18, 3.19). These adjustable planks would be set into position by divers such that the form closed tightly against the river bottom (figs. 3.20, 3.21). The forms were then lined with canvas or burlap to help contain the concrete. Once set and properly ballasted, the form was filled with wet concrete emptied by bucket from scows into a crib connecting to the foundation form. Because concrete is heavier than water, it flowed over the ballast rocks and cribbing, displacing the water, and set into a solid foundation bed, a technique known as béton en masse.

This method of filling a submerged timber crib with stones and some form of cement was employed a number of times in New York Harbor for subaqueous constructions. The hydraulic mortar utilized in these designs was combined with lime rich in silicates in order to achieve full underwater set. Small stones, granite chips, or other aggregate were also added. The usual béton mix was rich in Portland cement and resulted in a hard, dense concrete. Though some engineers of the period questioned the adjustable-form system and wondered if its complexity would be its undoing, the system did prevail, and all of the subpier foundations in Pier 1 are products of the McClellan approach. McClellan's successor, Charles K. Graham, had taken steps to replace the method midway with another he thought cheaper, but retreated from that decision, as explained in the 1875 annual report:

> This system of construction has been generally adhered to since my incumbency in office, and

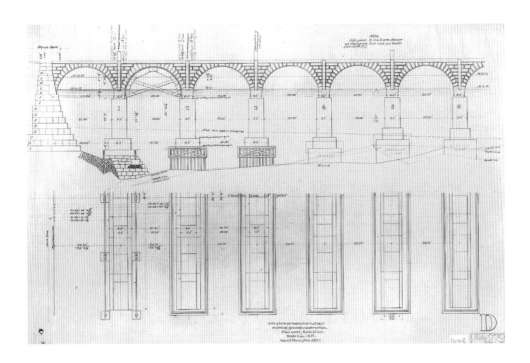

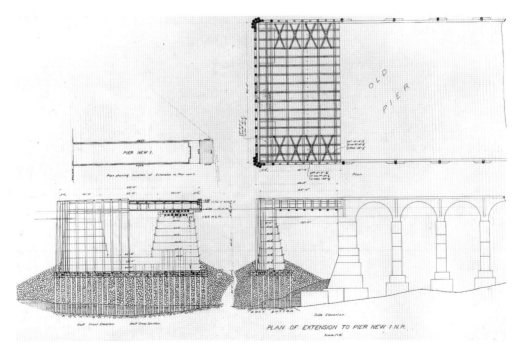

3.16 top
**SUB-PIERS AT INSHORE END OF PIER SHOWING GENERAL
CONSTRUCTION, PIER NEW 1, NORTH RIVER, MANHATTAN**
Elevation, plan. R. W. K., draftsperson. 1893. NYCMA.

3.17
EXTENSION TO PIER NEW 1, NORTH RIVER, MANHATTAN
Plan, elevations, section. Designer unknown. Circa 1910. NYCMA.

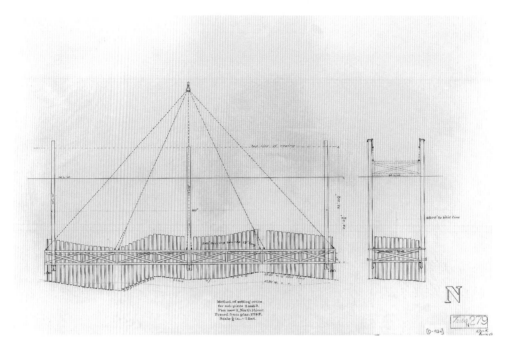

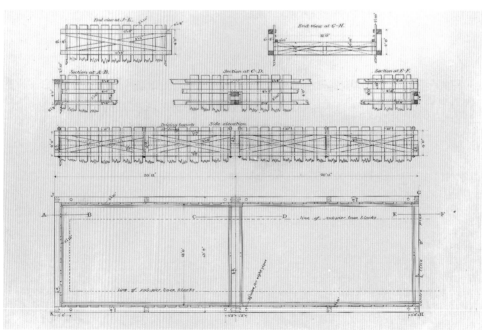

3.18 top
METHOD OF SETTING CRIBS FOR SUB-PIERS 2 AND 3, PIER NEW 1, NORTH RIVER, MANHATTAN
Elevation. R. W. K., draftsperson. 1893. NYCMA.

3.19
CRIB FOR SUB-PIERS 2 AND 3, PIER NEW 1, NORTH RIVER, MANHATTAN
Plan, sections, elevation. Designer unknown. Circa 1893. NYCMA.

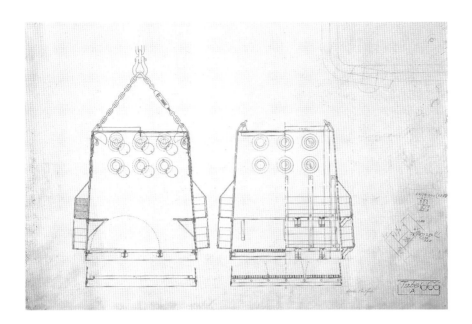

3.20 top
DIVING BELL
Sections, elevations. Designer unknown. Circa 1900. NYCMA.

3.21
DIVER
Photographer unknown. Circa 1900. NYCMA.

arches numbered 5, 6, 7, 8, 9, and 10 have been completed. I had contemplated the idea of employing a wall of pierre perdu (lost stone) in place of cribs, having used it successfully in the construction of eighty-four feet of wall to the northward of this pier, since my appointment, my intention being to carry this stone wall along the whole extent of the pier and weighting it with three times the amount which it was intended to carry in any probable use. Then, after three or four months, the weighting would be removed, the interstices filled with smaller stones, then laying six inches of concrete and upon that placing the base and pier blocks for the several arches. I am satisfied that this method, giving as it would have done a uniform foundation level, would have been more economical and quite as successful as the present system, but after having made a commencement I desisted ... and followed the plan ... as inaugurated by General McClellan. This is the only pier now being constructed entirely of stone and concrete masonry. It is not probable, owing to the expensive character of such structures, that another of the same kind will be undertaken.[4]

Despite this official forecast, the department would, in fact, erect one more pier with the block-and-bridge system: Pier A, built to house the department's headquarters (figs. 3.22, 3.23). Pier A's concrete arches were one foot thick at the crown, and longitudinal steel girders rested on the concrete cross-walls.

Several other important municipal harbor features were built in conjunction with Pier 1 and Pier A. In 1871, a temporary breakwater was installed to protect the small craft that briefly moored at the Battery. This structure proved entirely inadequate, and the Department of Docks authorized the construction of a permanent stone breakwater, known as the Naval Basin, enclosing a 220-by-130-foot area. Its wall was designed to be made of solid granite blocks, though this ashlar scheme was modified and the final structure incorporated béton en masse techniques with granite facing.

In 1903, the Fireboat Headquarters Pier was built on the south side of the Naval Basin. Pier A, the Naval Basin, and the new firehouse formed an impressive architectural assemblage that served as the nautical gateway to New York City. The monumental breakwaters were fitted with large navigation lights easily seen by vessels approaching the harbor after dark. The towers of the Pier A building and the Fireboat Headquarters framed the basin, and behind them rose the Whitehall Building and the skyline of lower Manhattan. Crews disembarking from the boats anchored in the harbor were required to come ashore via the Naval Basin.

One hundred and twenty years after its construction, the foundations of Pier 1 lie buried in the southern end of the modern landfill known as Battery Park City. Pier A still stands at the corner of West Street and Battery Place, one of the few surviving examples of nineteenth-century piers and piersheds. Its iron girders, though badly corroded, remain visible behind the rows of fenders and piles. The

3.22 top
PIER A, MANHATTAN
Photographer unknown. Department of Marine and Aviation. 1931.
NYCMA.

3.23
PIER A, MANHATTAN
Liselot van der Heijden, photographer. 1996.

structure is currently controlled by the New York State Department of Parks, and a variety of proposals for its use have been made. Although a major portion of the Naval Basin was filled in during expansions to the Battery, a segment of the original breakwater remains in place and acts as the pedestal for the Sculpture of the Mariners.

Riverwalls

For marginal wharves a retaining structure is required to support the earth or filling and must afford, either in itself or in combination with a platform of some kind, a vertical face of sufficient depth to permit vessels to lie close alongside. Such a structure must prevent erosion of the shore, withstand the impact of vessels, currents, and waves, and resist overturning, sliding, and deformation by the earth or other with its surcharge of merchandise.

—Carleton Greene, WHARVES AND PIERS

Port facilities primarily rely on retaining walls at the margins of a landform to stabilize the shoreline and establish deep water suitable for docking. The walls employed by the Dutch and their early successors consisted of timber sheet-piling or masses of loose stone, but both constructions had limitations. The loose stone could not be built into a vertical face, so those embankments generally needed a timber platform or extension to accommodate boat landings. The timber sheet-piling structures were neither stable nor durable. At any given time, one could expect a significant portion of these early wall structures to be undergoing repairs; more durable seawall techniques were needed. In 1865, civic interests were resolved to sponsor such renovations, and soldiers returning from the Civil War supplied a ready force of laborers. The Department of Docks' determination to build a continuous retaining wall along the shores of Manhattan resulted in one of the major civil engineering endeavors of the post–Civil War era. While a far more visible enterprise, the construction of the Brooklyn Bridge between 1867 and 1883, commanded more popular attention, the creation of riverwalls on the shores of southern Manhattan was unquestionably a project of comparable ingenuity and scale.

The principal design proposed by McClellan and adopted for the new walls called for 72-ton precast concrete blocks to be situated on dense fields of wooden piles (figs. 3.24, 3.25). The blocks were bound together with tension chains and faced with granite ashlars. The volume of masonry in one mile of the riverwall was approximately five million cubic feet, and a total of 19.5 linear miles would ultimately be built. No single scheme, however, was able to work under all conditions or survive the scrutiny of succeeding administrations. The walls that eventually lined the shores of the New York City waterways were built according to various plans, though much of the wall was, in some degree, indebted to the McClellan designs.

The engineering of these walls was complex and subject to many uncertainties: lateral water pressure, backfill, and live loads were constantly changing; groundwater levels on the land side of the wall, as well as tides, fluctuated levels; and the weight of construction materials diminished as they were submerged. Determining the static functions (the engineering term for physical behavior) for such dynamically loaded subaqueous structures significantly challenged the era's engineering capabilities. Graphic methods—the approximate delineation of internal stress using geometric-force diagrams, as opposed to analytical methods, which use mathematical formulas—were employed to determine external forces. From these graphic-force diagrams, necessary materials could be identified and a cross-sectional structure configuration developed and tested (fig. 3.26). After extensive experimentation, standardized seawall-calculation methods were developed and sanctioned by the Department of Docks. These methods would become engineering standards for the construction of ports.

The walls often incorporated a relieving platform (fig. 3.27)—again an instance in which New York innovations would be widely adopted—as indicated by a description in Carleton Greene's 1917 *Wharves and Piers*:

> One of the most remarkable sea- or bulkhead walls is that constructed by the Department of Docks in New York City, which in some places is built in mud 170 feet deep. It is of the relieving-platform type, supported on piles, which do not extend through the mud to hard bottom, with a vertical facing of concrete blocks extending seventeen feet below low water. This wall [was] originally designed in 1876.[5]

In this construction, a wooden platform was built atop piles at the height of the low-water mark on the inland face of the wall. The purpose of this platform was to diminish or eliminate both the lateral thrust of the backfilled earth (by reducing the amount of backfill material) and the vertical thrust from the stacking of cargo.

The earliest section of the wall could not be built with precast concrete blocks according to plan, as facilities for the production of precast units were still being devised and work needed to start immediately. Construction instead began using the better known and readily available methods of solid-stone masonry (fig. 3.28). In the 1872 annual report, this urgency was explained:

> The portion of the new riverwall south of Pier 1, North River, which was commenced during the past summer, is now completed nearly to the low-water mark. This part of the work is of granite, resting on a riprap foundation, carried down to firm bottom after dredging out the mud. From the exposed nature of the locality, and the very severe winter and spring, the work has been

3.24
PRECAST CONCRETE BLOCKS FOR RIVER CONSTRUCTION
J. P. Nordstrom, photographer. Circa 1890.

3.25 top left opposite
ISOMETRIC PROJECTION OF CONCRETE BLOCK
Detail. Department of Docks. 1891.

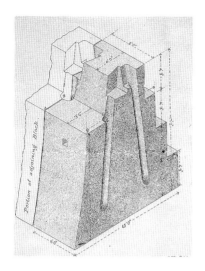

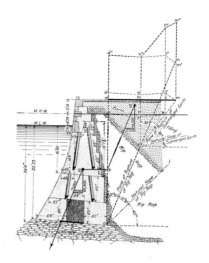

3.26 top right
PLATFORM WALL, WALLABOUT BASIN, BROOKLYN
Section. From Carleton Greene, *Wharves and Piers*, 1917.

3.27
VIEW OF FINISHED RIVERWALL NEAR SOUTH STREET, MANHATTAN
Photographer unknown. Circa 1900.

difficult and tedious. The necessity of preserving Pier 1 for the use of commerce, at present, has made it impossible to carry the new riverwall quite up to that pier. Granite was employed for the entire section of this portion of the work for the reason that it was not possible to complete the preparations for the maintenance and use of béton blocks in season. In the portions of the wall hereafter to be constructed it is intended to use large béton blocks to a very great extent.[6]

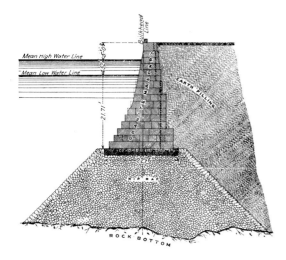

By 1875, the precast-concrete technology had been implemented:

The original plan for the construction of the seawall, devised by General McClellan, the then engineer in chief, is known as the béton block system, which consists of the formation of massive concrete blocks formed in molds, and manufactured in the open air, in such sizes as the nature of the work demanded. These blocks, when properly hardened, were lowered by the aid of the large floating derrick to a foundation of piles firmly driven, and then sawed off so as to form an even bed.[7]

For the riverwalls, variants of the original plan's precast-block system were adopted, but as wall construction proceeded around the island, builders encountered conditions that were not ideal for that method. Some engineers were eager to experiment with faster and more economical methods: along the upper East River, for example, the shallow rock made the use of wooden piles impractical, so a concrete wall was poured in place (fig. 3.29). Poured concrete walls were typically built with cofferdams, temporary watertight enclosures that could be drained and cleared of mud down to the bedrock to allow for unobstructed and dry construction. Wood forms, into which the concrete would be poured, were built directly inside the cofferdams. The cofferdams proved difficult to maintain, however, and the mass walls expensive to build, so another system was introduced that utilized concrete poured into bags and set directly underwater on the rock floor. The bags conformed to the irregular bed and to each other, creating a solid base upon which the original system's precast blocks could be placed.

Piers and Wharves

Once the riverwall construction was well under way and pieces of the permanent bulkhead had been established along stretches of the Hudson and East Rivers, the work of planning and building a new

3.28
RIPRAP WALL WITH UPPER PORTION OF GRANITE MASONRY, MANHATTAN
Section. From Carleton Greene, *Wharves and Piers*, 1917.

generation of pier structures began. As in Venice, with its intricate protection of tidal flow for natural cleansing, the Department of Docks was concerned about sanitation and knew how important it was to prevent the stagnation of water. For this reason the department determined that the pier

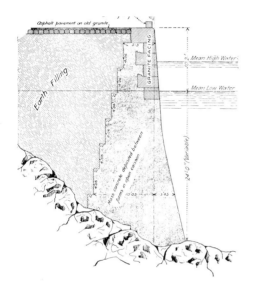

foundations would be open to permit the free passage of tides and river currents. Widening either river by several hundred feet would further allow for the circulation of water, sewage, and ice. In a city where raw sewage went directly into waterways, water-bred pestilence was a significant concern, and throughout the years of massive harbor construction the principle of protecting the natural movement of water was usually preserved. From the time the department decreed that the tidal flush be protected, no signif-

icant obstacle to the currents was erected until the 1975 installation of Battery Park City's northern retaining wall.

Manhattan's wharves and piers would line every available lot of usable shore on or near the harbor and assumed virtually every conceivable form. Marginal wharves, projecting platforms, basins, and dry docks were employed to enhance available waterfront space and improve access to commercial facilities on land. In addition to the stress of the natural environment, the variable weight of movement and handling of cargo, called the live load, put an enormous burden on these structures, far greater than typically imposed on nonmaritime buildings:

> The live load provided for in the designing of wharves varies from 75 pounds per square foot for those designed for handling passengers only, to 1000 pounds for heavy freight. It is difficult to prevent overloading by such heavy materials as pig lead (a common ballast material) or materials which are easily piled to a great height, such as sugar in bags, tin sheets in boxes, or sand and broken stone. Many wharves have failed from overloading, especially where they have deteriorated from age and decay. A heavy live load should be provided for rather than a light one.[8]

Pier 1, which took three years to build, demonstrated the long timespan and high cost of traditional stonework construction. Iron girders were introduced in the deck bridges of Pier A, which improved construction time, but the masonry-block

3.29
MASS CONCRETE WALL, EAST 116TH STREET, MANHATTAN
Section. From Carleton Greene, *Wharves and Piers*, 1917.

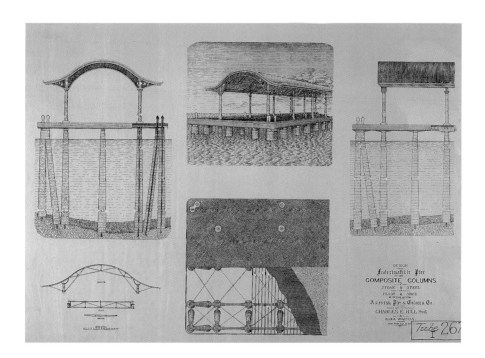

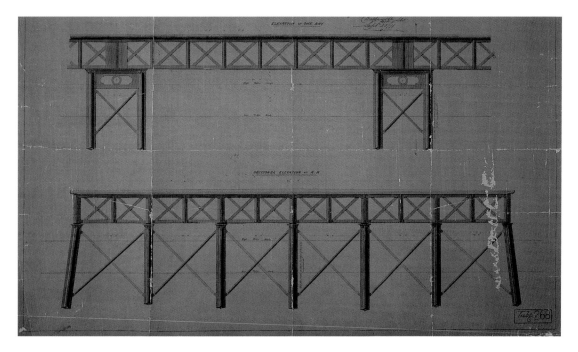

3.30 top
DESIGN FOR AN INDESTRUCTIBLE PIER UPON COMPOSITE COLUMNS
Perspective, sections, plans, details. American Pier and Column Co.
Aloha Vivarttas, designer. 1874. NYCMA.

3.31
PROPOSED SCREW PILE PIER FOR NEW YORK
Elevations. George Wells, designer. 1871. NYCMA.

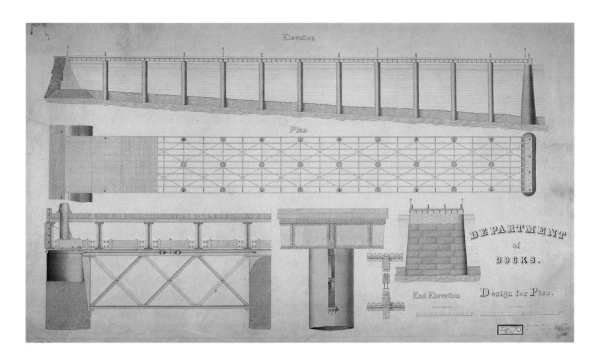

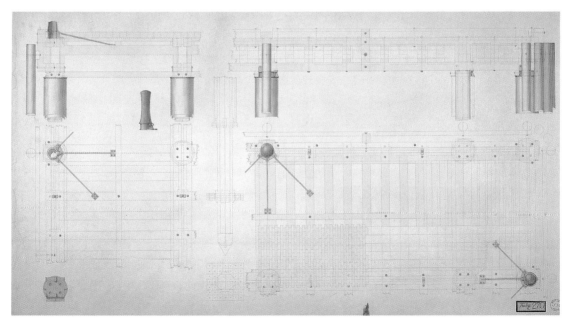

3.32 top
DESIGN FOR A PIER
Elevation, plan, details. Department of Docks. J. D. Van Buren,
assistant engineer. 1871. NYCMA.

3.33
PIER DETAILS
Department of Docks. Circa 1871. NYCMA.

foundations still required extensive labor. Solid filled pier structures provided one possible alternative to the construction problems of the block-and-bridge technique, but, while not as costly, solid piers interfered with the flow of tides and currents.

The Department of Docks' original 1870 call for plans had elicited numerous schemes for pier construction, many utilizing the emerging technologies of the period. The New York Pier and Warehouse Company proposed a series of iron pier structures resting on cylindrical iron pilings. The piershed itself was to be clad in cast iron and elevated above the platform on an open field of cast-iron columns. The American Pier and Column Company proposed a structure built with what it called Indestructible Composite Columns, wherein supporting piles would be assembled from stone disks bound together by continuous iron tension rods with the shed, deck, and roof to be constructed with sheet metal and iron trusses (fig. 3.30). Because iron piles, if too slender, would break under conventional pile-drivers, a system using screw piles was also proposed. (fig. 3.31) Piles would be assembled from cast-iron pieces and fitted with iron threaded screw tips. The piles would be turned, by hand or with horses, to bore into the mud. Screw piles allowed the iron components to remain slender.

The department, by obviating the need for the typical ramming installation,

itself designed several piers utilizing more modern building methods. One scheme called for girders to span iron-reinforced stone-block foundation piers—an industrial age version of the block-and-bridge construction method (fig. 3.32). Another construction proposed the use of shallow wood trusses resting on iron-and-concrete composite piles. Both of these plans incorporated wrought-iron tie-rods secured with cast fittings, placed diagonally along the pier framing (fig. 3.33). In 1879, a wrought-iron pier was built at Coney Island to accommodate steamboat landings. Sixty-foot iron piles were driven into the sand, cross-braced above water, and used as columns for a two-story piershed. Despite all the proposed applications of new industrial-age materials, however, only a handful of iron- or concrete-based pier structures would be built: timber would prevail as the primary material of construction.

During the 1880s and 1890s, the increasing size and number of ships, the demand for more plentiful pier space, and increased west-side shipping due to the Erie Canal made the Hudson River the logical place to construct the next generation of large piers. The river was sufficiently wide to build one-thousand-foot piers without infringing on the shipping channels, and the river's currents were slow enough that they would not impose unreasonable stress on the structures. But the Hudson posed special building problems that made wood the most suitable material for foundation building. In some places, the mud on the river floor was hundreds of feet deep. Pile foundations perform their function in one of two ways. In areas where the mud of the river floor is not too deep, the pile is driven down until it reaches rock or hardpan. In these cases, the pile acts as a fully braced column. In areas where the depth of the mud is so great that the pile cannot reach hard bottom, it is driven until the surface friction and cohesion between the pile and the mud becomes so great that the pile cannot be driven any deeper. In the Hudson River such friction piles had to be driven to an average depth of one hundred feet. In cases where the mud was too soft to develop adequate friction, laggings were added to the pile to increase surface area and therefore the resistance. These enormous pier constructions required approximately two thousand piles. In addition to these primary structural piles, a large pier required fender piles to protect against vessel impact, as well as mooring piles, adding another fifteen thousand linear feet of pile material. Framing for lateral bracing and deck construction could add one million more board feet. In order to accommodate the use of iron, composite, or concrete piles, the mud of the harbor bottom had to be shallow enough to permit the sinking of the piles to hardpan or rock. This would greatly reduce the number of piles required. But for the Hudson River with its deep mud bottom, larger piers made of these new materials were simply unable to compete economically or functionally with wood.

High-quality structural-grade wood was abundant and economical. Timber was harvested all across the continent. The rich resources of the forests and mills of the Great Lakes region had become available to New York City after the Erie Canal opened in 1825. The completion of the Panama Canal in 1914 provided access to the timber of the Pacific Northwest, where tall trees yielded durable piles up to 120 feet in length.

Other innovations privileged the use of wood in the Hudson River constructions. Piles were driven from floating drivers mounted on scows (fig. 3.34). The new steam-driven pile driver made it possible to construct pile piers quickly, increasing productivity from the drop-hammer rate of four piles per day to thirteen. The traditional disadvantage of timber—decay resulting from infestation by teredos, marine borers that tunnel into and devour wood fiber—was considerably lessened by a combination of accident and invention. Marine borers were such a serious problem that at times drastic remedies such as poisoning the harbor or setting off dynamite were considered. Both methods were used only in a limited capacity, as they not only eliminated marine borers but most other harbor biota as well. Ultimately, however, the waters of the harbor became so polluted that marine borers could no longer thrive. To bring dry rot and fungal decay under control, preservatives were newly available, in particular creosote, a distillate of coal tar, itself a by-product of steel production.

Timber structures proved to have another important advantage. Piers with piles and platforms of wood absorbed

impact energy better than those made from other materials. A fully loaded vessel coming into contact with the side of a pier, even at a very slow speed, carries enormous kinetic energy (fig. 3.35). If the pier cannot absorb the impact, the vessel will take the stress, thereby damaging or distorting hull plates. Likewise, the pier could suffer structural damage. Shipping companies were willing to pay a high premium to dock their vessels at piers less

likely to damage their craft. Elastic pier design became a general necessity as well as a municipal standard for New York City (figs. 3.36, 3.37).

The piling-and-platform pier was built according to several basic structures, which varied by the nature and materials of the piles, pile caps, and platforms. The most common form consisted of wood piles that extended above the high-water mark to culminate in wood caps and decks. Sometimes concrete decks and concrete caps were used in various combinations. In another common method, the wood piles were cut off near the low-water mark to support a permanently submerged wood platform that held earth or cinder fill. Variations of this configuration substituted reinforced-concrete posts, cross walls, and decks for solid filled deck structures. Further alternative methods employed either iron-and-steel or reinforced-concrete foundation structures in conjunction with cast-iron, wrought-iron, or steel piles.

Piers employing wooden piles extending to the deck were favored in New York. Construction was relatively simple: piles organized into dense grids were driven into the river bottom, cut off at five to seven feet above the low-water mark, and tied

3.34
PIER 94, NORTH RIVER, CAISSONS ON SOUTH SLIP,
CUNARD STEAMSHIP COMPANY
Stanley Oring, photographer. 1962. NYCMA.

together with a system of lateral bracing trusses and intermediate wood deck-beams. The deck typically consisted of layers of wood planking, which could be topped with concrete, stone, wood blocks, or asphalt to establish a smooth and durable working surface. Reinforced-concrete decks

offered protection from fire but often proved too heavy for use in areas with soft, deep mud.

Wood is prone to deterioration when subjected to repeated cycles of wetting and drying, and where wood is not continuously submerged, it is best to protect it from moisture altogether. Several pier-platform designs were intended to redress the problem of vulnerable pile heads. Pile caps served as armor and were primarily made of mass concrete, while other methods entailed the use of copper,

zinc, cast iron, or sprayed-concrete jackets. The Department of Docks conducted its own research into timber rot and preservation techniques. These investigations showed that properly selected and placed timber piles could successfully withstand the elements, although the elements were by no means confined to sea and river water:

The durability of a wooden wharf or pier depends to a very great extent on the care taken in the details of the design to prevent, as far as possible, decay caused by the wetting of the timber by the rainwater, horse urine, condensation, etc. To obtain this end, all places where water, dust, dirt, and rubbish can collect should be eliminated as far as possible. Pile heads where they project beyond the sides of cap timbers should be sloped off; all rainwater leaders extending down through the deck should be arranged so that the discharge will not fall on any timber; decks should be crowned and scupper holes provided in stringpieces and in the deck, wider on the outside than on the inside to prevent clogging; countersinks for bolt heads and washers in horizontal surfaces should be filled with pitch and all abutting surfaces should be drawn tightly together with screw bolts in order to reduce as much as possible the penetration of moisture between the adjacent pieces. Places on top of timbers on which dirt sifting through the seams in the deck can collect should be filled up solid

3.35
PIER DAMAGED BY VESSEL COLLISION, NORTH RIVER, MANHATTAN
Photographer unknown. Circa 1940. NYMCA.

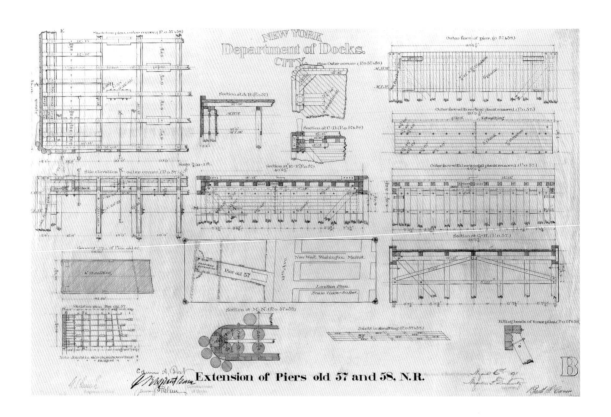

3.36
EXTENSION OF PIERS OLD 57 AND 58, NORTH RIVER, MANHATTAN
Partial plans, sections, details. Department of Docks. George Sears
Greene Jr., engineer in chief. 1891. NYCMA.

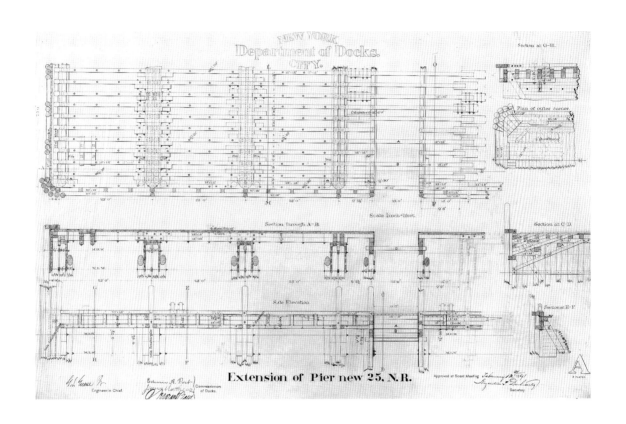

3.37
PIER 11 OR CEDAR STREET PIER, NORTH RIVER, MANHATTAN
This drawing shows the New York City municipal standard for wood
pier construction. General plan and cross-sections. Department of
Docks and Ferries. William G. Johnson. Circa 1890. NYCMA.

with chocks and fillers. Tenons, mortises, scarfs, laps, and all other surfaces of abutting timber should be brush-coated with wood preservatives, and pile heads should be liberally coated with asphaltic cement to make them shed water.[9]

With proper treatment the wood above the waterline could be expected to last for fifteen years. The pile caps and deck structure could be repaired or reconstructed once or twice during the useful life of the piles, allowing a pier a life expectancy of up to forty years.

Piersheds and Pier Enclosures

Until about 1890, piershed superstructures were usually timber frames clad in wood. Some cast-iron components were used for truss footings, brackets, and bearing plates, or wrought-iron tie-rods were used in combination with timber struts to fabricate trusses. The trusses that constituted the piersheds' frames were simple, in gabled Howe, Warren, or king-rod formations (fig. 3.38).

The same forces that made timber the primary material for pier platforms and foundations doomed it as a material for piershed framing. Wood piersheds were thought to be prone to fire, but it was weight, lack of elasticity, and cost that precluded wood as a viable piershed material. Heavy and rigid frames were required in order to support wood exteriors for the big open superstructures (figs. 3.39, 3.40),

and the large piers built on soft river mud could not accommodate that amount of weight. Light, flexible, and economical piershed-framing systems were a necessity, and by the 1880s, techniques for rolling structural steel sections had advanced enough to permit the production of large quantities of diverse profiles for commercial construction. New truss designs allowed for the rapid and economical erection of large-span, lightweight, steel-framed piershed structures (figs. 3.41–3.44). By 1900, the Department of Docks was no longer building wood-framed piersheds, a construction revolution that was reflected in all industries and categories of buildings.

Steel trusses and framing components could be ordered already engineered, cut to size, drilled for fastenings, and ready for assembly from rolling mills such as those in Bethlehem, Pennsylvania. These prefabricated systems could be erected with remarkable speed; the full eight-hundred-foot-long piershed frames of the Chelsea piers were erected in eight days (fig. 3.45). The steel framing extended above the roofline and served as hoisting towers along the piershed perimeters (figs. 3.46, 3.47).

By 1900, steel roof trusses could span up to 125 feet and offered the advantage of wide-open floor space by eliminating the need for load-bearing walls (figs. 3.48, 3.49). For two-story piersheds, plate girders were often used for the second-floor framing. In this configuration, additional intermediate support columns were used on the lower levels to keep the size and weight of the girders down, as in the Chelsea pier. Another typical technique used with wide piers involved the division of the piershed into three bays, with one primary space in the center and two smaller aisles on either side.

The combination of metal skin and lightweight steel frames provided flexibility to accommodate the structural distortion caused by vessel impact and uneven settling of pier platforms. Purely commercial piersheds were generally clad in sheets of copper, zinc, or galvanized iron. Easily worked and corrosion-resistant, copper was the most serviceable of these materials. Copper sheeting could be bent, stamped, and soldered to create practically any architectural facade element. Galvanized-iron sheeting, however, was the material most frequently used, as it was the least costly; lightweight, elastic, and noncombustible, it also met all structural requirements (figs. 3.50, 3.51). The main disadvantage of galvanized iron was its rapid deterioration in the presence of salt water, which necessitated periodic painting to prevent corrosion. Eventually, alternatives to pure galvanized iron were developed from laminates of steel, asbestos, and asphalt. The metal piershed enclosures, despite their industrial and utilitarian origins, were often elaborately ornamented. A surviving example of beautiful sheet-metal shed construction, although not a

particularly well-preserved one, is the Erie-Lackawanna Terminal in Hoboken, New Jersey.

While not fireproof, these new materials were noncombustible (figs. 3.52, 3.53), and although much thought and energy was devoted to fire protection for piersheds, the problem was never fully solved. The typical architectural approach to fireproofing—encasing steel in cement, terra cotta, or plaster—was costly, heavy, and inflexible. The advantage of lightweight steel framing was lost with the added weight of masonry fireproofing. The rigid cement encapsulation could not withstand the constant movement of the structures and was prone to break apart and fall off. The fire problem was to some degree solved by the invention of the automatic sprinkler system, but because piersheds were unheated, wet pipe systems were prone to freezing and consequently were often out of service. Moreover, the movement of the structures themselves could rupture pipes. These weaknesses became more critical as the piers fell into disuse. More than any other factor, failure to eradicate the danger of fire led to the disappearance of at least one-half of all the buildings on the New York City waterfront. Insurance-fraud arson added significantly to these losses (fig. 3.54).

The need for versatile and large cargo-bay doors resulted in many designs for movable wall and panel systems. The

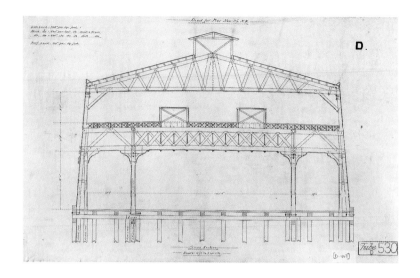

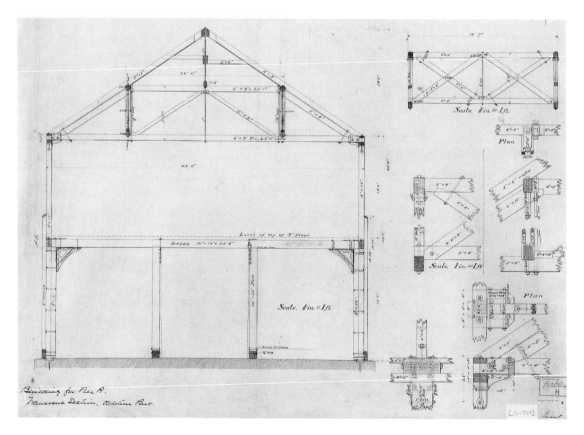

3.38 top
SHED FOR PIER NEW 25, NORTH RIVER, MANHATTAN
Cross-section. Branford L. Gilbert, architect. Circa 1885. NYCMA.

3.39
BUILDING FOR PIER A, TRANSVERSE SECTION, OUTSHORE PART, MANHATTAN
Section and details. N. J. V., draftsperson. 1885. NYCMA.

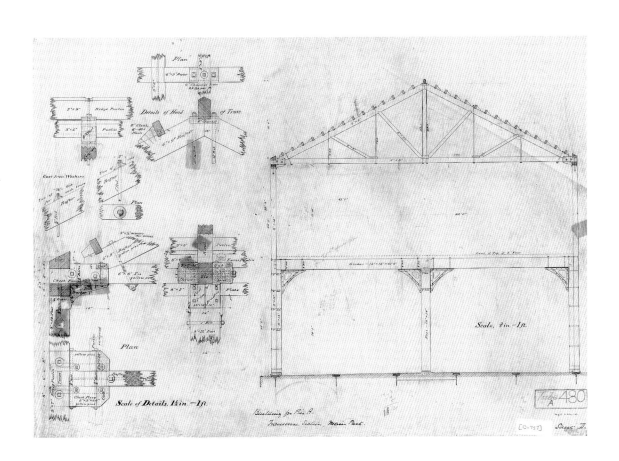

3.40
**BUILDING FOR PIER A, TRANSVERSE SECTION, MAIN PART,
MANHATTAN**
Section and details. N. J. V., draftsperson. 1885. NYCMA.

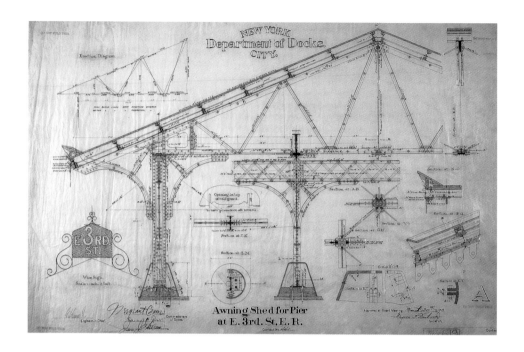

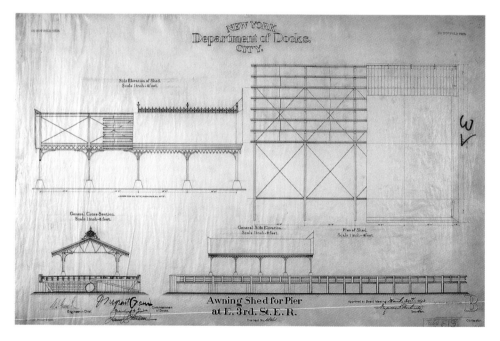

3.41 top
AWNING SHED FOR PIER AT EAST 3RD STREET, EAST RIVER,
MANHATTAN
Details. Department of Docks.
George Sears Greene Jr., engineer in chief. 1893. NYCMA.

3.42
AWNING SHED FOR PIER AT EAST 3RD STREET, EAST RIVER,
MANHATTAN
Elevations, plan, section. Department of Docks.
George Sears Greene Jr., engineer in chief. 1893. NYCMA.

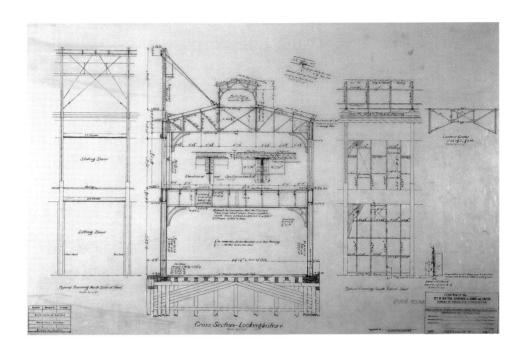

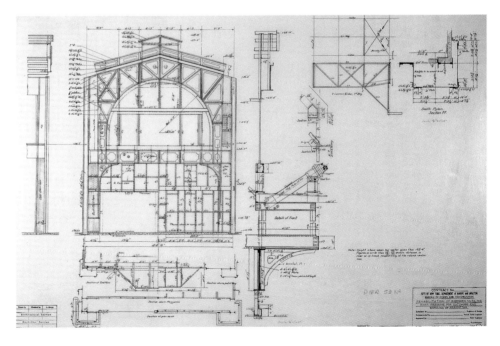

3.43 top
TYPICAL STEEL FRAMING AND CROSS SECTION OF BULKHEAD, PIER 53,
NORTH RIVER, MANHATTAN
Section, details. Department of Marine and Aviation,
Bureau of Design and Construction. Circa 1950. NYCMA.

3.44
REHABILITATION OF PIERSHED AND EXISTING FRAMING FOR
OUTSHORE END, PIER 53, NORTH RIVER, MANHATTAN
Elevation, details. Department of Marine and Aviation,
Bureau of Design and Construction. Circa 1950. NYCMA.

3.45
6TH DAY'S PROGRESS, CHELSEA SECTION, PIER 59, NORTH RIVER, MANHATTAN
Photographer unknown. 1908. NYCMA.

tons.

3.46 top
CONSTRUCTION PIER 87, NORTH RIVER, MANHATTAN
Photographer unknown. Circa 1920. NYCMA.

3.47
PIER 42, NORTH RIVER, MANHATTAN
Photographer unknown. Circa 1920. NYCMA.

3.48
PIER 33, EAST RIVER, MANHATTAN
Photographer unknown. Circa 1950. NYCMA.

3.49
INTERIOR OF PIER 27, NORTH RIVER, MANHATTAN
Photographer unknown. 1953. NYCMA.

3.50 top
EXISTING CONDITION OF NUMBER 1 BULKHEAD PRIOR TO DEMOLITION,
CHELSEA PIERS REDEVELOPMENT, NORTH RIVER, MANHATTAN
Mal Gurian Associates, photographer. 1967. NYCMA.

3.51
UNIDENTIFIED PIERS, EAST RIVER, MANHATTAN
Photographer unknown. Circa 1950. NYCMA.

3.52 top
FENDER SYSTEM, CENTER OF PIER 49, NORTH SIDE, NORTH RIVER, MANHATTAN
Photographer unknown. 1953. NYCMA.

3.53
PIER 28, SOUTH SIDE, NORTH RIVER, MANHATTAN
Photographer unknown. 1953. NYCMA.

side doors of the piersheds had to face the cargo hatches of the ships being unloaded. Because the positioning of these hatches was different on every boat, wall systems were devised that allowed the entire side of the piershed to be opened such that exterior walls were comprised entirely of doors and hatches. Variations employed panels that lifted vertically, horizontal sliding panels, vertical and horizontal swinging panels, and roll-up metal enclosures. The Chelsea piers used both vertical-swing and horizontal-sliding panels, each approximately twenty-two by twenty feet, which could be opened in different configurations to meet the requirements of diverse tasks (figs. 3.55, 3.56). Operating these doors was intended to be a one-person operation, in case a sudden storm or fire had to be shut out. There were often small personnel doors within the larger cargo doors (figs. 3.57, 3.58).

The large piersheds used for the transatlantic-steamship terminals, particularly those on the Hudson, shared certain architectural distinctions. The sheds typically housed two levels, with the upper floor providing passenger facilities such as waiting areas and the lower floor used for dispatching cargo and baggage. The upper spaces were often one continuous hall, hundreds of feet long, with exposed truss framing and illumination from raised-ridge skylights running the entire length of the roof. The facades generally conformed to one of several types. On the wider two-story piersheds, the inshore elevation was often a masonry wall with a large, arched opening that reached to the top of the second floor. Installed in these openings were window walls with doors for trucks and wagons on the ground floor as well as glass-wall assemblies above to enclose the waiting areas. The public entries were located on ground level beside the main freight and cargo doors. The facade corresponded to a kind of aisle-and-nave order that was generated from the plan within. These masonry facades offered a monumental and permanent image for the passenger-transportation companies (fig. 3.59).

Piersheds devoted exclusively to cargo were usually constructed of less permanent and substantial materials than the public terminals. The facades were organized in more traditional ways, with small-scale individual window openings as befitted the office space in the bulkhead wing of the structure. Facade details—sills, cornices, pediments, and pilasters—were executed in sheet metal (figs. 3.60, 3.61).

Although only a few were built, recreational piers were important concessions to noncommercial interests on the late-nineteenth-century waterfront. The city maintained at least four recreational piers on Manhattan Island. One such structure, built in 1897 at the foot of East 3rd Street, was envisioned and fought for by Jacob Riis and typified the form: a two-story, steel-frame shed with a covered but open upper level (figs. 3.62, 3.63). A similar recreational pier on East 24th Street, probably the largest of its kind, was an extension of the public bathhouse located there. It was modified in 1907 to become the New York Nautical School of the Department of Education (fig. 3.64). There was a recreational pier on the Harlem River (fig. 3.65) and a bathing pavilion on Far Rockaway, as well as three other structures on the Brooklyn shore, located at Second Street, Metropolitan Avenue, and the Coney Island beach. There were even a few floating swimming pools and sundecks on the waterfront (figs. 3.66, 3.67).

At the peak of port activity, thousands of harbor structures were built. The city and the water met along an intricate, many-layered edge. Virtually every foot of shoreline was occupied by some kind of maritime building: basins, docks, piers, wharves, and seawalls, as well as the headquarters of traders, haulers, shipbuilders, blacksmiths, rope makers, riggers, oyster merchants, brewers, carpenters, and all other conceivable maritime support trades. This horizontal city of piersheds and terminals, of railroad structures and industrial facilities, of shanties and flophouses, was an urban world unto itself. Its apparently haphazard and incomprehensible layout was diametrically opposed to the rational landscape of gridded streets and vertical towers that grew out of the rest of the city. It was a gateway village between the metropolis and the sea. For

many, this tidewater frontier town was the only New York they knew. It had its own hotels, bars, and brothels, as well as at least one floating church. The density and chaos of the New York City waterfront was an archetype of maritime urban space (fig. 3.68).

Remarkably, the architecture and construction of this waterfront city have for the most part escaped examination, because waterfront life is temporary by nature. People, places, and buildings come and go quickly. The water carries things to shore but often drags them away again. This hectic port world, with its ever-shifting business and transitory sights, was itself a version of the flotsam that accumulates and disperses at the shore. People, cargo, even whole enterprises, were constantly being deposited and settling briefly only to be towed out again. The boom of transportation activities, constant evolution of shipping techniques, rapidly advancing building technology, and the harsh environment in which these structures—with their consequently short lifespans—were expected to serve resulted in a sustained rhythm of building, demolition, rebuilding, and dissolution to which the humanity of the waterfront instinctively conformed.

The waterfront facades viewed by the public were often fabricated of little more than formed and shaped sheet metal, which easily replicated the appearance of permanent construction without possessing any real durability. Convention held that the impermanent, dockside structures should appear to be part of the stone-and-brick city beyond, and often it was only the thin veneer of inland facades that were embellished with the characteristics of an imitated style. Such illusory edifices suited the breathless pace of change on the waterfront. They are also the reason why so few examples of prime port architecture exist today (figs. 3.69–3.72). The epoch of the vigorous maritime waterfront is over, and the large-scale tokens of this once-teeming horizontal city's life have, for the most part, vanished as well.

NOTES

1. Stokes, p. 153.
2. Ibid., p. 309.
3. Ibid., p. 372.
4. DOD, 22 September 1875, p. 10.
5. Greene, p. 88.
6. DOD, 30 April 1872, p. 51.
7. DOD, 1 June 1875, p. 12.
8. Greene, p. 26.
9. Ibid., p. 33.

3.54
FIRE DAMAGE, UNIDENTIFIED PIER
Photographer unknown. Circa 1940. NYCMA.

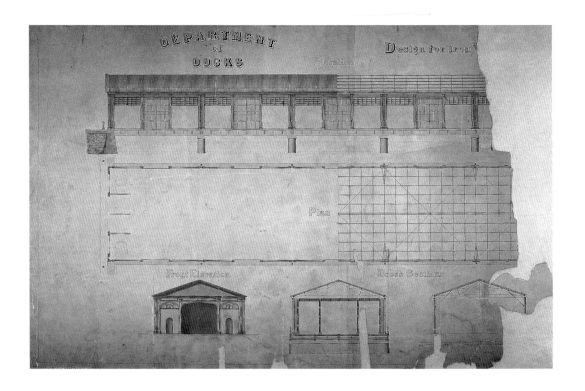

3.55 top
DESIGN FOR IRONWORK PIER
Elevation, plan, sections. Department of Docks. Circa 1880. NYCMA.

3.56
SHED, WHITE STAR LINE, PIER NEW 45, NORTH RIVER, MANHATTAN
Elevation. Designer unknown. Circa 1910. NYCMA.

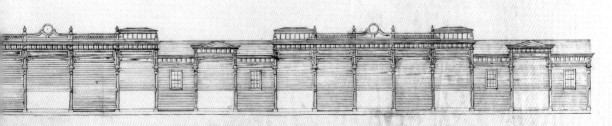

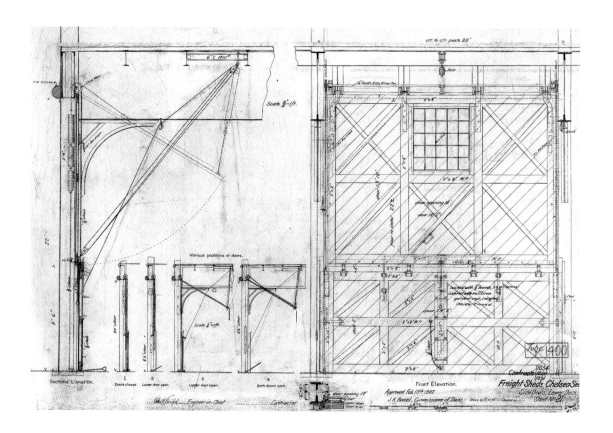

3.57
FREIGHT SHEDS, CHELSEA SECTION, SIDE DOORS, LOWER DECK
Front elevation, sectional elevation. J. A. Bensel, commissioner of docks;
Charles W. Staniford, engineer in chief; R. M. K., draftsperson. 1907. NYCMA.

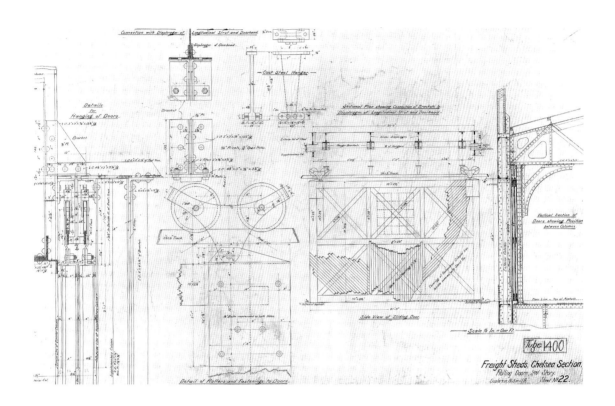

3.58
FREIGHT SHEDS, CHELSEA SECTION, ROLLING DOORS, SECOND STORY
Details. H. A. R., draftsperson. Circa 1910. NYCMA.

3.59 top
PIER 84, NORTH RIVER, MANHATTAN
Photographer unknown. Port Authority of New York. 1972. NYCMA.

3.60
EAST RIVER PIERS AT 20TH STREET, MANHATTAN
Photographer unknown. Circa 1930. NYCMA.

3.61
PIER 7, NORTH RIVER, MANHATTAN
Photographer unknown. Circa 1930. NYCMA.

3.62 top
RECREATION PIER 43 AT CHRISTOPHER STREET, NORTH RIVER, MANHATTAN
Photographer unknown. Circa 1930. NYCMA.

3.63
RECREATION PIER AT 3RD STREET, EAST RIVER, MANHATTAN
Photographer unknown. Circa 1920. NYCMA.

3.64
RECREATION PIER AT 24TH STREET, EAST RIVER, MANHATTAN
Photographer unknown. Circa 1930. NYCMA.

3.65 top
UNIDENTIFIED RECREATION PIER
Photographer unknown. Circa 1930. NYCMA.

3.66
RECREATION PIER AT 112TH STREET, EAST RIVER, MANHATTAN
Photographer unknown. Circa 1930. NYCMA.

3.67
UNIDENTIFIED RECREATION PIER
Photographer unknown. Circa 1920. NYCMA.

3.68
WEST STREET, MANHATTAN
Photographer unknown. Circa 1920. NYCMA.

3.69 top
PIER 101, WEST SIDE RAIL YARDS, MANHATTAN
Stanley Greenberg, photographer. 1993.

3.70
PIER, WILLIAMSBURG, BROOKLYN
Stanley Greenberg, photographer. 1993.

3.71 top
PIER 5, SUNSET PARK, BROOKLYN
Stanley Greenberg, photographer. 1992.

3.72
PIER 102, WEST SIDE RAIL YARDS, MANHATTAN
Stanley Greenberg, photographer. 1993.

EAST RIVER PARK AND DRIVE
Max Ulrich, photographer. 1939.
New York City Parks Archive.

4.1
BROOKLYN BRIDGE, FROM MANHATTAN
Photographer unknown. Circa 1910.
NYCMA.

TRANSFORMING THE EDGE
Overview of Selected Plans and Projects

Gina Pollara

Natural geography has long been recognized as the single most important factor in the rapid development and rise of New York Harbor to its preeminence as an international port (fig. 4.1). As a university professor visiting North America from Sweden observed in 1748:

> The situation of [New York] is extremely advantageous for trade: for the town stands upon a point which is formed by two bays; into one of which the river Hudson discharges itself, not far from the town; New York is therefore on three sides surrounded with water. . . . The port is a good one: ships of the greatest burthen can lie in it, quite close up to the bridge: but its water is very salt, as the sea continually comes in upon it; and therefore it is never frozen, except in extraordinary cold weather. This is of great advantage to the city and its commerce; for many ships either come in or go out of the port at any time of the year.[1]

Ironically, the topography that was so advantageous to New York City was also the feature most continually subjected to alteration. Prior to the 1870 establishment of the Department of Docks, significant landfill, shoreline, and underwater modifications had already taken place, the results of which are still recognizable today. Since these changes were largely determined by the needs of an expanding shipping industry, they parallel the evolution of water-related commerce in New York. As early

as 1664, for example, the kill that then separated Brooklyn from Red Hook was dredged to make a shorter "passage to the Gouwanus"[2] to allow ships laden with grain to reach the mills that flourished there.

The favorable geographic disposition of the Upper Bay and the lower East River to trade was nowhere more evident than on the east side of lower Manhattan, where the earliest settlements and port developments appeared. Prevailing winds allowed sailing vessels to navigate easily in and out of the port, and the east side provided commodious anchorages as well as shelter from the ice floes of the Hudson River. Port developments took longer to form on the west side. The construction of the first Hudson River pier was not begun until 1771, some 112 years after the small wooden dock—first proposed by Peter Stuyvesant in 1647 and completed in 1659—was built at Schreyers Hook, site of the present Pearl and Broad Streets.

In the earliest incarnation of the Manhattan shoreline, boats pulled up to Pearl Street, which was then called Dock Street, and were "aground at low water."[3] The water's edge continued along Dock Street (now Pearl), which became Queen Street after it crossed Hanover Square, until it met the present-day Cherry Street at Dover. The line then continued somewhat irregularly along Cherry, bulging out periodically to the current Water Street and beyond, until it cut back into the island along the old Corlears Street. Corlears no longer exists, but it was located parallel to and one short block northeast of Jackson Street. The shoreline then followed Lewis Street, now mostly covered by the Baruch Houses complex on the Lower East Side, after which the waterline continued inward, reaching as far inland as First Avenue at 18th Street (figs. 4.2–4.5).

The Dongan Charter of 1686 (named for the colonial governor of the time, Thomas Dongan) granted to the corporation of the city "all the waste, vacant, unpatented, and unappropriated lands within the city and island, extending to low-water mark in all parts,"[4] effectively establishing the limits of the city to the outer edges of the land exposed at low tide. This allowed for the sale of water lots by the corporation to its citizens, a practice begun in this same year that encouraged development of the waterfront. A "New York water lot" was a parcel of land that "lay between the marks of high tide and low tide, and was therefore under water half the time."[5] Later these lots would be leased from the city, but whether leased or sold the corporation retained the right to dictate improvements to the area. If citizens wished to buy, lease, or improve upon a water lot, they would have to petition the governing body, which

would often grant the request with a directive to modify the parcel of land in a way that would conform to existing adjacent public spaces. The petitioner would then be obliged to execute such public works at his own expense. For example, a grant of land at the lower end of Queen Street (now a part of Water Street) to Gerardus Beeckman in 1722, specified that he had to "make and keep a public slip 24 feet wide . . . and a street facing the river of 30 feet wide."[6] In addition, when the growth of commerce or public need required the erection of embankments and wharves or new streets, the city would direct its residents to erect such works —under the supervision of its surveyors and according to their exact specifications—with the further obligation that they keep such structures in good repair, often all at their own expense. They could not "claim any property or interest" in the works, which "remained to the use of the City."[7]

In spite of its hospitable terrain, enlarging and transforming the shape of New York City has been a persistent endeavor since the earliest times. Landfilling was the primary means of shoreline modification up to the nineteenth century, and earth and stone taken from the leveling of hills and the construction of basements and streets provided early sources of materials, though rubbish was often deposited as well (fig. 4.6). Successive landfilling operations accounted for the exten-

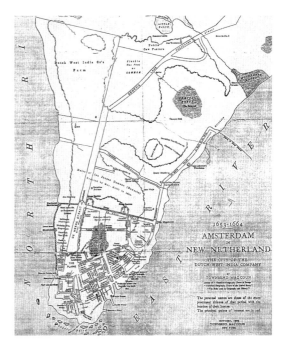

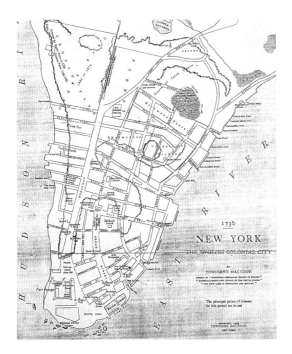

4.2 top
1609, ISLAND OF MANNAHTIN AT THE TIME OF ITS DISCOVERY
4.3
1730, NEW YORK, THE ENGLISH COLONIAL CITY
Townsend MacCoun. 1909.

4.4 top
1653–64, AMSTERDAM IN NEW NETHERLAND, THE CITY OF THE
DUTCH WEST INDIA COMPANY
4.5
1807, NEW YORK CITY AND MANHATTAN ISLAND
Commissioners Appointed by the Legislature. P. Maverick, engraver.
Townsend MacCoun. 1909.

sion of Manhattan's east and west banks, the elimination of marshy areas—such as those at 14th Street, which reportedly almost bisected the island at high tide—and the persistent enlarging of the Battery at the tip of Manhattan (fig. 4.7). The original fort at the Battery, whose modern

of the modern City of New York."[9] Significantly, this plan extended the street grid far into the East River, in effect mandating the city's reliance on the well-established expedient of landfill. In its concerted effort to furnish an extensive and coherent city plan, with its inevitable

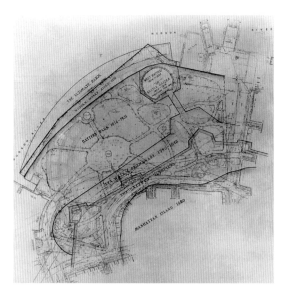

boundaries at the time of Hudson's discovery in 1609 were under water at high tide, stood upon a mere two acres of land. But, by 1800, about 729 acres of new land had been added to the southern tip of Manhattan.[8]

Given what was to come, however, those early efforts were modest and arose haphazardly out of scattered public need rather than any unified municipal design. The Commissioner's Plan, adopted in 1811, laid out the existing street grid of Manhattan and is considered "the advent

effects on the shoreline, the Commission could be said to anticipate the Department of Docks, an agency that brought a systematic and comprehensive approach to the development of the New York City waterfront. The department represented a continuation as well as an institutionalization of a process begun before its establishment: the radical and often dramatic reshaping of many areas of New York City.

The transformations of the island became more ambitious as technological innovations such as steam power made

4.6
BATTERY PARK
Map showing landfill since 1650.
New York City Parks Archive.

4.7
BATTERY PARK
Map showing landfill increments. 1939.
New York City Parks Archive.

them realizable. Behind such growing ambition was the mid-nineteenth- and early-twentieth-century attitude of confident superiority to both history and nature that spawned such grand schemes as the total redesign of the city of Paris and the audacious incursion that was the carving of Mount Rushmore. Far from being inviolable, the physical environment—whether built by one's ancestors or god-given—was perceived to be both inexhaustible and at the disposal of the living generation, an attitude that was borne out by projects undertaken in the waters around New York.

The Hell Gate

The body of water called the East River that connects the Upper New York Bay with the Long Island Sound is not technically a river, but a saltwater estuary or tidal strait subject to tidal fluctuations that are influenced by its varying terrain. The ocean tide washes into both the top and bottom of the strait, and it takes approximately three hours longer to travel the length of the Long Island Sound and reach the top of the East River than it does to flow up the sixteen miles of river to meet the sound. The result of this difference, aided by rocks and reefs in the area, is that "whirlpoolle" that the Dutch called the "Hellegat."[10] The navigational hazards of this strait, where the Long Island Sound meets the Upper East River and the Harlem

River, were well-known and documented early on (fig. 4.8). In 1670, Daniel Denton described a "narrow passage [where] there runneth a violent stream both upon flood and ebb, and in the middle lieth some islands of rocks, which the current sets so violently upon that it threatens present shipwreck; and upon the Flood is a large Whirlpool, which continually sets forth a hideous roaring, enough to affright any stranger from passing further, and to wait for some Charon to conduct him through."[11]

In spite of this knowledge, it was not until the mid-nineteenth century that surveys to determine the area's hydrographic profile were begun in order to draft plans for underwater modifications that would allow safe passage. In 1848, Lieutenant Commander David D. Porter, who had studied the situation, reported to the superintendent of the United States Coast Guard Survey that the removal of Pot Rock, "the principal obstruction in the Hell Gate," would by itself make those rough waters "less dangerous by half." Porter further recommended the removal of Halletts Point, a projecting reef off Astoria, Queens, that extended forty yards into the eastern channel of the Hell Gate and was "the most accessible obstruction."[12] Porter also mentioned other dangerous rocks such as Bald-headed Billy, the Frying Pan, Rylanders Reef, and Blackwells Rock, the names of which attest to the familiarity of the terrain (fig. 4.9). By 1851, a program

4.8
HELL GATE, EAST RIVER FROM BLACKWELLS ISLAND TO LAWRENCE POINT
United States Coast and Geodetic Survey. 1909.
New York City Department of Environmental Protection Archive.

of surface-blasting was begun that proved to have little effect.

In 1866, the United States government placed Major General John Newton of the United States Engineer Corps in charge of the operations, and a new approach was attempted: "By the aid of drill scows and other apparatus he suc-

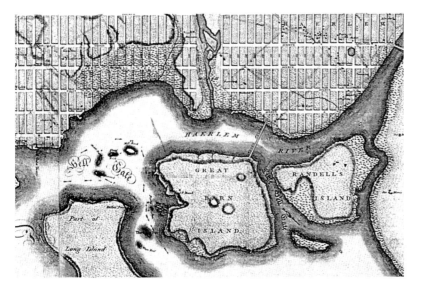

deal of rock has already been blasted out and cleared away. Of about 165,000 cubic yards of rock to be removed, at least 42,000 have been taken out. For removing the rest the rock is being tunneled and pierced in every direction [fig. 4.10]. When this is accomplished a tremendous blast will be made with 7,000 pounds of nitroglycerine equal in force to 70,000 pounds of gunpowder.[14]

The great explosion to remove the reef took place on September 24, 1876, as reported in the *New York Evening Post* (fig. 4.11):

Fifty-two thousand pounds of explosives were fired off at one touch of a button by General Newton's daughter. The day was Sunday, a cloudy, sullen day. Many of the inhabitants of the city feared destruction of property, but the only damage done was to a few windows and to fish in the river.[15]

ceeded in partly removing the Frying Pan Rock in Hell Gate; the Pot Rock, in the same channel, and Ways Reef, near Halletts Point."[13] An account written at the time noted the scope of the endeavor:

Few people are aware of the stupendous work going on at Hell Gate and of the important results that may be expected to ensue from it. The removal of rocks there, so as to make a perfectly free and safe channel for the largest vessels, was a vast undertaking. In this age, however, hardly anything seems impossible to engineering skill. . . . A vast

Similar work on the Flood Rock also in Hell Gate, which had begun in 1875 and was interrupted, then resumed. On October 11, 1885, nine acres of the rock were destroyed by dynamite. The task of dredging the blasted material proceeded slowly, and nearly two years later the *New York Times* reported that the work was still underway even though "the dredger has double crews and is at work night and day." The paper noted that "no wrecks

4.9
NEW YORK CITY AND MANHATTAN ISLAND
Commissioners Appointed by the Legislature. P. Maverick, engraver. 1807.
NYCMA.

4.10 top
PREPARATIONS AT BLASTING SITE, HALLETTS POINT REEF IN HELL GATE
Photographer unknown. 1876. NYHS.

4.11
THE GREAT EXPLOSION OF HALLETTS POINT REEF IN HELL GATE
Photographer unknown. 1876. NYHS.

have been known in Hell Gate since the explosion, where before they were of daily and, in fact, tidal occurrence."[16] Sixty thousand cubic yards of rock had been removed to clear a channel 350 feet wide and 18 feet deep across the reef, and the work was as yet incomplete.

This and other waterfront alteration projects, bold in themselves, entailed significant technological innovations, and their importance in the field of civil engineering was widely recognized at the time. These "engineering triumphs," as the *New York Herald* called them, were displayed in the form of models painstakingly manufactured over the course of two years for exhibition at the 1893 World's Fair in Chicago. Of the eight models shown there, five were devoted to the Hell Gate, and as the *Herald* recounted:

> One [model] shows a section of rocks near Halletts Point as it appeared before the first explosion in the fall of 1876. . . . By turning a crank the surface is made to rise, revealing underneath it the galleries made by blasters and . . . holes plugged with dynamite cartridges, the cofferdam, and the whole work as it appeared when all was ready for the blast. . . . Another model represents a general view of Hell Gate as it appeared before 1869, when operations were begun by the government. . . . The model is in effect a relief map giving the height of the rocks above the water at low-water mark. A clear notion is obtained of the situation of the rocks relative to outlying territory [as] portions of Wards Island and Halletts Point [are] delineated. . . . Flood Rock, the Hen and Chickens, the Gridiron, and smaller jagged points of rock that formerly warned navigators are faithfully reproduced.[17]

Despite the immense scale of this project, it was only one of many ongoing attempts to rework the form and hydrography of New York City's rivers.

The Harlem River

In their natural forms, the Spuyten Duyvil Creek and the Harlem River were "little, insignificant streams" that made Manhattan an island by separating it from the mainland. The waters of the Hudson and the Harlem Rivers were connected by the Spuyten Duyvil Creek and the "little channel, scarcely deep enough for craft"[18] that existed at Highbridge, the head of navigation of the Harlem River (fig. 4.12). The importance of these narrow waterways for passage around the island was acknowledged early, as evidenced by instructions given to the area's inhabitants in 1699: they were allowed to build a mill on the river "provided that they do not hinder the passage of boats and sloops round Manhattan's island."[19]

Although most of the improvements carried out by the Department of Docks were concentrated in lower Manhattan, where overcrowded conditions and the need to accommodate larger vessels demanded immediate attention, the department recognized the significance of the Harlem River to the interrelated system of American water commerce, and included its development in their early pier and bulkhead plans. The department described in its annual report of 1871:

> [The Hudson River] is navigable for 150 miles above the city, and by its connecting channels affords water communication with the western states and the chain of the Great Lakes. Through the upper and lower bays [it] communicates directly with the ocean. . . . The East River . . . gives a good

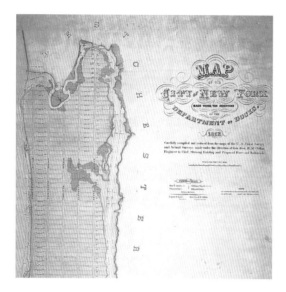

communication from the Hudson to Long Island Sound. . . . The Harlem River . . . gives two-and-one-half miles of good waterfront to the city, and presents the means of obtaining, at a reasonable cost, a second and convenient channel of communication for small vessels between the upper waters of the Hudson River and the Long Island Sound.[20]

Cutting through the mouth of the Harlem River to connect Flushing Bay with the North River was a prevalent idea at the time, because such a channel was a logical extension of the global shipping network initiated by the 1825 opening of the Erie

Canal. Such a connection allowed ships, arriving with goods from the continental interior destined for foreign ports, to avoid sailing the much longer Hudson River route around Manhattan to reach the open sea. Proposals made to the Department of Docks in 1870 in response to their open call for waterfront improvement plans recognized the utility of developing the Harlem River as a two-way link to this international system. In notations on his drawing "Plan for Constructing a Magnificent Floating Dock" submitted to the department, Samuel B. Nowlan called for the installation of a "breakwater and draws passing from Manhattan Island, to Randalls and Wards Islands and thence to Lawrence Point, Queens County, with 4 draws and locks to be closed on the retiring tide and opened at full tide for receiving ships of any draught of water with openings of 75 feet" and also proposed to widen Harlem River 100 feet "from Flushing Bay to Spuyten Duyvil so that ships from Europe can be put in direct communication with the Pacific Union Railroad and receive their cargo of teas from China and Japan ending at anchor on the Hudson River from the New Jersey coast in 16 days from California."

In envisioning the Harlem River Ship Canal, the Department of Docks considered three different routes to cut through Manhattan Island in order to make a navigable waterway of the Harlem River. One route, "by way of Shermans

4.12
NEW YORK CITY
Department of Docks. General George McClellan, engineer in chief. 1872.
NYCMA.

Creek and Tubby Hook," would have severed the upper portion of the island above what is now Washington Heights, far south of the selected solution, "by way of Dyckmans Creek and Spuyten Duyvil." The alternate "by way of Kingsbridge"[21] was dismissed as much too costly. Even after the department settled on cutting through Dyckmans Meadow along the very narrow and shallow Dyckmans Creek, the construction of the canal was a protracted process exacerbated by jurisdictional struggles, problems with the acquisition of land and water rights, slow construction, and even bad weather. In 1875, the department reported that the progress had been hindered because the New York state legislature had delegated authority over the project to both the Department of Docks and the Department of Public Parks. Even after the legislature granted permission to the federal government to improve the Harlem River and Spuyten Duyvil Creek in April 1876, movement was slow. The final plan for improvement was not adopted until 1878, and in 1879, anticipating the completion of the canal, the engineer, General Egbert L. Viele wrote:

> The business capacity of the Harlem River is yet to be developed. . . . We are soon to realize the fact that this fine river is the proper terminus of the Erie Canal. When the contemplated improvements of this river are completed, a commercial channel will be opened that will render unnecessary the transportation of the canal freight the entire length of the island and around the Battery, to interfere with the shipping and the ferries. It will, instead of making this long detour, be discharged into warehouses and elevators on the Harlem River and at Port Morris, whence the foreign shipping can receive it. The grain and lumber trade of the city will center here, and a large amount of business, now crowded into the lower end of the island, will be transacted at this point. The facilities offered by rapid-transit railways have made all this not only possible, but certain.[22]

Viele's optimism was premature, however, as the following decade would be devoted not to construction but to revisions of the plan, cost estimates, and the acquisition of riparian rights. Work finally began in 1889. Dams were erected at both ends of the cut to keep water out and to allow stone walls lining both sides of the canal to be built. Cribwork and pilework revetment were erected along the banks of the Harlem River. On March 19, 1893, the *New York Herald* complained that "the canal is not finished yet, and when the dams are torn down this fall it will still be far from complete," but conceded future rewards: "As to the benefit to commerce, that can hardly be estimated. It is not unreasonable to suppose that within the next fifty years every foot of the shoreline on the Harlem Ship Canal will be utilized for shipping purposes." The *Herald's* view of the project's effect on aquatic life, with its priority on commercial rather than ecological losses, is strikingly unlike our modern perspective:

The life of the bobtail clam, which has had its haunts in the marshy meadows of the Harlem River, is fast drawing to a close. Within six short months the luscious bivalve will cease to exist there, except in the memories of the inhabitants of Fordham Heights, Kingsbridge, and vicinity. No more will the blithesome clam digger, clad in long rubber boots, a short fustian coat, and a red necktie, hie himself to the flats when the tide is out and dig himself a bucketful of this fruit for breakfast. The removal of dams in the long talked of ship canal will put an end to his occupation. It will take away the vocation of the angler for eels, and from a romantic, placid, lagoonlike estuary it will transform the stream into a canal with swift-running currents, in which few of the present inhabitants of its waters can exist. Here and there along the banks of the big ditch a few small submerged nooks may be left in their pristine state, but the locality will never again be the happy hunting ground it has been in the past.[23]

another fishing ground upon account of the city of New York"[24] (fig. 4.13).

The cut made through Dyckmans Meadow separated the fifty-two acres of land now known as Marble Hill from the physical island of Manhattan. That area, whose borders were defined on the north, west, and east by the looping Spuyten Duyvil Creek, became an island when the canal was cut through its southern side,

and remained so until about 1910 when the rest of the creek was filled in. To this day, a trace of this origin remains: though physically joined to the Bronx on the mainland, Marble Hill belongs administratively to the borough of Manhattan.

On June 17, 1895, a procession of vessels formally opened the Harlem Ship Canal. Construction had entailed the removal of 550,000 tons of rock; the excavation of 162,000 cubic yards of earth; the dredging of 1,000,000 cubic yards of earth; and the building of 5,000 cubic yards of retaining walls. In his speech at the celebration banquet, New York City mayor William Strong voiced the sentiments of the day: "This canal has spoiled my fishing ground, but still, I am willing to do away with

Brooklyn

Despite infill and expansion efforts, Manhattan was eventually handicapped by its status as an island. With increased traffic from the Erie Canal, with ships and rail-

4.13
HARLEM RIVER
Photographer unknown. 1886. NYHS.

ways in need of extensive support facilities, and with the appearance of longer vessels with deeper drafts, the relatively small area the island provided became congested and finally insufficient to support this growing industry. The demand for land that could accommodate both huge storage facilities and the machinery needed to load and unload goods pushed the focus of the port across the river to Brooklyn, where enormous tracts of land, many of them under water, were available for development.

The engineering feats accomplished in the waters around Manhattan Island were dwarfed by those achieved in the waters off Brooklyn. Projects carried out in the 1800s added literally hundreds of acres of port-related facilities to Brooklyn that included enormous basins, dry docks, storage warehouses, and thousands of feet of piers. Since these works took place before the consolidation of Greater New York in 1898, many of them were privately planned, financed, and built, though after 1870 the Department of Docks often served in a supervisory capacity. Part of the aim of the consolidation was to integrate the fragmented system of waterfront improvement administered by separate authorities spread throughout the different municipalities. This step was yet another attempt to envision the potential of the waterfront on a grand scale.

The fifty acres of land that originally formed the Red Hook were transformed by the construction of both the Atlantic Basin and Docks, and the Erie Basin. Originally described in 1712 as "bounded on the east by a creek; on the south, by the Gouwanus Bay; on the west, by Hudson's River; and on the north, by the East River,"[25] the area is now firmly attached to Brooklyn. The uplands that formerly existed in present-day Carroll Gardens, Cobble Hill, and Boerum Hill adjoined salt meadows and marshes that further separated Red Hook from the main land mass of Brooklyn. These areas were leveled, and the land pushed out into the East River and used as fill, to allow streets to be laid out and buildings to be erected. This expansion encouraged commerce and supported an influx of population for servicing the growing shipping industry.

The construction of the Atlantic Dock and Basin, which opens onto the Buttermilk Channel separating Brooklyn from Governor's Island, was proposed in 1839 by the merchant and entrepeneur Colonel Daniel Richards, who not only owned the land, but planned and paid for the project as well. Work commenced in 1841 and produced a forty-acre basin of water along with wharves and warehouses. Built upon "shoal water land," it was an ambitious undertaking, since the entire forty acres planned for the basin were very shallow at low tide and had to be significantly dredged in order to accommodate vessels with a draft of twenty feet. The excavated earth was then used to create

4.14 top
ERIE BASIN WITH BUSH TERMINAL PIERS AND SUNSET PARK, BROOKLYN
Thomas Airviews, photographer unknown. Circa 1886. NYCMA.

4.15
ERIE BASIN, RED HOOK, GOVERNORS ISLAND, AND LOWER MANHATTAN
Fairchild Aerial Surveys, photographer. 1951. NYCMA.

4.16
PORT AUTHORITY GRAIN TERMINAL, RED HOOK, BROOKLYN
Stanley Greenberg, photographer. 1991.

4.17 top
DRY DOCK, BROOKLYN NAVY YARD
Stanley Greenberg, photographer. 1991.

4.18
DRY DOCK INTERIOR, BROOKLYN NAVY YARD
Stanley Greenberg, photographer. 1991.

4.19
BROOKLYN NAVY YARD
Stanley Greenberg, photographer. 1991.

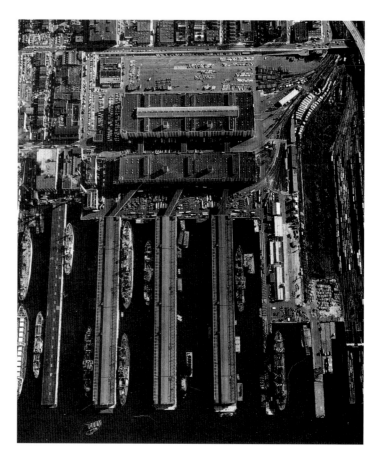

4.20 top
BUSH TERMINAL PIERS, BROOKLYN
Tip of Erie Basin in foreground. Photographer unknown. Circa 1950.
NYCMA.

4.21
BROOKLYN ARMY TERMINAL, SUNSET PARK
United States Army, photographer. Cass Gilbert, architect. Circa 1950.
NYCMA.

4.22 top
BROOKLYN ARMY TERMINAL, SUNSET PARK
Photographer unknown. Cass Gilbert, architect. Circa 1970. NYCMA.

4.23
BROOKLYN ARMY TERMINAL, PIER 2, SECOND FLOOR, SUNSET PARK
Stanley Greenberg, photographer. 1994.

4.24
HUDSON AND EAST RIVERS FROM WEST 67TH STREET TO BLACKWELLS ISLAND
United States Coast and Geodetic Survey. 1909.
New York City Department of Environmental Protection Archive.

4.25 top
SUGAR PLANT, RED HOOK, BROOKLYN
Stanley Greenberg, photographer. 1993.

4.26
SUNSET PARK CONTAINER PORT, BROOKLYN
Stanley Greenberg, photographer. 1993.

the land on which the surrounding ware-houses were built with enough additional material to fill in another forty acres of adjacent lands. In fact, the water had been so shallow that "cows were in the habit of standing in it to cool themselves and appeared to the viewer from the uplands as if they were almost over to Governors Island, and gave rise to the quaint notion that the cows actually waded over to Governors Island."[26] The first warehouse was erected in 1844, with other storage facilities added as needed until they covered some twenty acres of made land, totalling some sixty acres.

Even so, the Atlantic Basin was one of the smaller harbor improvements and never included the dry dock facilities and barge terminals that were central to other projects. Erie Basin, another privately developed human-made project created from submerged lands, opened in 1864 and encompassed 135 acres. Sheltered from the waters of the Upper New York Bay by a 2,500-foot breakwater, it became one of the world's leading grain ports (figs. 4.14–4.16).

Similarly immense landscaping projects created the Brooklyn Navy Yard out of extensive mud flats in Wallabout Bay. This was one of the first large-scale projects to be developed in the borough with the earliest purchase of lands by the United States government occurring in 1801. The facility was successively enlarged until, by the time of the Second World War, it covered 145 acres and included six dry docks for ship conversion and repair (figs. 4.17–4.19). At the turn of the century, the Bush Terminal piers to the south of Red Hook formed another major warehouse facility along the waterfront (fig. 4.20). Begun in 1890 with one pier, the complex eventually occupied 200 acres and became what its founder, Irving T. Bush, had intended—an "industrial city within a city."[27] The Brooklyn Army Terminal, completed in 1919 and noted for its design by Cass Gilbert, was a military ocean-supply facility in Sunset Park that covered 97 acres (figs 4.21–4.23).

The Brooklyn waterfront developed in this way until, during its heyday in the late nineteenth and early twentieth centuries, its economic prosperity rivaled and then surpassed that of Manhattan (fig 4.24). It extended from Newtown Creek in Greenpoint at its northern border, south past Gowanus Bay, to the Army Terminal in Sunset Park, until the whole of it combined to create one vast configuration of huge shipbuilding and repair facilities, sugar refineries, and enormous storehouses for bulk items such as coffee and grain (figs. 4.25, 4.26).

The Era of Robert Moses

The imagination required to foresee such vast transformations originally sprang from the diffuse achievement of individual intentions. Yet a singular voice emerged with the ambition of one person, Robert Moses. Regardless of one's view of the ultimate social, economic, and environmental impact of his legacy on New York City and its inhabitants, the controversial Moses has to be seen as one of the last in a long line of planners who consistently envisioned and built on a massive scale. From 1924 to 1968, Moses held a variety of civil-servant positions with both the city and state of New York—a total of twelve in all—that allowed him to conceive of and control huge projects that literally reconfigured most of New York City and a substantial part of Long Island. As parks commissioner, president of the State Parks Council, and finally, head of the Triborough Bridge and Tunnel Authority, Moses supervised the construction of a vast network of expressways, parks, and public housing (fig. 4.27). For better and for worse, he was a late practitioner of the kind of audacious landscape manipulation that characterized nineteenth-century civic projects. Unlike predecessors such as General John Newton, Moses had to contend with an active and growing awareness of the environmental impact of his projects, in response to which he euphemistically represented his harbor works as "waterfront reclamation." In a review and defense of the topographical changes to New York City implemented under his tenure, Moses argued:

> Instead of blocking off waterfront from the public, the most casual honest survey will show that 106 miles of waterfront property have been opened up and preserved for public use. In accomplishing this, 15,857 acres of waterfront property, an area greater than Manhattan Island, were acquired or created by filling operations.[28]

He further enumerated that:

> In 1934 there were 14,827 acres of park in the city, of which 928 acres represented land under water. In 1962 there were 35,450 acres of park land, of which 9,268 acres represented land under water. . . . To accomplish this was no mean task in a congested city like New York . . . but this makes the reclamation we accomplished all the more notable. To condemn the persistent, forthright, and carefully studied restoration is nothing short of an outrage.[29]

Though ecological concerns had been voiced in the nineteenth century, environmental damage was accepted as an unfortunate but unavoidable consequence of any "improvement." Moses remained loyal to the position that other kinds of benefits deserved priority over those to the environment, although for larger sectors of the mid-twentieth-century public, such damage was gradually becoming intolerable.

During his tenure as parks commissioner, Robert Moses' projects were driven primarily by the need to provide anchorage or to connect his complex network of bridges and expressways. Often it seemed as though the creation of parkland was simply a by-product of the need to link segments of highway, a suspicion confirmed by the way Moses frequently secured funding for his proposals. Mislabeling projects gave Moses access to sources of financing that otherwise would have been unavailable. Inwood Hill Park, at the top of Manhattan Island, is one such example. The park was resculpted by Moses during the 1930s as part of his West Side Improvement Plan, which included the expansion and overhaul of Riverside Park as well as the creation of a highway

along the western edge of Manhattan that would cross the Harlem River on a new bridge, the Henry Hudson, to join the Saw Mill River Parkway (fig. 4.28). Running a six-lane highway through Inwood Hill Park—at the time a lush, three-hundred-acre wilderness—and classifying it as a park access road made up for a shortfall in monies, allowing the entire project to be completed with funds designated for park improvements. The original Inwood Hill Park was sacrificed, along with Manhattan's last freshwater marsh and the hamlet

of Spuyten Duyvil (figs. 4.29, 4.30).

Similar massive alterations were made to Randalls and Wards Islands in order to provide foundations for the immense structure of the Triborough Bridge (figs. 4.31, 4.32). Though these islands, including the fifty-two-acre sand bar southeast of them known as the Sunken Meadow, had been surveyed in 1874 by the Department of Docks, only minimal modifications had been made before Moses' involvement. Instead, the islands had long been used for the city's unwanted. They provided sites for potter's fields and garbage dumps, and eventually institutions for juvenile delinquents, tuberculosis patients, and the mentally ill, as well as one of the largest municipal sewage treatment plants. In the mid-1930s, Moses began the process of joining the two islands. He razed the institutional buildings and filled in the Sunken Meadow, attaching it to Randalls Island. As described by Moses biographer Robert Caro:

> A hundred yards out from the shoreline of Jackson Heights, giant pile-drivers, mounted on giant barges, pounded steel bulkheads into the muck at the bot-

4.27
JACOB RIIS PARK, MARINE PARKWAY BRIDGE CONNECTING QUEENS
AND BROOKLYN
Photographer unknown. Circa 1940.
Triborough Bridge and Tunnel Authority Special Archive.

tom of Flushing Bay. Then long strings of barges piled high with sand from the Rockaways made their ... way up the East River, through Hell Gate, and into the bay to dump the sand behind the bulkheads. Long convoys of dump trucks ... [deposited] shale and stone in with the sand. And the mixture became a mass solid enough to hold concrete.[30]

Moses created over one hundred acres by moving 2,300,000 cubic yards of excess excavation taken from building projects in Manhattan and highways in the Bronx. He

transformed the islands into parks that would be overshadowed by the four concrete arms of the Triborough Bridge. Little Hell Gate, the shallow tidal creek that originally separated the islands, was gradually filled in and all but eliminated.

Other landfill operations administered by Moses throughout the city created highways and parks linked together—

peripheral roadways edged by green— such as the Shore Parkway in Brooklyn (now called the Belt Parkway) and the East River Drive (now the Franklin Delano Roosevelt Drive), with its related East River (fig. 4.33) and Carl Schurz Parks (fig. 4.34).

Orchard Beach in the Bronx's Pelham Bay neighborhood was one of a few notable exceptions to Moses' standard roadway-and-park model. When purchased by the city in 1883 as part of a parks initiative, Pelham Bay Park fell outside the city limits. The area that would become Orchard Beach consisted originally of distinct land masses: a peninsula called Rodmans Neck; and a trio of islands, Hunters Island and the Twin Islands (fig. 4.35). The plan for the development was drawn up in 1936 by the accomplished architect Aymar Embury II, who was also involved in building the Henry Hudson and Triborough Bridges. Working under Moses, Embury and his colleagues provided a plan that would create a mile-long, crescent-shaped beach from the waters of Long Island Sound (fig. 4.36). As described by Moses, "Through major land- and water-filling operations, and pure white sand floated up from Sandy Hook, a

4.28
HENRY HUDSON BRIDGE AND SPUYTEN DUYVIL PENINSULA
Photographer unknown. Circa 1939.
Triborough Bridge and Tunnel Authority Special Archive.

4.29 left
**HARLEM SHIP CANAL, HENRY HUDSON BRIDGE, AND WEST SIDE
PARKWAY UNDER CONSTRUCTION**
Photographer unknown. Circa 1935.
Triborough Bridge and Tunnel Authority Special Archive.

4.30
UPPER MANHATTAN AND THE BRONX
Allied Map Co., photographer. The Department of City Planning. 1984.
New York City Department of Environmental Protection.

4.31 top
WARDS AND RANDALLS ISLANDS
Fairchild Aerial Surveys, photographer. Circa 1936.
Triborough Bridge and Tunnel Authority Special Archive.

4.32
WARDS AND RANDALLS ISLANDS
Allied Map Co., photographer. The Department of City Planning. 1984.
New York City Department of Environmental Protection.

large beach was created—one of the most heavily used public beaches in the city"[31] (fig. 4.37).

The primacy of ecological concerns dominating post-Moses waterfront development signaled the end of the proactive nineteenth-century approach. With the notable exceptions of Battery Park City and the aborted Westway project, the scale of municipal works—both built and proposed—grew more modest. Rather than suggesting new landfill, projects both large and small—such as the Harlem River–Bronx State Park Plan or the Sherman Creek State Park— concentrated on reclaiming former industrial waterfront and recycling existing structures for residential and recreational use (figs. 4.38– 4.40). Waterside, a residential high-rise complex built over the East River in the early 1970s, demonstrates another type of ecological compromise. Rather than building on landfill, this complex was erected on a concrete platform over concrete piling in the East River so as not to entirely destroy natural underwater habitats or interrupt the flow of the river (figs. 4.41, 4.42). As a result of these kinds of projects, the hard edge of the city that resulted from Moses' accumulated system of highways has softened. The Queens

West project, currently under construction at Hunters Point, will "preserve the ragged edge, incorporating spatial variety and even some old industrial relics of the existing waterfront"[32] (figs. 4.43, 4.44).

The era of large-scale incursions upon the waterfront appears to be coming to a close and the future of the shoreline lies more with leisure than with industry. Yet, over the course of two centuries, through both strategically destructive and constructive interventions, the contours and topography of New York City have undergone a conspicuous physical evolu-

tion engineered entirely by humans. Those centuries belong not only to the history of the city, but to the history of imagination itself.

4.33
EAST RIVER PARK AND WILLIAMSBURG BRIDGE BETWEEN MANHATTAN AND BROOKLYN
Skyviews, photographer. 1964.
Triborough Bridge and Tunnel Authority Special Archive.

NOTES

1. Stokes, pp. 611–12.
2. Ibid., p. 236.
3. Ibid., p. 373.
4. Ibid., p. 338.
5. Rosebrock, p. 8.
6. Stokes, p. 498.
7. Ibid., p. 372.
8. Squires and Barclay, p. 12.
9. Bonner, p. 356.
10. Stokes, p. 125.
11. Ibid., p. 274.
12. Ibid., p. 1813.
13. Ibid., p. 1965.
14. Ibid., p. 1951.
15. "Little Old New York," *New York Evening Post,*
    15 January 1925.
16. Ibid.
17. "Harbor Models for the Fair," *New York Herald,*
    19 March 1893.
18. "Digging Out the Harlem Canal," *New York Herald,*
    19 March 1893.
19. Stokes, p. 419.
20. DOD, 26 April 1871, pp. 33–34.
21. "Harlem River Improvement," *New York Herald,*
    31 January 1879.
22. Stokes, p. 1969.
23. "Digging Out the Harlem Canal."
24. "Harlem's Union of the Waters," *New York Herald,*
    18 June 1895.
25. Stiles, vol. 1, p. 61.
26. Ibid., vol. 3, p. 576.
27. Jackson, p. 171.
28. Moses, p. 23.
29. Ibid., pp. 1–3.
30. Caro, pp. 392–93.
31. Moses, p. 9.
32. Herbert Muschamp, "Queens West: Why Not Something
    Great?" *New York Times,* 22 May 1994.

4.34
CARL SCHURZ PARK AND GRACIE MANSION, MANHATTAN,
BLACKWELLS (ROOSEVELT) ISLAND, QUEENS
Skyviews, photographer. 1964.
Triborough Bridge and Tunnel Authority Special Archive.

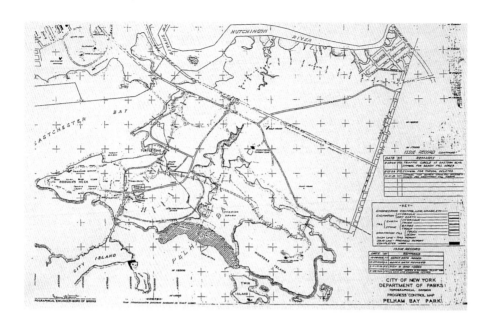

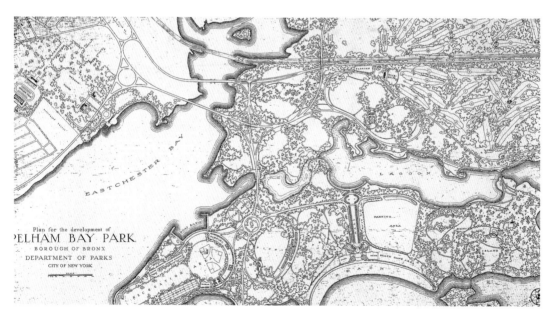

4.35 top
PELHAM BAY PARK (ORCHARD BEACH)
Progress control map. City of New York, Department of Parks,
Topographical Division. A. A. Anderson, chief topographical engineer.
1936.

4.36
**PLAN FOR THE DEVELOPMENT OF PELHAM BAY PARK
(ORCHARD BEACH)**
Department of Parks. Aymar Embury II, designer. 1935–36.
New York City Department of Parks and Recreation, Map File Division.

4.37
ORCHARD BEACH AND PELHAM BAY
Allied Map Co., photographer. New York City Department of City
Planning. 1984.
New York City Department of Environmental Protection.

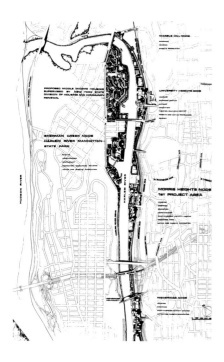

4.38 top
PROPOSAL FOR HARLEM RIVER AND BRONX STATE PARK
Site plan. State Park Commission for the City of New York. Paul
Friedberg, landscape architect. 1968–72.

4.39
POWER PLANT, SHERMAN CREEK, MANHATTAN
Photographer unknown. Circa 1920.
NYCMA.

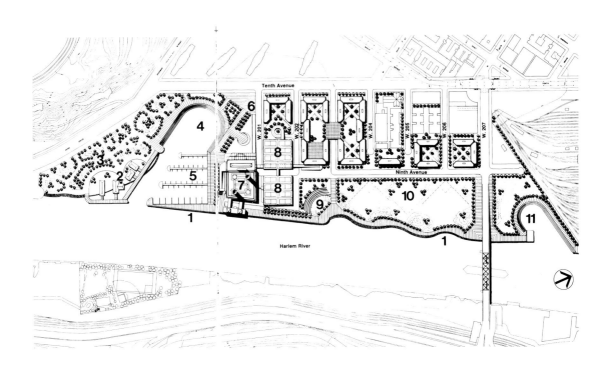

4.40
PROPOSAL FOR SHERMAN CREEK STATE PARK
Site plan. Richard Dattner, architect. 1975.

4.41 top
WATERSIDE COMPLEX, EAST RIVER, MANHATTAN
Construction showing concrete pilings.
Davis, Brody and Associates, architects. 1972.

4.42
WATERSIDE COMPLEX, EAST RIVER, MANHATTAN
Davis, Brody and Associates, architects. Circa 1974.

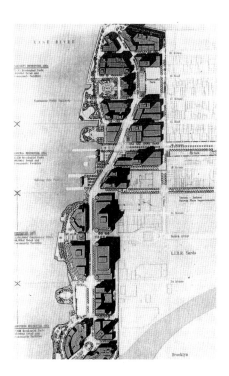

4.43 top
QUEENS WEST, EAST RIVER
Queens West Development Corporation. Gruzen, Samton, Steinglass, architects; Beyer, Blinder, Belle, associated planner and architects. 1990–93.

4.44
LONG ISLAND RAILROAD BARGE TERMINAL, HUNTERS POINT, QUEENS
Stanley Greenberg, photographer. 1993.

"QUEENS OF THE PIERS"—THE SHIPS: *QUEEN MARY, FLANDRE, OLYMPIA, UNITED STATES, AMERICA,* AND *INDEPENDENCE*
Piers 84–90, North River, Manhattan. Wide Word Photos. 1954. NYCMA.

5

5.1
RIVERSIDE PARK
J. S. Johnson, photographer. Circa 1900. NYHS.

EVOLVING PURPOSES
The Case of the Hudson River Waterfront

Michael Z. Wise, Wilbur Woods, and Eugenia Bone

> But look! here come more crowds, pacing straight for the water, and seemingly bound for a dive. Strange! Nothing will content them but the extremest limit of the land; loitering under the shady lee of yonder warehouses will not suffice. No. They must get just as nigh the water as they possibly can without falling in. And there they stand— miles of them—leagues. Inlanders all, they come from the lanes and alleys, streets and avenues— north, east, south, and west. Yet here they all unite.
>
> —Herman Melville, MOBY-DICK

The history of development along the Hudson River waterfront has been characterized by conflicts between private and public purposes, and between government and local communities (figs. 5.1, 5.2). Despite these different interests, commercial concerns defined waterfront improvement into the 1960s, when the Hudson River ceased to function as a major port (fig. 5.3). The definitions for this improvement varied widely, but there were nonetheless undeniable economic motivations that encouraged the progress of commercial development along the Hudson River through the first half of the twentieth century. In contrast, the post-shipping-era waterfront is experiencing an identity crisis. There is no consensus on how the waterfront should be used—whether for urban or natural uses, or a combination thereof—and power struggles for leadership have crippled even the most modest proposals.

In the nineteenth century, the waterfront was a scene of crime, prostitution, disease, and dilapidated housing, but with great commercial potential, responding to this degraded environment was not a matter of conflict for New Yorkers public or private. The plans that led to the original construction of the Chelsea piers (fig. 5.4), like many of the great waterfront development projects of the past, had the luxury of originating in reaction: New Yorkers were unanimous in wanting dangerous, decrepit areas improved, and the economic opportunities of the era made the direction of such improvement obvious. As the twenty-first century approaches, however, New York is searching for vision in a vacuum. The commercial need for a Hudson River port has all but disappeared. There is no longer anything to react to along the Hudson River waterfront, except the fact that one of the greatest urban-planning opportunities in the world lies sterile, fallow, and crumbling.

The History of the Hudson River Waterfront

The earliest Manhattan development along the banks of the Hudson River began in 1699, when the city granted property

5.2 top
NORTH RIVER PIERS, MANHATTAN
Photographer unknown. Circa 1900. NYCMA.

5.3
NORTH RIVER PIERS, MANHATTAN
Photographer unknown. Circa 1930. NYCMA.

5.4
CARGO BARRELS, PIER 57, CHELSEA PIERS
Photographer unknown. Circa 1920. NYCMA.

owners between Cortlandt and Cedar Streets possession of the waterfront that abutted their land (fig. 5.5). Grantees were obligated to build wharves and level the banks for roadway access, though they often failed to do so. At the time, the southwest part of the island was primarily

residential; the East River docks dominated shipping. In 1701, a Common Council committee was instructed to survey the waterfront and build slips, wharves, and streets in order to organize port activities, and by 1789 the Outer Streets and Wharves Acts initiated public control of the water's edge.

In the first half of the nineteenth

century, Hudson River development was focused on wresting control of the waterfront from private hands and establishing an organized port. The east-side docks were too small for long ships, so shipping had migrated to the west-side piers in the early 1800s, and the Randall Plan of 1807 solidified municipal control of the shores. This established public standards that promoted the orderly coexistence of shipping enterprises. The plan's mandate was to develop the waterfront for commercial purposes only. As early as 1810, the city was buying lots and developing them—often at a loss. By 1830, New York City was the country's preeminent port, and commercial interests reigned. As the city grew, landfill material was dumped haphazardly, often inhibiting the navigation of waterways. No parks were planned for the waterfront, and all attempts to create public recreational spaces were rejected as being incompatible with commercial opportunity. (The first waterfront park, the Jones Wood, was proposed in 1851, but never realized.)

During the latter half of the nineteenth century, an essential conflict arose that would become a perennial west-side waterfront theme: commercial and industrial use versus alternative public functions (figs. 5.6, 5.7). Up until 1856, when permanent pier- and bulkhead lines were established, the Hudson River waterfront had developed in a piecemeal way, resulting in sewage and silt buildup as well as human

5.5

MAP SHOWING HIGH- AND LOW-WATER MARKS AND ORIGINAL CITY GRANTS OF UNDERWATER LAND MADE TO VARIOUS PARTIES BETWEEN 1686 AND 1873, BATTERY TO 51ST STREET, HUDSON AND EAST RIVERS; ALSO PIER- AND BULKHEAD LINES ESTABLISHED FROM 1750 TO 1873
Plan. Department of Docks. General Charles K. Graham, engineer in chief; John Meehan, assistant engineer; David T. Keiller, compiler and draftsperson. 1873. NYCMA.

5.6
PIERS 46 AND 47 AT WEST STREET, NORTH RIVER, MANHATTAN
Photographer unknown. Circa 1900. NYCMA.

congestion. Businesses such as slaughter-houses and hide-curers prevailed, creating a breeding ground for typhus, cholera, and yellow fever. The residential streets were slums. A web of autonomous agencies, each with some jurisdiction over the waterfront, paralyzed development.

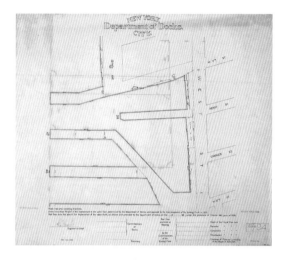

Inevitably, the piers sank into disrepair.

In response to this chaos, the Department of Docks, was given authority over the waterfront and proposed and realized a number of port facilities. The greatest achievement in Hudson River waterfront development history was arguably the construction of the Chelsea-Gansevoort Piers (fig. 5.8). The project, initiated in 1880, called for new docks to ease downtown crowding and accommodate the larger passenger liners (fig. 5.9). For both economic and aesthetic reasons, New York wanted large, modern, beautiful piers to celebrate the powerful position the city held in the world marketplace. The architectural firm of Warren and Wetmore created grand exteriors with allegorical sculpture embedded in concrete and pink granite (fig. 5.10). The long-span steel trusses supporting the piersheds were breakthroughs in industrial-design systems (fig. 5.11). Although it took thirty years for the entire plan to be completed, the Chelsea piers represented the confluence of technological advances, commercial realities, and cultural ideals—a unity of municipal and civic will.

Farther north, Frederick Law Olmsted's Riverside Park had been built along the steep slopes below Riverside Drive from 72nd Street to 129th Street. Completed in 1880, the park was intended to block the view from Riverside Drive of an unsightly railroad in the hopes of lur-

ing wealthy homebuyers to the area. The railroad still passed through the eastern edge of the park, however, an undesirable glitch for local real-estate developers. Combined with the northward extension of the bulkhead that implied an increase

5.7
PIER IMPROVEMENTS, PIERS 46 AND 47, WEST STREET, NORTH RIVER, MANHATTAN
Plan. Department of Docks. Circa 1890. NYCMA.

5.8
CHELSEA PIERS, MANHATTAN
Original design. Warren and Wetmore, architects.
From Carleton Greene, *Wharves and Piers*, 1917.

in commercial maritime activity, the local community put its collective foot down and demanded that the railroad be covered and the park enlarged, with the stipulation of no further railroad expansion. In 1894, Riverside Park was extended to the water's edge, with two strips of waterfront reserved for the Department of Docks.

In the first half of the twentieth century Hudson River waterfront development was impacted greatly by the rise of local advocacy groups and the domination of Parks Commissioner Robert Moses. Planning for the northern expansion of Riverside Park began in 1917, and many schemes were suggested for hiding the remaining section of railroad and redeveloping the park. Public tennis courts and similar recreational facilities that might  attract outsiders were thought to be a potential detriment to the neighborhood, and were opposed by local real-estate concerns. Other ideas were defeated by a variety of interested parties: local chambers of commerce, landowners, the tenacious Women's League for the Protection of Riverside Park, the railroad, and the Parks Department itself. However, automobile congestion along Riverside Drive brought pressure to use the new park-extension areas for additional roadways, and in the end, Robert Moses forced that plan through. In 1938, the extension of Riverside Park, which included the 79th Street boat basin and the Henry Hudson Parkway, was completed (fig. 5.12).

Elsewhere along the waterfront, development was winding down. By the late 1930s, shipping had begun to fade from Manhattan's western edge. The option of rapid automobile travel over the George Washington Bridge, completed in 1931, or through the Holland and Lincoln Tunnels, opened in 1927 and 1937 respectively, cut into west-side passenger-ferry traffic. At the same time the smaller cargo vessels of the early part of the century (figs. 5.13, 5.14) were replaced by giant container ships that were better able to load and unload on the expansive shoreline of New Jersey. The advent of jet airplanes further diverted maritime activity from the west side.

The latter half of the twentieth century finds the waterfront in its most profound crisis. With no commercial strongmen or unified public will, the waterfront is practically returning to its pre–Department of Docks state of disfunction.

For a financially pressured city that wants or needs certain parcels of land developed for economic reasons, the most expedient option is to allow private development, which often results in zoning waivers, tax abatements, and other lures

5.9 top
CHELSEA SECTION PIERS 54 AND 56
Typical elevation. Warren and Wetmore, architects; J. H., draftsperson;
Approved by G. E. H. 1907. NYCMA.

5.10
CUNARD WHITE STAR, PIER 56, CHELSEA PIERS
View from the Miller Highway. Photographer unknown. Circa 1930.
NYCMA.

Progress, Chelsea Section, Pier 58 '08. June 20.

5.11
CONSTRUCTION OF PIER 58, CHELSEA PIER, NORTH RIVER,
MANHATTAN
Photographer unknown. 1908. NYCMA.

of questionable value to the long-term economic health of the city. It has also left New Yorkers with few public spaces. Private developers cannot be relied upon to produce public goods, and the benefits of special government treatment are often marginal.

The social initiatives of the 1960s made large sums of federal money available for urban renewal, and nonmaritime

commercial waterfront planning began. In 1963, the city commissioned a comprehensive proposal for the entire Hudson River waterfront, from the Battery to West 72nd Street, involving extensive landfill at the lower portion (fig. 5.15). Prepared by the engineering firm Ebasco Services, the plan called for a new convention center to extend from West 38th to 43rd Streets, as well as a heliport (fig. 5.16).

The plan was never fully implemented, though it did establish the basic structure for the landfill at Battery Park City (figs. 5.17, 5.18) and laid the groundwork for what would later become the Jacob K. Javits Convention Center.

In the meantime, millions of dollars were squandered by the city on ineffective bids to salvage the seventy-nine unused piers along the Hudson in the hope that this effort would revitalize commercial shipping. Some structures were modernized for use by shipping companies that never availed themselves of the facilities. Other piers burned or simply rotted away. One pier became a docking point for a floating jail, another was reconfigured into a municipal impoundment lot for illegally parked cars, and a third serves as a city bus depot.

In 1966, the City Planning Commission put forth a further proposal known as the Lower Manhattan Plan (figs. 5.19, 5.20), which called for expanding the entire southwest waterfront with landfill with the extension of existing streets to waterfront parks and plazas (fig. 5.21). A conference on the waterfront's future was held that same year in response to the

5.12
RIVERSIDE PARK AND HENRY HUDSON PARKWAY, MANHATTAN
Skyviews, photographer. 1964.
Triborough Bridge and Tunnel Authority Special Archive.

5.13 top
CAR FLOATS (LIGHTERS), PIER 1, NORTH RIVER, MANHATTAN
Photographer unknown. Circa 1920. NYCMA.

5.14
PIER 86, NORTH RIVER, MANHATTAN
Photographer unknown. Port Authority of New York. 1972. NYCMA.

neglect and divided authority that had added to the degradation of the waterfront (fig. 5.25). Then–Manhattan borough president Percy Sutton's call for public access to the waterfront resonates three decades later.

Of the many Hudson River projects both abandoned and completed during the second half of the twentieth century, the one with possibly the greatest impact on New Yorkers' quality of life and a major motivator behind the subsequent reevaluation of the waterfront's possibilities, was the massive cleanup effort instigated by the Clean Water Act of 1972. Ironically, this goal could only have been possible with the decline of commercial port activities in New York City. Twenty-five years after the act's passage, the waters of New York are significantly cleaner. Certain key-indicator biota have returned to the harbor due in part to the decrease in shipping and industry, but this regeneration is primarily a result of reforms in sewage treatment. The Hudson River's restoration of health suggests that its primary post-shipping-era use will most likely accommodate New Yorkers' great need for recreational options.

The North River Pollution Control Plant

One direct response to the Clean Water Act, the $1.1-billion North River Pollution Control Plant, was installed on Harlem's west shore and processes 165 million gallons of raw sewage every day (fig. 5.26). The plant was originally intended to have been located on the Upper West Side, but residents mobilized to block its construction, and it gravitated to the less-affluent neighborhood running from West 137th to West 145th Streets. After plans for the plant itself had been drawn up, including a facade of concrete arches designed by Ted Long of Associated Engineers, additional architects—among them Philip Johnson, Gruzen and Associates, and Bond Ryder—were asked to devise schemes to camouflage the rooftop (fig. 5.27). In 1967, Johnson proposed what he called a major aesthetic monument on the waterfront. This involved the placement of fifteen acres of water displays, including four two-hundred-foot-high fountains, atop the plant, with a swath of greenery to span the Henry Hudson Parkway and link to the slope beneath Riverside Drive.

After neighborhood groups were consulted, planners chose an alternative scheme, proposed by Bond Ryder, that called for a twenty-eight-acre recreational facility connected to Riverside Drive by two bridges. In 1971, full designs for the plant were confirmed, and construction on the platform started the following year and was completed in 1978. In 1979, architect Richard Dattner was selected to design the plant's park, which, with funding and approvals, took five years. Construction on the plant's working facilities was implemented in two phases: the

Advanced Preliminary Treatment Facilities were begun in 1983 and in operation by 1986; and the Secondary Treatment Facilities were started in 1985 and completed in 1990. Construction on the park commenced in 1987, nearly twenty years after the Harlem site had been chosen for the plant itself. The $128-million park opened atop the plant on May 27, 1993 (fig. 5.28).

The plant has emitted unpleasant odors since it began operation. Under duress from community-group lawsuits, state and city authorities have made some progress in combating the problem through a series of modifications that are expected to cost over $50 million. But the park above the plant has been a huge success. In an area much in need of recreational facilities, Riverbank State Park drew over 1.4 million visitors in its first year of operation. It offers a variety of sports and recreational amenities. But in terms of a greater urban plan, the park remains an island separated from the rest of the urban fabric, as it can be reached only by special bridges from Riverside Drive at 138th and 145th Streets and by an elevator and stair tower that link its northern end to the lower part of Riverside Park.

Battery Park City

Launched as an urban-renewal development in 1966, Battery Park City was created on the site of deserted city-owned piers. Constructed with earth and rubble excavated from the foundation of the nearby World Trade Center, the ninety-two-acre landfill was completed in 1976 (fig. 5.22). Under a 1979 master plan developed by architects Alexander Cooper and Stanton Eckstut, the existing Manhattan street grid was extended into the new area in an effort to integrate the development with the rest of lower Manhattan (figs. 5.23, 5.24). Despite these efforts, West Street, an eight-lane highway on the landfill's eastern border, remains a barrier separating the new complex from the existing urban fabric.

Battery Park City, which consists primarily of office space and luxury housing, was built by the Battery Park City Authority. According to former Urban Development Corporation chairman William Stern, the original rationale for the project was that it would create jobs, produce government revenue, and be a catalyst for downtown development. After numerous proposals and revisions (fig. 5.29), a scheme was adopted that accommodated the 1980s development strategy: to rely heavily on the building of huge corporate headquarters on the site (fig. 5.30).

The project was funded with $200 million in state-issued bonds, a public expenditure justified by "guarantees made by its government organizers that rental revenues would be partly redirected toward middle- and low-income housing projects throughout the city's five bor-

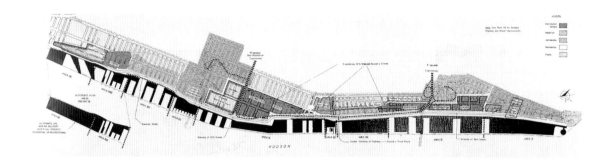

5.15–5.18: THE PORT OF NEW YORK COMPREHENSIVE ECONOMIC STUDY, MANHATTAN DEVELOPMENT PLAN 1962 TO 2000
Department of Marine and Aviation, City of New York. Ebasco Services Inc., business consultants; Moran, Proctor, Mueser and Rutledge, consulting engineers; Eggers and Higgins, architects. 1962.

5.15 top
PLAN OF PROJECT ADJACENT UPLAND AND WATERFRONT DEVELOPMENT TO THE YEAR 2000
Courtesy of Ann L. Buttenwieser.

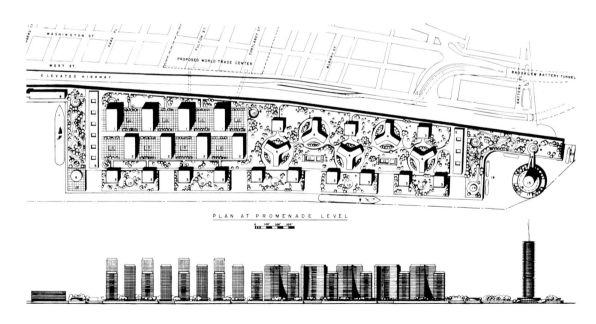

5.16 opposite
PROPOSED RECREATIONAL CENTER AND CONVENTION HALL, BETWEEN WEST 38TH AND 45TH STREETS
Perspective. Rudolf Associates, renderer.
Courtesy of Ann L. Buttenwieser.

5.17, 5.18 above
PROPOSED DEVELOPMENT BETWEEN BATTERY PARK AND CHAMBERS STREET
Perspective and plan. Rudolf Associates, renderer.
Courtesy of Ann L. Buttenwieser.

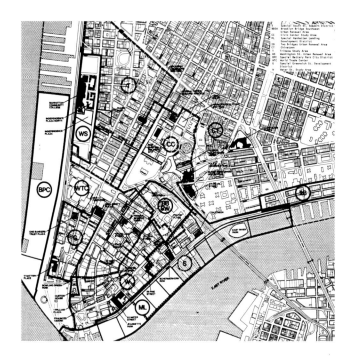

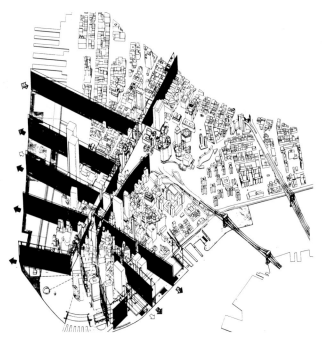

5.19–5.21: LOWER MANHATTAN PROJECTS
Mayor's Office of Lower Manhattan Development, Department of City
Planning, Battery Park City Authority. Wallace, McHarg, Roberts and
Todd; Whittlesey, Conklin and Rossant; Alan M. Voorhees and
Associates. 1966–73.

5.19 top
PROJECTS PLAN

5.20 opposite
VISUAL CORRIDORS

5.21
LOWER MANHATTAN

oughs," according to a September 20, 1993, story in the *New York Observer*.[1] At that time, the authority stated that profits from Battery Park City had helped back bonds for the construction and rehabilitation of 1,400 housing units elsewhere in New York City.

Battery Park City now comprises eighteen buildings with 4,800 middle- to upper-income apartment units, as well as the World Financial Center with its four office towers and 125-foot-high vaulted glass winter garden, designed by Cesar Pelli Associates. One-third of Battery Park City consists of parks and open space, including a 1.2-mile riverfront esplanade. Artists were invited to contribute to the design of specific park features with "conceptions [that] subordinate personal artistic style to the functional requirements

of particular sites," as described by Ken Johnson in *Art in America*.[2] Hudson River Park at the northern tip of Battery Park City was completed in 1992, and the new building for Stuyvesant High School opened there the same year. At Battery Park City's southern end, ground was broken in 1994 for a hexagonal Holocaust Memorial Museum designed by Kevin Roche (fig. 6.25, p. 263).

The Road Along the River

Perhaps the longest-running saga in the Hudson River waterfront development involves the ramshackle thoroughfare along Manhattan's southwestern edge, formerly the elevated Miller Highway. The Miller Highway was named for Julius Miller, the Manhattan borough president from 1922 to 1930 who championed it. Built along the Hudson River from Canal Street to 79th Street in the 1930s, the highway eased congestion and provided motorists with a continuous glimpse of the river, although it blocked the view from other vantage points, such as the dozens of east-west streets it crossed (figs. 5.31, 5.32). Lined with ornate bronze lamps and bas-reliefs designed by sculptor René Chambellan, the Miller Highway remained in use until December 15, 1973, when an overloaded dump truck broke through the roadbed and forced the artery to close between the Battery and 42nd Street. The abandoned elevated structure,

5.22
LOWER MANHATTAN
Allied Map Co., photographer. Department of City Planning. 1984.
New York City Department of Environmental Protection.

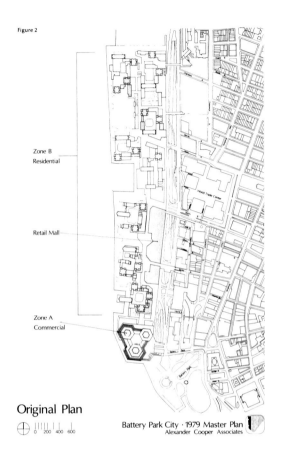

Figure 2

Zone B
Residential

Retail Mall

Zone A
Commercial

Original Plan

Battery Park City · 1979 Master Plan
Alexander Cooper Associates

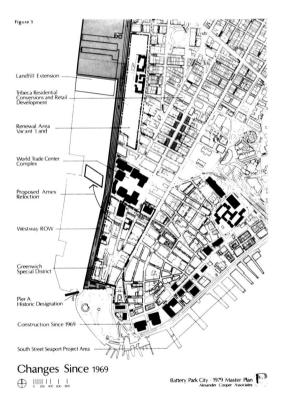

Figure 3

Landfill Extension

Tribeca Residential
Conversions and Retail
Development

Renewal Area
Vacant Land

World Trade Center
Complex

Proposed Amex
Relocation

Westway ROW

Greenwich
Special District

Pier A
Historic Designation

Construction Since 1969

South Street Seaport Project Area

Changes Since 1969

Battery Park City · 1979 Master Plan
Alexander Cooper Associates

5.23, 5.24
BATTERY PARK AND BATTERY PARK CITY
Battery Park City Authority. TAMS Gibbs and Hill Associates, architects
and engineers; Alexander Cooper Associates. 1969–79.
Battery Park City Authority.

5.25
STREET-CLEANING DUMP, WEST 134TH STREET, NORTH RIVER
Photographer unknown. Department of Docks and Ferries. 1910. NYCMA.

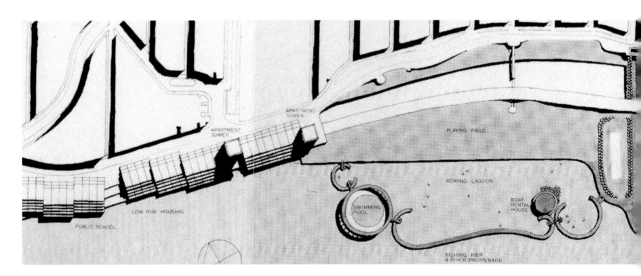

5.26 top
**RIVERSIDE PARK AND NORTH RIVER POLLUTION CONTROL PLANT
(UNDER CONSTRUCTION), MANHATTAN AND NEW JERSEY**
Allied Map Co., photographer. Department of City Planning. 1984.
New York City Department of Environmental Protection.

5.27
PROPOSED PARK
Site plan. Gruzen and Partners, architects, planners, engineers.
Circa 1975.

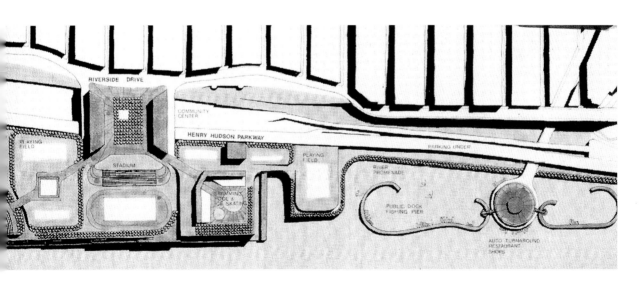

5.28
RIVERBANK STATE PARK
Norman McGrath, photographer. Richard Dattner, architect; TAMS
Engineering; Abel, Bainnson, Butz, Associates, landscape architects.
1993. Richard Dattner, architects.

5.29 top
DEVELOPMENT BETWEEN BATTERY PARK AND CHAMBERS STREET
Original plan, perspective. Rudolph Associates, renderer.
Circa 1965.

5.30
BATTERY PARK CITY
New York State Department of Transportation, photographer. 1989.
Hudson River Park Conservancy.

with its treacherous ramps connected to West Street, served for many years as a makeshift track for joggers, bikers, and walkers. The ground-level portion of the roadway was repaved to provide temporary traffic service for five to ten years and was still in use in 1996, though large sections of the highway have been demolished.

The massive federal project known as Westway was designed to replace the Miller Highway and reclaim the decrepit harbor area. Proposed in 1974, Westway had become by the mid-1980s one of the nation's most disputed public-works projects. Five main proposals were developed, each with different roadway configurations. Variations included underground and street-level highways, outshore layouts (where the highway was to be located on the edge of new landfill), and inland routes (fig. 5.33). With a price tag of $2.3 billion, the fatal plan for Westway involved extensive landfill; the construction of a new 4.2-mile, six-lane highway; and parkland, housing, and commercial development atop its 181 acres (figs. 5.34, 5.35). Westway would have connected with both the Brooklyn Battery and the Lincoln Tunnels. It was a grand but fatally flawed scheme because it failed to recognize and consider the necessity of community support.

In 1981, the United States Army Corps of Engineers issued a dredging and landfill permit for Westway, and President Ronald Reagan presented New York City mayor Ed Koch with a check for $85 million for the Westway right-of-way. For the federal government, Westway offered an opportunity to integrate the national highway systems with America's largest urban center. In 1982, Federal District Court judge Thomas Greisa blocked the landfill permit because the Army Corps of Engineers had failed to assess the landfill's impact on striped-bass hatcheries. Environmental-impact hearings were held in 1984, and in 1985, the Army Corps of Engineers issued a new landfill permit. The courts overruled this permit too, and, citing congressional opposition, New York leaders decided to discard the Westway plan and apply the total federal commitment for $1.7 billion to mass-transit funding and the construction of a scaled-down highway. Opponents of Westway, who saw the development plan as an egregious example of government operating for the benefit of powerful special interests like large construction concerns and to the detriment of local neighborhood communities, had sponsored eleven years of litigation.

The federal government would not reclaim the $85 million it had already paid for Westway's right-of-way immediately. New York City and New York State made a deal with the federal government whereby the right-of-way land would be preserved from commercial development and used to create public spaces, like a much-needed lower Manhattan park. However, New York State would, on behalf of both

5.31, 5.32
MILLER HIGHWAY AND NORTH RIVER PIERS, MANHATTAN
Photographers unknown. Circa 1950. NYCMA.

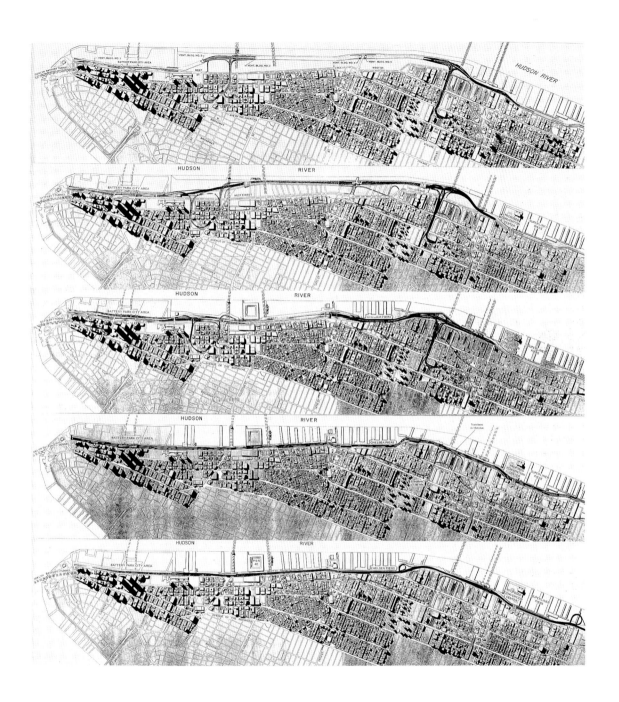

5.33
WEST SIDE HIGHWAY PROJECT
System Design Concepts; Marcou, O'Leary and Associates; Skidmore, Owings and Merrill; Parsons, Brinckerhoff, Quade and Douglas; New York State Urban Development Corporation. Department of City Planning; New York City Transportation Administration; Federal Highway Administration; United States Department of Transportation. 1971–74.
Route 9A Reconstruction Group, New York State Department of Transportation.

the city and state, request a waiver of the payback in September 1995. That month, city comptroller Alan Hevesi filed suit against Governor George Pataki in state supreme court. The suit's intention was to block New York State from repaying the $85 million, and the obligation it implied to build a park, to the federal government because, by returning the federal grant, New York State would in effect unburden itself of the responsibility to build park space and would have the freedom to develop the west-side waterfront in any manner it chose. Mayor Rudolph Guiliani, a supporter of the state's position, has insisted that large developments that are opposed because of their presumed negative impact on neighborhoods would not be built along the west-side waterfront. Other city officials, however, have disagreed. In the *New York Observer,* Hevesi stated, "It's disingenuous for the state to suggest we trust their plans even as they're reneging."[3]

Westway has since been replaced by plans for a far more modest, tree-lined boulevard (fig. 5.36) known as New York State Route 9A. The planned seven-lane roadway was nicknamed "Lessway" by Robert Ronayne, the former executive director of the New York State Department of Transportation's Route 9A Project. At hearings on five possible variations in May and October 1993, a proposed $380-million reconstruction of the existing road received the most support.

The five-mile urban boulevard is planned as a surface highway divided by a tree-lined median and flanked by a walkway and bike path to the west. The S-curve of the current highway at 23rd Street would be straightened out. Decorative elements such as lampposts, public art, and park benches would ornament the corridor. The equivalent of forty percent ($680 million) of the original Westway trade-in funds are slated for Route 9A, of which $380 million will go to Route 9A and $300 million to the Hudson River Waterfront Park. Construction began in 1996.

Public suspicion regarding the planning of Route 9A has been constant. Fears that the improved thoroughfare will be nothing more than an incentive for developers to build up the western edge of Manhattan have been repeatedly addressed. For example, Route 9A officials had to assure local activists that water and sewage lines would not be upgraded to carry the greater loads necessary to accommodate large-scale development. Tom Fox, former head of the Hudson River Park Conservancy, the authority created to implement the ninety-three-acre park, told the *New York Times,* "There's such a fear of government run amok that an attempt to have it focus on creating public works is treated with great suspicion."[4] In response to this controversy, the Route 9A Project's Community Participation Program was initiated by the Department of Transportation in 1986 in an effort to keep citizens fully informed about the route's design and planning.

Indeed, the complexity of the decision-making process for public-works projects, combined with the relative modesty of the Route 9A plan, does suggest that New York City is confined to implementing low-impact development. New York senator Daniel Patrick Moynihan, arguing that Westway could have been a Central Park–like achievement for twentieth-century New York, said shortly after the plan's defeat, "It says something about us that we can't do these things anymore. . . . I fear the kind of preservationism that preserves out of fear that nothing equivalent [to what has been done in the past] could be done in the present."[5]

Hudson River Park

Along the western edge of the proposed Route 9A, the waterfront from the northern edge of Battery Park City to 59th Street is slated to be converted into the Hudson River Waterfront Park, a four-mile stretch to encompass a 270-acre strip of land between the river and Route 9A, with an average width of eighty feet (fig. 5.37). The park has been designed by a team of landscape architects, Quennell Rothschild Associates and Signe Nielsen, and construction is to proceed as segments of Route 9A are completed. The $300-million park involves no landfill and will not alter the existing topography of the waterfront.

It would provide bicycle paths and a riverfront esplanade, while restoring thirteen piers for public access under the auspices of the Hudson River Park Conservancy. The passenger-ship terminals between West 48th and 52nd Streets, used mostly by cruise liners in warm weather months, are to be refurbished.

Intense battles among planners, developers, lawmakers, and citizens groups have arisen over how much commercial use of the piers and waterfront areas should be permitted. The Hudson River Park Conservancy vows that it will not create a mall and only intends a park along the river. Given the likelihood of heavy cutbacks at the state level, however, commercial development of some sort is likely to be required to help pay for the park. Fears that the ratio of park to commercial development could favor the latter were heightened in April 1995 when Peter Keogh, who worked in the real-estate field for many years as an engineer and lawyer, took over as conservancy chief.

The Hudson River Park Conservancy is a unique public authority since it cannot issue bonds or override zoning. It requires public participation in its decision making, and its scope is limited to implementing the West Side Waterfront Panel Plan. The conservancy was created because Governor Pataki and Mayor Guiliani felt that such a specialized municipal organization was necessary to build a park in a location spanning several distinct com-

5.34
WESTWAY PARK
Alternative plan. 1971–74.

5.35
WESTSIDE HIGHWAY PROJECT
Plan. 1971–74.

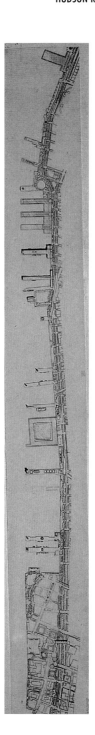

5.36
ROUTE 9A
Plan. 1993.

5.37
HUDSON RIVER WATERFRONT PARK
Plan. 1990.

munities and where more than a dozen different government agencies have existing operations or jurisdictions. The conservancy is a subsidiary of the New York State Urban Development Corporation, which is not bound to the same restrictions as the conservancy. Worried community groups fear that the conservancy misrepresents its true intentions when it promises not to allow large commercial development along the waterfront, because at any time, the Urban Development Corporation could step in and make unpopular decisions, absolving the conservancy of accountability.

Three areas called "nodes of development" have already been identified by the conservancy as ideal sites for commercial projects that would fund the maintenance of the park: the 42nd Street area, where Circle Line and cruise ships currently dock; the Chelsea Piers, which are already being developed (fig. 5.38); and Pier 40, currently a forty-acre parking lot and storage facility at the western end of Houston Street. Hotels, commercial offices, and residences are banned in the park, but commercial recreational uses will be encouraged. According to the conservancy's plan, revenues from projects within the park will be used only for the park itself.

A midtown maritime district is planned for the waterfront at 42nd Street, entailing renovation of the plaza where excursion boats and the Intrepid Sea, Air, Space Museum reside as well as construc-

tion of an open-air amphitheater. The Con Edison refueling facility and the Department of Sanitation's marine transfer operations, both of which are water-dependent, will continue to operate. Piers 94 and 97 are designated as public spaces. A new three-block recreation area will connect DeWitt Clinton Park to the Hudson shore. Also slated is a permanent floating heliport on the *Guadalcanal*, a six-hundred-foot-long, fifty-five-foot-high former navy heliport ship, which is opposed by local community groups because the craft would be docked parallel to the shore, and would thus block waterfront views from the tip of Pier 84, currently the only public pier in the Clinton neighborhood.

The conservancy cites the Chelsea Pier complex as a model commercial development for a waterfront park that can generate revenue. These four piers, between West 17th and 23rd Streets, once served as arrival and departure points for great ocean liners like the *Mauritania* and the *Ile de France*, and have been undergoing conversion into a one-million-square-foot center for sports, film production, and public recreation. Each of the four piers extends over six hundred feet into the Hudson River. Two will be enclosed, and a five-block-long building will link the piers on the shore.

Pier 40 is arguably the most disputed "node of development" in the Hudson River Park plan. Nearby neighborhoods—

Chelsea, Greenwich Village, SoHo, and TriBeCa—are in desperate need of park space. The local community board and its waterfront advocacy organization, the Federation to Preserve the Greenwich Village Waterfront, are adamant that the pier not be developed for commercial use, citing the pier as the area's only potential park locale. The community board has held firm that it will only approve its own

park plan, which calls for razing Pier 40 to street level and creating an open green space. The federation believes it can finance the plan with Route 9A easement money (the contested $85 million for Westway's right-of-way) and other federal funding. Both the conservancy and Douglas Curry, president of the Route 9A Project, consider the federation's financ-

ing proposals unrealistic.

While governmental forces admit the district is in dire need of park space, Pier 40 has been judged an excellent site for the commercialization necessary to help fund the whole of Hudson River Park. According to Hudson River Park Conservancy president Peter Keogh, it is inevitable that Pier 40 will be commercially developed. With this conflict between community and city interests, Pier 40 has become the flashpoint for what Keogh has described as the potential "Balkanization" of the Hudson River waterfront.

The Railroad Yards

The site of the former Pennsylvania Railroad yards, along the riverfront between West 59th and 72nd Streets, remains the largest piece of land available for development in Manhattan (fig. 5.39). Proposals for the area from Donald Trump represent perhaps the most conspicuous instance in which the city has invested its faith in a private developer for financial rescue. First dubbed Trump City, renamed Television City, and eventually redesigned and known as Riverside South, the project's many incarnations are a monument to Trump's tenacity and grand ambitions.

5.38
CHELSEA PIERS, HUDSON RIVER, MANHATTAN
New York State Department of Transportation, photographer. 1989.
Hudson River Park Conservancy.

In 1985, Trump provoked an uproar with his initial plan to build a $3-billion residential development project at the former railroad yards site. The focal point of that grandiose vision was to have been the world's tallest edifice, with forty-eight more stories than the Empire State

Building. The project has since been progressively scaled back.

The sixteen proposed buildings now range in height from fifteen to forty-nine stories, containing a total of 5,700 apartments. They would be situated along a 21.5-acre riverfront park, extending from 59th Street up to the current southern edge of Riverside Park, at 72nd Street (fig.

5.40). A portion of the West Side Highway would be pushed inland to accommodate the park.

In July 1994, Trump's inclusion of a group of Hong Kong investors in the Riverside South project appeared to provide a major push toward the development's realization. The new team hired architect Philip Johnson to design the first four buildings of the complex, for which Skidmore, Owings and Merrill is creating the master plan. Even with public amenities including the park, many Upper West Side residents fear that Riverside South will only add to neighborhood congestion, particularly at the already overtaxed subway station at 72nd Street and Broadway. Concern has also been sparked by Trump's plan to funnel Riverside South sewage to the North River Pollution Control Plant, which does not yet have the capacity to handle the increased load.

The Cost of Democratic Participation

Imperfect as they are, Riverbank State Park, Battery Park City, and the earlier example of Riverside Park illustrate that only modest steps in waterfront development may be possible. Current ecological taboos in waterfront development, such as landfill; a dramatically drained public infrastructure budget; community associations with agendas of their own; public suspicion of government duplicity, especially in giving municipal assets to private

5.39
NORTH RIVER PIERS AND WEST SIDE RAIL YARDS, MANHATTAN
Site of proposed Trump City project.
Photographer unknown. Circa 1950. NYCMA.

to developers; and the ambitions of individual organizations and agencies to give their own exclusive definition to the waterfront: all these factors have con-

RIVERSIDE SOUTH PARK

spired to paralyze the decision-making process. The task of reconciling such competing forces was described by the Manhattan Regional Planning Association as early as 1930:

> It is not within the power of any one body to carry into effect a plan for any portion of the waterfront of Manhattan, there are concerned in the control of this waterfront federal, state, and municipal authorities. Numerous private corporations and persons are concerned in its ownership and development. The preparation of any plan with the expectation of public action in putting it into effect is impractical. The expense that would be involved even with the highest degree of cooperation between the owners and the public authorities would be enormous. The making of plans for definite application has to proceed in the usual piecemeal way, although these partial plans should be fitted into a comprehensive plan of the city.[6]

The days of Robert Moses and his author-

itarianism are gone. In its place, New York City has a participatory system that is characterized by an inability to create consensus. New York City's decrepit waterfront is a testament to the high cost of democracy. But some progress has been made.

After years of delay, in 1993 the city council proposed new waterfront zoning laws regulating permissible uses on the waterfront. Development of the Hudson River waterfront is contingent upon the plans proposed in the New York City Comprehensive Waterfront Plan.

The New York City Comprehensive Waterfront Plan

In August 1992, Mayor David Dinkins held a news conference to announce the release of the New York City Comprehensive Waterfront Plan, the first citywide plan, prepared by the Department of City Planning, to address the longest and most diverse shoreline of any city in the nation. The plan was labeled a "discussion document" and was meant to stimulate dialogue among New Yorkers about the future of their waterfront, as well as offering a vision of what the waterfront could become. Many New Yorkers responded positively to the proposal, but others felt it

5.40
RIVERSIDE SOUTH PARK
Plan. Thomas Balsley Associates, landscape architects; Mel Chin, Joyce Kozloff, Mary Miss, Fred Willson, artists; Skidmore, Owings and Merrill; Willen, architects. 1993. Riverside South Associates.

went too far, or not far enough, in protecting or promoting certain interests. A widely attended public hearing on the plan in October 1992 demonstrated the importance New Yorkers attach to their waterfront, and participants voiced a broad range of concerns.

The plan recognizes the existence of many sections of the waterfront that remain dormant and derelict, or inaccessible for public use and enjoyment. It is intended to provide a long-range framework to guide land-use along the city's entire shoreline, a vision that would address environmental concerns as well as needs for working port facilities, waterside public access, open space, housing, and commercial activity (figs. 5.41, 5.42).

Increased access to the waterfront relies to a great extent on the concept of the public-trust doctrine, an inveterate legal theory establishing the state government's claim to hold tidal waters and submerged land in trust for the benefit of the public. Historically, common law based on custom and usage has held that property rights for private waterfront ownership ended at the mean high-water line. The state had clear titles to the "wet sand" between high- and low-water marks, to subaqueous land, and to the water itself. This right-of-access is based on the conviction that the foreshore and waters have unique characteristics associated with a public purpose.

Six months after the release of the Comprehensive Waterfront Plan, the first of a number of supporting elements was added to amplify and implement revitalization efforts. The Waterfront Zoning Reform was proposed in early 1993 as a draft amendment to existing zoning resolutions. Upon adoption by the city council in October 1993, the new waterfront zoning addressed issues such as public access, visual corridors, floating structures, design controls unique to a shoreline location, and the desirability of fostering water-related uses. The Department of City Planning issued detailed studies of the twenty-two local sections of the waterfront, called "reach studies," compiled into plans by borough. These studies give both officials and the public more thorough information about particular sites where land-use changes are recommended. They also highlight the importance of landmark structures and other historic elements that evoke the city's past as a port, seaside resort, and home to those who valued or needed proximity to the waterfront.

The reach studies for Manhattan, for example, propose to ring the island's waterfront with an "emerald necklace" of parks and bicycle paths. In some cases, this would entail closing gaps between existing public spaces; elsewhere, the creation of entirely new green areas.

During the two-year course of the plan's development, the Department of City Planning held meetings to hear the views of public officials, government agencies, community boards, and civic and neighborhood organizations. The department organized and worked closely with the citywide Waterfront Plan Advisory Committee to identify and debate issues affecting the waterfront's future. That panel represents diverse interests, with membership comprised of advocates for natural resources, open space, industry, housing, and economic development. It includes representatives of such groups as the Municipal Art Society, the Parks Council, the Real Estate Board of New York, the American Institute of Architects, the Port Authority, and the Regional Plan Association, as well as state, federal, and local agencies and elected officials. Public review and discussion intensified as the proposed draft of waterfront-zoning resolutions went through the city's formal land-use review procedure in 1993.

The new zoning brought several of the Comprehensive Waterfront Plan's recommendations closer to actualization. First, the zoning calls for all new residential and commercial developments in medium- and high-density waterfront areas to set aside fifteen to twenty percent of their land area for publicly accessible open space, to be devised according to urban-design controls but maintained by the property owner. Visual and physical corridors must be created or preserved to prevent the waterfront from being walled off. Underwater land between the bulk- and pierhead lines will be excluded from floor area calculations, thereby protecting the waterfront from overly dense and out-of-scale development. To encourage more water-dependent uses, excursion and fishing boats as well as ferries are permitted to operate in a wide variety of commercial zones that have appropriate controls for size and parking.

The most controversial aspects of the zoning were proposed limitations on the height and form of waterfront buildings. Only two options had previously existed for controlling these factors: contextual zoning and height-factor zoning, neither of which were designed specifically for waterfront locations and both of which lacked the flexibility needed for typical large, irregular waterfront lots. Contextual zones are based on the city's grid and result in lower building with higher coverage. Height-factor regulations encourage tall buildings that could wall off the waterfront. As adopted, the waterfront zoning stipulates a minimum-coverage requirement as well as height limits in order to avoid "tower in a park" designs whereby building height is out of scale with its surroundings.

Implementation of the Comprehensive Waterfront Plan will continue after the Waterfront Revitalization Program —a framework of twelve local and forty four state policies for regulating waterfront land use and development—has been revised to reflect the master plan. The Department of City Planning is currently altering and enhancing this framework, articulating different regional characteristics in order to give specificity to

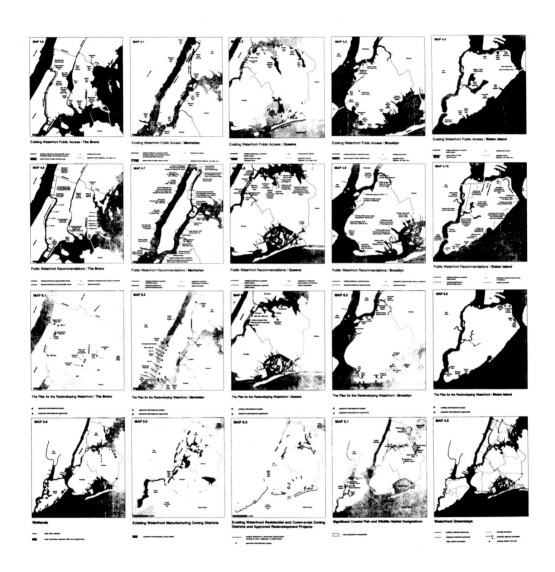

5.41
NEW YORK CITY COMPREHENSIVE WATERFRONT PLAN
Use, resource, and recommendation maps from the discussion documents. 1992.
New York City Department of City Planning.

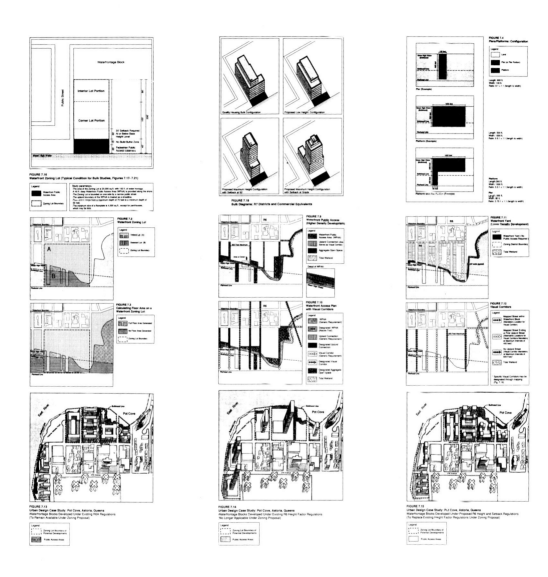

5.42
NEW YORK CITY COMPREHENSIVE WATERFRONT PLAN
Proposed zoning principles from the discussion documents. 1992.
New York City Department of City Planning.

the policies' applications. These revisions to the Waterfront Revitalization Plan will be adopted after a public review process.

The Comprehensive Waterfront Plan identifies potential redevelopment sites, many of which will require further rezoning, for new housing and commercial activity. To implement these recommendations, future zoning changes may be proposed by the city, private landowners, elected officials, community boards, or local organizations. The timing of these initiatives will depend on the availability of resources. A number of sites, including those slated for the Riverside South and Brighton by the Sea complexes, were approved for large-scale development prior to the adoption of the new waterfront zoning and will not be subject to those regulations. In reviewing these projects, however, the City Planning Commission did insist that generous amounts of open waterfront space be made available for public access. As of 1996, the Department of City Planning was in the process of rezoning priority areas such as Red Hook and Mill Basin in Brooklyn, and Northern Hunters Point and the downtown Flushing waterfront in Queens.

Public funding, another element of the Comprehensive Waterfront Plan's implementation strategy, is recommended both immediately and in the future for the preservation of natural areas, for public-access development, and for infrastructure support for the working and the redeveloping waterfronts. Taken together, these investment proposals are well beyond the city's immediate financial abilities. Even so, by aggressively seeking state and federal funds, and by carefully targeting the city's capital resources, many of the plan's investment priorities are advancing.

Over the next decade, the city intends to spend more than $6 billion for water-quality improvements. This commitment follows upon the substantial work undertaken over the last twenty years to transform the city's waterways into healthy ecosystems, benefitting fish and wildlife resources, waterfront development, and recreation. The Federal Intermodal Surface Transportation Act has promised over $23 million to plan and construct pedestrian and bicycle greenways along the waterfronts of all five boroughs. State and local funds are being used to acquire and protect natural wetlands and habitats around Jamaica Bay; Udalls Cove in Douglaston, Queens; and in South Richmond, Staten Island. Some private development is also moving forward, such as the reopening of Staten Island's Howland Hook Containerport, one of two such facilities in the city, after a ten-year hiatus.

If the new zoning laws are enacted, river views like those seen from the Henry Hudson Parkway would no longer be an exception on the west side. Yet despite this legislative drive to recover the waterfront, there remain numerous public challenges to aspects of the overall plan. Financing for the transformation is still in dispute, a situation exacerbated by the budgetary cutbacks that followed Republican victories in 1993 and 1994 at city, state, and federal levels. Whether the waterfront transformations will be fully realized is thus uncertain. With the exception of Battery Park City, the Chelsea Piers, and Riverbank State Park, development along the Hudson has been stymied by a welter of court orders, public protests, and budgetary constraints.

The Hudson River waterfront remains one of the great opportunities for renewal in urban America. Few places in the country offer such ample resources that, if thoughtfully used, could so enhance regional culture. The possibilities are too great to think that beneficiaries must be limited to a narrow segment of the population. It is not difficult to imagine the substantial economic advantages that could accompany large-scale improvements in the composition of the waterfront. Ecological vigilance and traditional public parks can readily coexist with the kind of renewed industrial, commercial, and transportation infrastructures that the city so desperately needs. But to realize any such harmonious vision of urban activities, all of the interests involved will have to think more broadly rather than from the confines of their own biases and make democracy work.

NOTES

1. Lauren Ramsey, "Battery Park City: Quiet Enclave on the Edge of Manhattan," *New York Observer*, 20 September 1993.

2. Ken Johnson, "Poetry and Public Service," *Art in America*, March 1990.

3. Michael Powell, "Adieu Westway Bucks!" *New York Observer*, 25 September 1995.

4. David W. Dunlap, "Jostling for Position on the Riverfront," *New York Times*, 11 July 1993.

5. Alan Finder, "Westway, A Road That Was Paid With Mixed Intentions," *New York Times*, 22 September 1985.

6. Manhattan Regional Planning Association, *From Plan to Reality*, vol. 1, 1933. p. 135.

HUDSON RIVER PARK

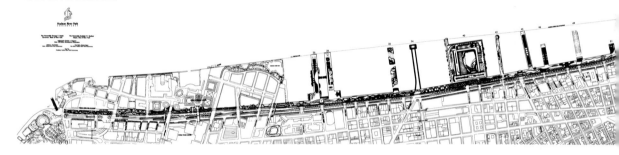

HUDSON RIVER PARK
Proposal. Quennell Rothschild Associates, landscape architects and lead design consultants
with Signe Nielsen in conjunction with Hudson River Park Conservancy. 1995.

6

6.1
INTERIM BIKE PATH AND ESPLANADE, HUDSON RIVER
Liselot van der Heijden, photographer. 1996.

MODEST ENDEAVORS
Reclaiming the Shoreline

Michael Z. Wise

Where longshoremen once toiled, in-line skaters glide. High-rise apartment buildings loom over the former moorings of transatlantic schooners, and landscaped esplanades grace the wharves upon which immigrants took their first steps into the New World. Ever so slowly, the New York City waterfront is changing (fig. 6.1).

The drive to reclaim the city's derelict shoreline, rotting piers, and abandoned marine terminals was guided by the 1993 adoption of the Comprehensive Waterfront Plan, the first city-wide shoreline proposal (fig. 6.2). The plan guaranteed common access to New York City's largest sweep of nature by mandating that private developers provide public space in new waterfront developments, and by barring new construction from blocking views of the water itself.[1]

But the vast expanse of the city's 584-mile waterfront combined with its diversity—disparate physical and economic conditions, from industrial to residential to wetlands— would seem to defy a coordinated policy. Indeed, little appears to have changed along the city's watery edge since the plan was adopted by the City Council on

October 25, 1993. The comprehensive program was the initiative of departing Democratic mayor David Dinkins; under Mayor Rudolph Giuliani's subsequent administration as well as the 1994 Republican dominance at state and national levels, there has been considerably less encouragement for public-sector development projects.

The momentous task of reclaiming New York City's forgotten edge has been thwarted by the region's entrenched, late-twentieth-century emphasis on inland improvements; New Yorkers have turned away from their seafaring origins to focus on building interior commercial districts

6.2
PIERS 7 AND 8, NORTH RIVER, MANHATTAN
Photographer unknown. Circa 1920. NYCMA.

and public spaces like Central Park, Prospect Park, and the Brooklyn Botanic Garden. As always, financial exigencies compound the lack of political will in unlocking this underutilized natural resource. Given that the city was strug-

gling to close a 1996 budget gap estimated at about $2 billion, with New York State facing a $4-billion shortfall, creative financing will prove imperative in waterfront progress.[2]

Even with ingenious economic solutions and centralized support, recent experience indicates that it takes more than big money to bring a significant waterfront proposal to fruition: grassroots community support is essential, to be ignored only at great peril. Community-led campaigns thwarted Westway and nearly doomed the Riverside South devel-

opment proposed for the Upper West Side. Having honed their skills in these battles, New York City citizens groups are demonstrated "giant killers," in the words of Gene Russianoff, staff attorney for the Straphangers Campaign, which opposes a proposed new Yankee Stadium on Manhattan's western waterfront.[3]

After the debacle of Westway, the use of landfill to extend the city's perimeters has become taboo. Similarly, the proposal for a large mixed-use development called Riverwalk, planned for Stuyvesant Cove along the East River, was withdrawn in 1990 due to environmental concerns, as the project would have stood largely atop thousands of piles in the river (fig. 6.3).

With the exception of the proposed Queens West development across the East River from the United Nations and Donald Trump's scaled-back Riverside South, the megaprojects of the 1980s are dead, victims of a real-estate market slump that devastated plans for the city's edge. Vastly more modest plans that focus on converting the waterfront into recreational facilities or natural parkland have risen in their stead. By definition, truncated ambitions fall short of firing civic imagi-

6.3
RIVERWALK
Model. Davis, Brody and Associates, architects; Wolfgang Hoyt, Esto, photographer. 1987.

nation. But while most of these projects are barely noticeable on their own—if and when they are realized—their cumulative implementation could do much to transform the face of the waterfront.

Despite these delays, one fundamental metamorphosis has made incremental progress possible and is likely to spur still more—the successful cleanup of New York Harbor water over the past two decades. Since the 1970s, the city has upgraded and expanded its network of fourteen sewage treatment plants, thereby reducing discharges of liquid waste into rivers and bays (figs. 6 4, 6.5). Surveillance to thwart the illegal discharge of industrial waste has been heightened, and a fleet of garbage-skimming boats now removes several hundred tons of floating debris from the water each year.[4] The harbor is cleaner than it has been in years, according to a report prepared by the New York State Water Resources Institute at Cornell University. The two-year study, released in June 1995, pointed to the revival of bird colonies and the reopening of previously contaminated city beaches for swimming.

Waterfront advocates rightly urge vigilance in assuring that the effort continues. Despite progress, the harbor remains among the most toxic in the nation, the Cornell study also found, since it has yet to recover from previously unrestricted dumping of heavy metals and other hazardous substances. And during rainstorms, excess water runoff that cannot be pro-

cessed by sewage treatment plants continues to flush trash, road oils, and chemicals directly from dirty streets into local waters.[5] Riverborne silt has also been choking New York Harbor's bays and tributaries. The mud, much of it contaminated with toxins, is routinely dredged by the United States Army Corps of Engineers and dumped into the Atlantic Ocean some six miles off the New Jersey shore. But since the mud harms marine life, federal law prohibits dumping the most severely contaminated material. Searching for an alternative solution, Congressman Jerold Nadler in April 1996 proposed depositing the silt in Brooklyn between existing piers along its dwindling commercial waterfront. Nadler argued that the fill could be used to create a new container port.[6]

The progress of water-quality improvement has been matched by a reanimation of waterborne activity in the harbor (fig. 6.6). Before the construction of tunnels and bridges, ferries once crisscrossed the Hudson and East Rivers, with as many as 125 lines operating around New York City. By 1968, the Staten Island Ferry, wholly operated by the city of New York, was the only ferry still in regular operation on New York's waters. Now, against all expectation, ferry service is on the "upswing," according to Alan Olmsted, director of ferry services for the Department of Transportation.[7] Olmsted dates the revival to 1986, when New Jersey

6.4 top
RIVERBANK STATE PARK AND NORTH RIVER POLLUTION CONTROL PLANT
Stanley Greenberg, photographer. 1996.

6.5
RED HOOK WATER POLLUTION CONTROL PLANT, BROOKLYN
Stanley Greenberg, photographer. 1992.

6.6
CHELSEA PIERS MARINA
Liselot van der Heijden, photographer. 1996.

entrepreneur Arthur Imperatore began operations between Weehawken and Pier 78 at West 38th Street in Manhattan. Four private companies now run service along a dozen routes, with total passenger trips averaging about twenty-four thousand on weekdays. Ridership has risen every quarter since 1986. It is growing an additional five to ten percent every year as new routes are implemented. This unforeseen development, entirely market-driven, opens the possibility for other ways to revive the waterfront that have yet to be considered by city planners or developers. By bringing boats and people back into daily contact with the water's edge, ferry service is likely to energize future waterfront projects.

The ferry revival has been made possible through the use of increasingly rapid and efficient vessels, and by linking scheduled ferries with bus and minibus services that bring passengers from docking points to inland destinations. The largest ferry company, New York Waterway, operates a fleet of over fifty buses in tandem with its twelve boats. Additional routes are planned from the Upper East Side along the East River to

Wall Street and La Guardia Airport, and along the Hudson from Nyack and Yonkers to Manhattan. In addition, the planning commission may allow smaller boats to operate a water-taxi system either with scheduled or for-hire operations, said Joseph Rose, the chairman of the Department of City Planning.[8]

To accommodate the resurgent ferry traffic and foster its continued growth, the city plans to rebuild Pier 11 in downtown Manhattan and has commissioned a new ferry terminal to be built

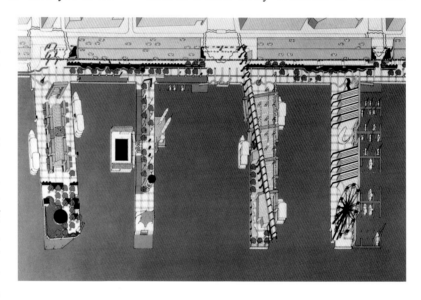

atop it (figs. 6.7, 6.8). Pier 11, jutting into the East River one block south of Wall Street at Gouverneur Lane, is now used by about fifteen hundred passengers a day. Designed by Manhattan architects Henry Smith-Miller and Laurie Hawkinson, the new terminal will service up to eight

6.7
EAST RIVER PIERS
Study. Quennell Rothschild Associates, landscape architects. 1991.

thousand passengers a day when it is completed in June 1998. The architects have devised a lightweight glass-and-steel waiting area for passengers, with parts of its long and narrow facade capable of pivoting open in warm weather. Since it will be used by passengers traveling from the

financial district to La Guardia Airport as well as by commuters to Brooklyn and New Jersey, the pier incorporates such design references as elements of an aircraft landing strip. This new pier is intended to be a future-oriented gateway on the city's shore, bringing a new mien to what was thought to be an all-but-defunct mode of transport. The Smith-Miller and Hawkinson design befits a transit hub for the new millennium and contrasts sharply with the preservationist stance taken in the South Street Seaport complex.

South Street Seaport was envisioned by the Rouse Company, the development outfit based in Columbia, Maryland, that was also responsible for Faneuil Hall Marketplace in Boston and Harborplace in Baltimore. Rouse's Baltimore and Boston projects were carried out in conjunction with public development authorities that had broad-based powers to promote change. In New York, the Rouse scheme was put into effect by local authorities equipped with a narrower mandate, and the seaport did not affect change beyond its immediate vicinity. For the time being, South Street Seaport stands as an isolated transformation. Where the Baltimore and Boston projects are beloved by their citizenry, South Street Seaport has come to be scorned by many New Yorkers, a convenient punching bag for community activists fearful of a theme-park trend in commercial activity along the shoreline.

The South Street Seaport was originally planned as part of the Manhattan Landing project, a $1.2-billion development unveiled in 1972 that encompassed six million square feet of new office space, 9,500 apartments, a hotel, and a park with

6.8
PIER 11 PASSENGER FERRY TERMINAL
Smith-Miller and Hawkinson, architects. 1996.

a 150-foot-wide public promenade from the Battery to the Brooklyn Bridge. All these facilities were to have been built atop platforms over the East River, extending Manhattan's landmass eighty-eight acres beyond the bulkhead line.[9] Recession and the municipal financial crisis of the late 1970s doomed Manhattan Landing, and South Street Seaport was realized on its own in an area designated a historic landmark district and already the site of the South Street Seaport Museum.

The seaport was created in two phases: the Fulton Market and two restored blocks of historic buildings opened in 1983, and a three-story red steel-and-glass shopping mall called Pier 17 in 1985 (fig. 6.9). The complex relies heavily on patronage from out-of-town tourists and has suffered from lower Manhattan's economic decline. In the early years of its operation, an effort was made to draw tenants whose food or products somehow testified to the past maritime activity of the site. Seafood may still be on the menu, but the latest tenants—including the Gap, Banana Republic, Sharper Image, plus shops selling T-shirts and Christmas decorations year-round—are little different from retailers found at malls across the United States.

Fulton Market, designed by Benjamin Thompson and Associates, has ultimately failed to achieve any special sense of place.

Outside decks have proven far more appealing than the dreary interior food court and retailing areas. The publicly accessible deck space around Pier 17 does provide New York's best vantage point for admiring the Brooklyn Bridge, if one can ignore the canned music playing from

speakers throughout the seaport (fig. 6.10). This indistinctive, anywhere-USA atmosphere may feel more integrated with the city once the South Street complex is finally linked up with its Manhattan environs via a planned bikeway and pedestrian path along the East River, currently being promoted by the city's Economic Development Corporation. Additionally, the area's local community board has urged further commercial development to enhance the waterfront, and a sixty-foot-wide esplanade is planned along the bottom of Manhattan,

6.9
SOUTH STREET SEAPORT, PIER 17 FROM BROOKLYN BRIDGE
Stanley Greenberg, photographer. 1996.

where the new Whitehall Ferry Terminal is to be built.

The Whitehall Ferry Terminal serves the Staten Island Ferry, and in 1985 the City Development Authority sought to replace the old facility with a high-rise office tower incorporating a new terminal

at its base (figs. 6.11–16.13). A plan called South Ferry Plaza, involving developer William Zeckendorf and designed by Kohn Pederson Fox, was selected (fig. 6.14). Zeckendorf defaulted on the deal in January 1991, and a fire later that year heavily damaged the existing terminal. In the face of a slump in the real-estate market, the city abandoned the proposed office tower and held its first public architectural competition in many years. The competition treated the erection of this major new civic building as an important

event, a justified approach given that the terminal serves some seventy thousand commuters and sightseers every day. In November 1992, a jury chose a design by the firms Venturi, Scott-Brown and Associates and Anderson/Schwartz Architects. Their design centered on a massive clock, 120 feet in diameter, with the seal of New York City emblazoned on its face (fig. 6.15). Mayor David Dinkins predicted that the structure would "become a bold new symbol for the city,"[10] but it was a little too whimsical for some politicians. Staten Island borough president Guy Molinari described it as "more suitable for a model village under someone's Christmas tree."[11]

Financial constraints sounded the death knell of a bold, if jokey, design. The Giuliani administration's decision to allow automobiles back on the ferry has required the reconfiguration of the two-and-a-half-acre plaza fronting the terminal in order to accommodate cars and a bus loop.[12] Federal, state, and local funding has been cut; consequently the originally proposed budget of $120 million was reduced to approximately $73 million. The architects have been forced to excise the clock face and a vaulted waiting hall in favor of a diluted design, a remarkably feeble shed of glass and gridded green metal that attempts to blend in with the neighboring Battery Maritime Building. This plan could be revised again—the architects have presented another tongue-in-cheek scheme incorporating an

6.10
SOUTH STREET SEAPORT, PIER 17
Stanley Greenberg, photographer. 1996.

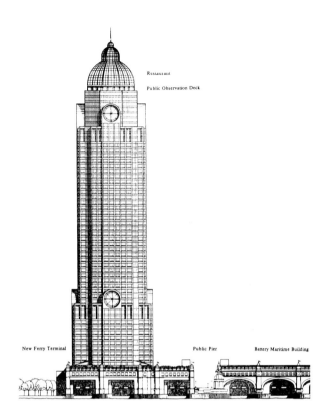

Restaurant

Public Observation Deck

New Ferry Terminal   Public Pier   Battery Maritime Building

6.11 top
SOUTH FERRY PLAZA
Proposal, south elevation. Fox and Fowle and Frank Williams, associate architects. 1985. New York Economic Development Corporation.

6.12
SOUTH FERRY PLAZA
Proposal, plan. Fox and Fowle and Frank Williams, associate architects. 1985. New York Economic Development Corporation.

6.13 top
SOUTH FERRY PLAZA
Proposal, aerial view. Clark, Tribble, Harris and Li, architects. 1985.
New York Economic Development Corporation.

6.14
SOUTH FERRY PLAZA
Proposal, aerial view of model. Kohn Pedersen Fox Associates,
architects. 1985. New York Economic Development Corporation.

American flag into the facade—before construction is due to start in 1998.

By far the most ambitious waterfront project under construction is the Queens West development, slated for seventy-four acres of Hunter's Point waterfront directly across the East River from the United Nations. The $2.3-billion proposal calls for the construction of nineteen buildings to include apartment houses, a hotel and conference center, offices, and retail space. It also entails the creation of twenty acres of public space and recreational areas, including a 1.25-mile-long riverfront esplanade with spectacular views of the Manhattan skyline. By mimicking that skyline in low-density Queens, however, the development will set itself apart from its immediate environs, not unlike the Battery Park City complex that served as its initial inspiration. The Queens West development will be less severe than Battery Park City, and will not have a highway like Manhattan's West Street to slice it away from its surroundings, but the towering new buildings—at least one of which is forty-two stories high—will throw up walls of their own in a neighborhood where the average building height does not exceed four stories.

Sponsored jointly by the state of New York through its Empire State Development Corporation, the city of New York via its Economic Development Corporation, and the Port Authority of New York and New Jersey, Queens West

originated in the early 1980s when Battery Park City first showed signs of becoming a commercial success. The initial master plan, prepared by Gruzen Samton Steinglass and Beyer Blinder Bell in 1984, called for buildings placed close to the water's edge and arranged in a highly formal manner with seven to eight acres of decks protruding over the river to create an evenly scalloped shoreline (fig. 6.16). But after the 1987 stock-market collapse and subsequent real-estate slump, the project was redrawn with slightly reduced density. Buildings were pulled back from the water to allow more public space, which would be delineated by the shoreline's natural geography.

An alternate master plan calling for substantial cuts in density has been put forward by a consortium of neighborhood activists known as the Hunters Point Community Coalition. Designed by architect Bonnie A. Harken, the complex would have no buildings taller than twenty stories and its southern tip would be left open as public park[13] (fig. 6.17). In the view of the Queens West Development Corporation, a state subsidiary administering the larger proposal, such a scaled-back version could not be financially viable. The coalition, in turn, charges that the development corporation's calculations are based on overvalued property estimates for publicly held land. In a bid to placate community opponents, the Queens West Development Corporation built a sixty-by-six-hundred-foot park, located a few blocks away from the waterfront itself, on the site of a derelict railway cut.[14] The park, opened in 1995, provides basketball and handball courts as well as shaded seating and tables. The trendy, razor-edged steel furniture could have been more humanely contoured, but otherwise the park itself is a valuable addition to the area and is a harbinger of public amenities to come with the larger complex.

In April 1996, construction began on the first major component of Queens West, a forty-two-story cooperative apartment tower designed by Cesar Pelli. Pelli has also designed a second tower, to be located just to the north, but the first structure could end up a lone beacon on the site, as prospective occupants have not yet been identified. The high-rise seems an overblown development for the locale, both aesthetically and in terms of current demand. It would be desirable for subsequent elements of the Queens West master plan to undergo modification and reduction before the project is taken further.

Queens West's original hopes of winning tenants from United Nations agencies appears unrealistic given the organization's recent efforts to scale down its bloated bureaucracy. Developers might do better to try luring medical businesses that could benefit from proximity to New York and Bellevue Hospitals on the East River's opposite bank. Transportation connections to Manhattan are good: Queens West is one subway stop away from Grand Central Station, and ferry service to and from East 34th Street began in early 1996, taking only four minutes to cross the river.

To preserve a reminder of the area's industrial past, the first Pelli tower will open onto a waterfront park centered on a pair of original gantries poised over float bridges that were once used to transfer freight cars from river bridges to railway tracks. The gantries' long-legged silhouette has also been adopted as the official logo of the development, a forlorn, disingenuous symbol given Queens West's scale and decidedly postindustrial character. The use of these relics in the park, to be known as Gantry Plaza and to be designed by Weintraub and di Domenico with Thomas Balsley Associates, appears as an incongruous fig leaf. A more promising art project, however, could be the erection of a massive statue of the borough of Queens' namesake, Catherine of Braganza. Painter and sculptor Audrey Flack has proposed a monumental thirty-six-foot-high bronze figure of the seventeenth-century Portuguese princess who became the Queen of England, striding purposefully forward atop a fifty-four-foot-high base. The colossus, an all-too rare example of heroic figurative public sculpture in our day, has the potential to become a true source of pride for Queens residents. Unfortunately the monument's realization cannot be guaranteed, as funds are being raised privately.[15]

6.15
WHITEHALL FERRY TERMINAL
Venturi, Scott-Brown and Associates with Anderson/Schwartz,
architects. 1992. New York Economic Development Corporation.

6.16 top
QUEENS WEST
Proposal, model. Gruzen, Samton, Steinglass, architects, planners, with
Beyer, Blinder, Bell, architects. David Hirsch, photographer. 1984.

6.17
QUEENS WEST, ALTERNATE SCHEME
Bonnie A. Harken, architect. 1994.

Sculpture spurred another Queens waterfront revitalization at the 4.2-acre site now known as the Socrates Sculpture Space and Park. Located just across from the northern end of Roosevelt Island at Halletts Cove, the park's land had served as a marine terminal and then a dump for rubble from the 63rd Street subway-tunnel excavations. The private Athena Foundation later leased the site from the city and transformed it into an outdoor showplace for large-scale sculpture. The Manhattan skyline serves as a dramatic backdrop in a setting originally developed by two sculptors, Mark DiSuvero and Isamu Noguchi, who kept nearby studios. Since the park's founding in 1986, management of the property has returned to the city's Parks Department. The endeavor demonstrates how small-scale, private innovations can effect change along the water's edge.

Modest changes are indeed taking place around the waterfront, often in out-of-the-way areas. On the Bronx coast opposite Rikers Island, for example, a new three-hundred-foot long fishing pier has been opened, constructed of recycled plastic. Bicycle paths are being extended throughout the city. As mentioned in Chapter 5, the reach studies proposal of an "emerald necklace" of parks will close some gaps between existing public spaces and create entirely new ones elsewhere. Although landfill is now off-limits as a planning tool, less obtrusive steps are

being taken to extend the edge. The Parks Department plans to construct a cantilevered platform over the Hudson River along the West Side Highway between 83rd and 91st Streets, where the highway runs so close to the water that building public pathways would be impossible without broadening the shoreline or moving the road itself.

On the east side, the Parks Service is working to improve the East River Esplanade from 63rd to 125th Streets. Already, the esplanade between 85th and 95th Streets has been entirely rebuilt with new paving, rails, benches, and plantings. These improvements were funded by developers who, in exchange, were allowed to build apartment houses at twenty percent greater density than normally permitted. Further south, at East 60th Street, an abandoned marine transfer station was converted into a public open-air pavilion in 1993 and connected to the East River esplanade. Funded by New York Hospital in a deal involving its recent mammoth expansion, the structure has not been successful. Known as the 60th Street Pavilion, it provides public seating in the shadow of the Queensboro Bridge. The upper platform of the former transfer station is crowned with an aluminum sculpture by artist Alice Aycock. The intent is laudable, but Aycock's sculpture is a lackluster jumble and the open space beneath it uninviting because of the grating rattle of the bridge's steel plates.

Many as-yet-uncompleted, smaller waterfront projects were funded under a five-year federal transportation bill known as the Intermodal Surface Transportation Efficiency Act, passed by Congress in 1991 to enhance local transportation-related activities. Eligible uses of the money include the installation of bicycle and pedestrian paths, rehabilitation of historic transportation buildings, and preservation of abandoned transportation corridors. Approximately $10.8 million in federal funds has been earmarked through the act for over twenty New York City waterfront projects, with the stipulation that local authorities match at least twenty percent of the funding for any approved projects. Such projects include the bicycle and pedestrian path running between South Street Seaport and the southern tip of Manhattan at Wall Street; Hudson River waterfront improvements along the edge of Riverside Park; Harlem Beach, a proposed twenty-block ribbon of recreational green along Harlem River Drive (fig. 6.18); and the restoration of the Coffey Street Pier, to be opened to the public, in the Red Hook section of Brooklyn.

Vast stretches of waterfront land have been acquired by the Parks Department over the past decade as part of a more concerted and centralized drive to preserve and reclaim natural areas and wetlands. These include salt marshes that are to be kept as nature preserves in Jamaica Bay and Staten Island. Environ-

mentalists hail the acquisitions, but others question whether the city has overreached its ability to maintain public spaces and, even if it could, whether open space is the best use of the land.

A major new challenge to the public sector has been posed by the United States Coast Guard's decision to vacate Governors Island, below the southern tip of Manhattan. The Coast Guard announced in October 1995 that it will close its base on the 175-acre island by the end of 1998.[16] The oldest continually operated military post in the United States, the base is one of the region's most important defense installations and the largest Coast Guard facility in the country. The base, with its glorious views of the lower Manhattan skyline, will be one of the city's most desirable real-estate opportunities when decommissioned (fig. 6.19). Originally sold by the Manahatas Indians to the Dutch for two ax heads, a string of beads, and some nails, Governors Island has been valued at $500 million.[17] The Coast Guard's departure could presage a significant expansion of the public realm or lead to the creation of a different sort of private enclave. Until now, the island could be reached only by ferry and helicopter with Coast Guard permission. Some of its buildings have already been landmarked, and city ownership is thought likely to prevent fundamental alteration to the unspoiled town, which includes a McKim, Mead and White–

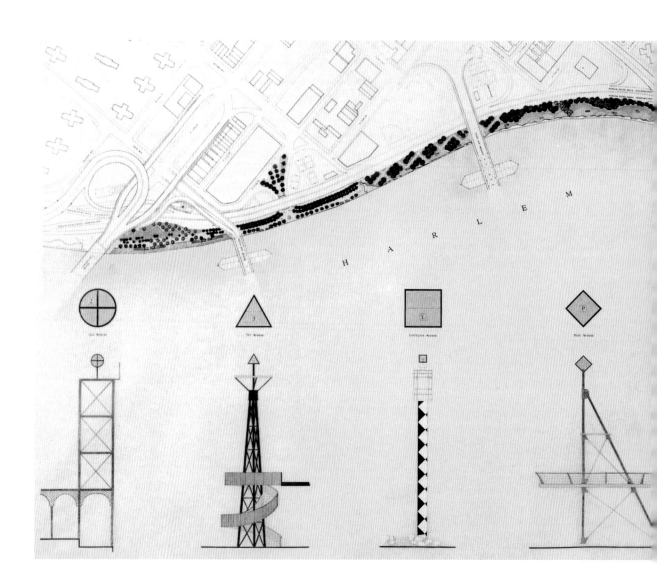

6.18
HARLEM BEACH, HARLEM RIVER
Proposal. Quennell Rothschild Associates, lead consultants, landscape
architects. Circa 1992.

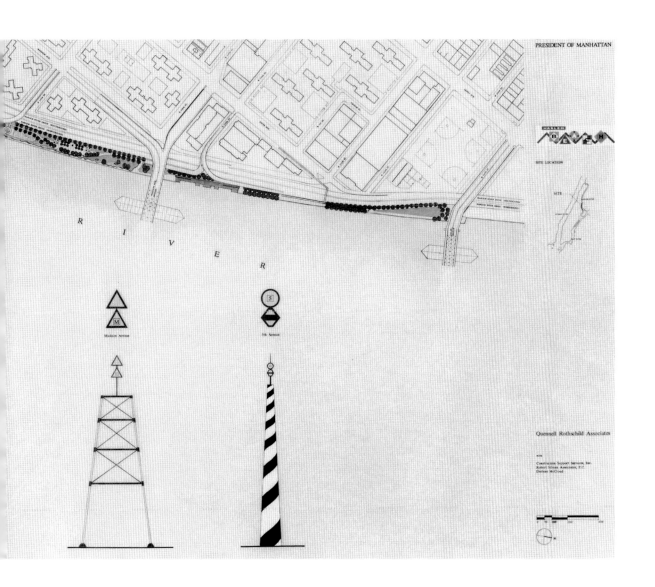

designed army housing block over one thousand feet long as well as a hotel, bowling alley, movie theater, and nine-hole golf course, all in the shadow of Manhattan.

Acquiring additional open space is seductive, but the tremendous scale of waterfront property and its upkeep renders wholesale transformation of the shoreline into public parks highly unrealistic, particularly in the current and foreseeable economic climate. "No government has ever shown a capacity to take care of parks of that dimension regardless of whether money was an issue," says Rosina Abramson, a former executive director of the City Planning Commission who helped draft the Comprehensive Waterfront Plan as well as a former president of the Queens West Development Corporation. Even if the requisite funds were at hand, argues Abramson, "It is very shortsighted and very limited to think of only one use for the waterfront. If you understand the nature of cities and the future of cities and the strengths and weaknesses of a city like New York, I don't think you can or should take the waterfront out of its economic development strategy."[18]

While any industry along the water should be environmentally sound and buffeted by public space, it is still desirable to strive for a range of uses. In some areas manufacturing remains appropriate, and in at least one case, industry can even benefit the environment. As of August 1995, a nineteen-acre site in the South Bronx's old Harlem Rail Yard, just north of Randalls Island, is to house a $280-million plant that would produce recycled paper from New York City's trash (fig. 6.20).

One new variable is the Giuliani administration's drive to attract superstores to the city. An initiative has called for extensive changes in zoning regulations to allow large retail stores to locate in manufacturing areas without going through an extensive review process. Zoning restrictions limit the height of non-water-dependent structures on existing piers to forty feet, but the effort to bring in large retailers could still have a major impact if the stores are allowed elsewhere along the shore. "The loophole for big-box retailers may come back to

6.19
GOVERNOR'S ISLAND, LOWER MANHATTAN, BROOKLYN PIERS, AND ATLANTIC BASIN
Allied Map Co., photographer. Department of City Planning. 1984.
New York City Department of Environmental Protection.

haunt us," says Ellen Ryan, the Municipal Art Society's director of issues and planning.[19]

The Comprehensive Waterfront Plan provides a valuable framework for guiding development along the coast, but more remains to be done. Zoning changes,

including language expressing municipal aspirations as to what should happen on particular sites, have yet to be applied to the official zoning map, which gives teeth to the text. As it now stands, the burden of making zoning-map changes is left to private waterfront developers, as well as the cost of undertaking the complicated environmental review process. City Planning Commission chairman Joseph Rose terms this burden one of several "serious obstacles to reuse of the waterfront."[20] But in the current economic climate, there has

been no flood of projects submitted to the commission for review, and the program has yet to be tested under optimal market conditions. There are also concerns that mandated public access could be subject to challenge following a 1995 Supreme Court ruling that set limits on a local government's ability to require property owners to relinquish part of their land to public purposes in exchange for permission to build or expand. In *Dolan* v. *City of Tigard, Oregon*, the court held that there must be a "rough proportionality" between a zoning law that restricts development and the harm that the development might cause.[21] Mindful of the ruling, Rose stated that the commission would seek to be as flexible as possible: "We're receptive to the notion of modifications that are required on a site-by-site basis."[22]

Confrontations between environmentalists and developers combined with a lack of coordination among public agencies continue to complicate the process of waterfront change. Progress is further hampered when the array of bureaucracies with shoreline jurisdiction mutate periodically into new entities, and administrative officials change with each political administration. The protracted waterfront battles and subsequent delays have

6.20
MOTT HAVEN RAIL YARDS, BRONX
Photographer unknown.Circa 1910. NYCMA.

fortuitously spared New York City from several ill-considered projects. But an ad hoc approach to waterfront development has its pitfalls, most notably in a lack of coordinated implementation that leads to surplus costs and deficient aesthetic cohesion, seen most recently in the construction of Route 9A along the Hudson. Work on the highway began in spring 1996, when plans for Hudson River Park remained stalled. Building these two physically parallel projects in tandem would have led to substantial savings and ensured visual unity, but Governor George Pataki has stalled on committing state funds for the park (figs. 6.21–6.23). The standoff is indicative of unresolved civic attitudes regarding the future of the waterfront in the first place. Nevertheless, incremental progress is slowly altering the long-neglected shoreline for the better. Rather than bemoaning the lack of speedy change, planners and architects must cut through bureaucratic paralysis. They must seize the slowdown in the real-estate market and its negative effect on development as an opportunity to rethink how the waterfront can best be used for a variety of purposes (figs. 6.24, 6.25). They must reimagine any development as an occasion to enhance the beauty and prestige of the city at large, and ultimately, to once again engage the edge.

NOTES

1. James C. McKinley Jr., "Proposal to Double-Park Area on the Shore," *New York Times*, 12 August 1992.

2. "More Budget Pain for the City," editorial, *New York Times*, 20 April 1996.

3. Richard Perez-Pena, "The Future Home of Yankee Stadium? It's All in the Traffic Patterns," *New York Times*, 14 April 1996.

4. Andrew C. Revkin, "Strides Seen in New York Harbor Cleanup," *New York Times*, 15 June 1995.

5. Ibid.

6. Jerold Nadler and Michael R. Long, "Make Brooklyn a World-Class Seaport," *New York Times*, 13 April 1996.

7. Alan Olmsted, interview with author, 25 March 1996.

8. Joseph Rose, interview with author, 2 April 1996.

9. R. Stern, p. 215.

10. David W. Dunlap, "Face of Future for Ferry Terminal Is 120 Feet Tall and Has Two Hands," *New York Times*, 6 November 1992.

11. Ibid.

12. Marvine Howe, "Staten Island Ferry Revives a Battle of Boroughs," *New York Times*, 3 April 1994.

13. David W. Dunlap, "Queens West Begins With a Park," *New York Times*, 18 September 1994.

14. Douglas Martin, "Welcome to Donnybrook Park," *New York Times*, 25 March 1996.

15. Joseph P. Fried, "Catherine of Queens?" *New York Times*, 26 July 1992.

16. Parks Council, "Governors Island New York's Next Great Park?" *Openspace*, winter 1996.

17. Don van Natta Jr., "Coast Guard Plans to Leave Governors Island," *New York Times*, 17 October 1995.

18. Rosina Abramson, interview with author, 28 March 1996.

19. Ellen Ryan, interview with author, 2 April 1996.

20. Joseph Rose, interview with author, 2 April 1996.

21. *Dolan* v. *City of Tigard, Oregon.*

22. Joseph Rose, interview with author, 2 April 1996.

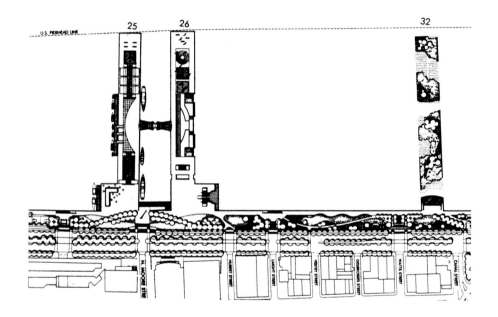

6.21–6.23: HUDSON RIVER PARK
Proposal. Quennell Rothschild Associates, landscape architects and lead design consultants with Signe Nielsen in conjunction with Hudson River Park Conservancy. 1995. HRPC.

6.21
Pier 25, public pier including town dock; Pier 26, public pier including educational estuarium and small boat launch; Pier 32, wildlife islands and "get down" to allow access to water.

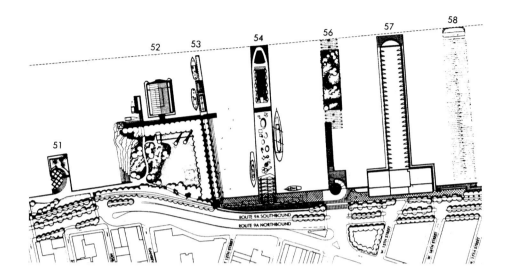

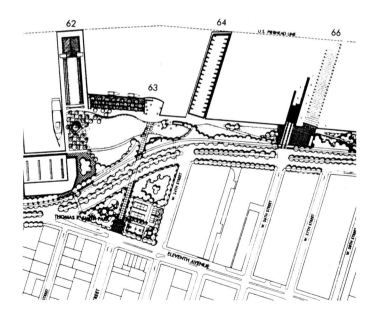

6.22 top
Pier 51, public pier and water play area; Piers 52 and 53, "Gavensport Peninsula," current sanitation department pier redesigned for recreation, including beach on southern side and fireboat house on north; Pier 54, public pier with emphasis on waterfront history; Pier 56, wildlife island with viewing area; Pier 57, bus garage; Pier 58, pile field.

6.23
Piers 61, 62, and 63, Chelsea Piers and Chelsea Waterside Park; Pier 64, recreational pier; Pier 66, pile field and railroad float bridge on south side.

6.24
HOLOCAUST MEMORIAL PARK AND PIER A
Liselot van der Heijden, photographer. 1996.

6.25
HOLOCAUST MEMORIAL MUSEUM
Liselot van der Heijden, photographer. Kevin Roche, architect. 1996.

CHRONOLOGY

The Native American inhabitants of the areas that eventually became New York City were linguistically connected to the Algonquians. They used the waterways for fishing as well as travel. Some historians have proposed that an existing chain of swamps, ponds, and streams formed a waterway that linked the Hudson and East Rivers.

1524   Giovanni da Verrazano is the first European to discover New York Harbor.

1525   Esteban Gomez visits New York Bay.

1609   Henry Hudson explores the Upper Bay and the Hudson River.

1614   Adriaen Block sails Long Island Sound, discovers Block Island, and makes the first map of Manhattan.

1621   The Dutch West India Company is formed.

1625   The first permanent European settlement is made in lower Manhattan and named New Amsterdam.

1626   Governor General Peter Minuit purchases Manhattan Island from the Native Americans (for the Dutch West India Company) for an estimated twenty-four dollars.

1634   Settlements begin in Brooklyn.

1638–42   The first ferry operates, between Manhattan (near Dover Street) and Fulton Ferry, Brooklyn.

1639   Areas of the Bronx are purchased by the Dutch West India Company from the Native Americans but are not settled until 1641, by Jonas Bronck. David de Vries and others settle in Staten Island, but are subsequently driven out by Native Americans.

1645   The first permanent settlement in Queens is established at Vlisingen (Flushing).

1647   Peter Stuyvesant's administration begins. He and his council recommend the construction of a pier into the East River at approximately the present-day Pearl and Broad Streets. This pier will be completed in 1648 or early 1649 and known as the Little Dock or Schreyers Hook Dock.

1653   New Amsterdam receives charter establishing municipal government. Peter Stuyvesant builds a fortified wall, river to river, at the present-day Wall Street, to keep out the British, who were trading rivals of the Dutch.

1654   The "Waal" or bank of the East River in front of the city hall (Pearl Street and Coenties Alley) was washed away, and the city government decides to protect the new bank with sheet piles.

1655   The first ferry house is built on the Brooklyn side of the East River.

1656   The city court requires the residents along the East River to comply with the earlier order of 1654 to line the bank with boards, or to pay to have the work done by the city. Stuyvesant and council declare the beach at the present Whitehall and Pearl Streets the first public marketplace in New Amsterdam.

1658   The city council permits construction of a new pier at the current Moore and Pearl Streets. The pier, known as the Wijnbruch (wine-bridge, or wine-dock) or weighhouse pier, was completed in 1659. It was first extended in 1660, and many times thereafter.

1659   Wharfage regulations are established.

1661   Oude Dorp becomes the first permanent settlement on Staten Island.

1664   The British capture New Amsterdam, and rename it New York. Citizens petition the colonial government for permission to dredge the kill between Brooklyn and Red Hook at their expense. Approval is granted.

1665	Thomas Willett becomes the first mayor of New York.
1673	The Dutch retake New York.
1676	A new dock, known as the "Great Dock," is completed at Schreyer's Hook between Coenties Slip and Whitehall Street. This dock was repeatedly enlarged, and served as the only place of dockage until 1750.
1680	The council orders that "Spiting Devil" be considered as a site for the erection of a bridge.
1686	The Dongan Charter transfers from the British Colonial Authorities all decisions concerning unencumbered land to the municipality, which effectively establishes its jurisdiction over the waterfront. This essentially allowed for the extension of the city's shoreline through landfill operations.
1691	The city orders buyers of land between the Wijnbruch and the Great Dock (the current Moore Street and Whitehall Slip) to make a street. This is the current Water Street, opened in 1694.
1693	Kingsbridge is built across the Harlem River, connecting Manhattan Island to the mainland.
1699	The city grants property owners between Cortlandt and Cedar Streets possession of the waterfront that abutted their land. Owners of waterfront property were required to build wharves and level banks for roadway access. This is the beginning of the development of the Hudson River shorefront.
1701	In order to regulate the port, a committee of the common council orders that the waterfront, built slips, wharves, and streets be surveyed.
1713	The first ferry to Staten Island from Manhattan is established.
1720	The common council orders the hiring of persons to repair the wharves and clean the mud out of the docks.
1723	A storm destroys most of the city's dock facilities and vessels, as well as many onshore structures. The city begins reconstruction.
1750	The common council approves a plan to build a pier on the west side of Coenties Slip. This becomes known as the "Albany Pier."
1771	The city begins to construct the "Corporation Dock," a stone structure near Castle Clinton, and the first dock on the Hudson River. It is completed in 1775.
1789	The common council passes the Outer Streets and Wharves Act, which initiates the policing of public control of the water's edge.
1801	The Brooklyn Navy Yard opens. This area in Wallabout Bay will continually be enlarged and developed.
1807	Robert Fulton launches the first steamboat, called the *Clermont*. The Randall Plan, which solidified municipal control of the shores, is issued.
1811	The Commissioners Plan for the future growth of New York City is adopted. This plan laid out the street grid of New York (also known as the Randel Plan), extended its boundaries into the water, and solidified municipal control over the waterfront.
1824	The first dry dock in the United States is built on the East River at East 10th Street.
1825	The Erie Canal opens. By the 1830s shipping is increasingly concentrated on the West Side of Manhattan with the Hudson River as the principal commercial shipping lane. In the same period, New York City becomes the leading port in the United States.
1834	A bistate commission defines the boundary between New Jersey and New York in the Hudson River and New York Bay.

1841	Construction of Atlantic Basin in Brooklyn begins.
1846	The Hudson River railroad is established.
1848	Surveys are made of the Hell Gate to determine a complete hydrography.
1851	Surface blasting of the rocks at the Hell Gate in the East River commences. Jones Wood, a waterfront park between 70th and 75th Streets on the East River, is proposed.
1852	The city decides to fix a permanent exterior street along the shore of the Harlem River between the East River or Sound and the North (or Hudson) River and to extend the existing streets and avenues to this street.
1853	By this time, New York has 112 piers; 55 are on the North River, and 57 on the East, some of them extending nearly an eighth of a mile into the river.
1855–56	The Commission for the Preservation of the Harbor makes recommendations for the establishment of pier and bulkhead lines. These are adopted by the New York State legislature but not by New Jersey.
1856	Diamond Reef, which lies at the north end of Governor's Island and extends about 200 rods into the channel, is removed.
1857	The Board of Alderman intervenes for the first time in waterfront construction. After this date, no one is allowed to build a pier without permission from the city.
1859	The Cooper Union opens.
1860	The Fort Lee Ferry is established from 130th Street in Manhattan to the opposite shore in New Jersey.
1864	Construction of Erie Basin in Brooklyn begins.
1866	General John Newton, of the U.S. Engineer Corps, assumes charge of the Hallett's Point blasting operations.
1867	The Brooklyn Navy Yard undergoes expansion; construction begins on the Brooklyn Bridge and on Riverside Park on Manhattan's West Side.
1870	The city and state legislature establishes the New York City Department of Docks (DoD) and appoints General George McClellan as engineer in chief.
1871	The DoD and the city adopt McClellan's plan to improve the waterfront by encircling the island with a masonry riverwall and building wooden piers. The plans for the construction of Pier 1, a masonry pier, are approved.
1873	McClellan resigns from the department, and Charles K Graham takes his place as engineer in chief.
1875	Graham resigns; George S. Greene replaces him as engineer in chief.
1876	Hallett's Point Reef in the Hell Gate is blasted away. The United States Government grants approval to improve the Harlem River and Spuyten Duyvil Creek.
1877	Pier 1 is completed.
1878	The plans for improving the Harlem River and Spuyten Duyvil Creek are adopted.
1880	George S. Greene proposes to develop the area along the Hudson River between Perry and West 19th Streets by constructing a new riverwall and twenty-one piers. This plan is known as the "Chelsea Piers." Riverside Park is completed.

1883 The Department of Docks proposes to revise the waterfront improvement plan to include developing the area between Grand and East 34th Streets on the East River. The Brooklyn Bridge opens.

1884 Plans for Pier A, including a building that would house a police station and the Department of Docks headquarters, are approved and construction begins. The department proposes, and the city approves, a plan to develop the waterfront above 86th Street on the East River to Third Avenue on the Harlem River. Corlears Hook Park on the East River is completed.

1885 Pier A is completed. Flood Rock in the Hell Gate is destroyed by an explosion supervised by General John Newton.

1887 The dredging of the Hell Gate to create a navigable channel is largely complete.

1888 The Federal Rivers and Harbors Act gives the U.S. Army Corps of Engineers control over all navigable waters in the United States including the sole power to determine bulkhead and pierhead lines.

1889 The city approves the plan to develop the East River above 86th Street. Construction begins on the Harlem Ship Canal.

1890 The U.S. Army Corps of Engineers sets new pierhead lines.

1894 Riverside Park is extended to the edge of the Hudson River.

1895 The Harlem River Ship Canal opens. The city establishes public recreation piers.

1897 George S. Greene retires, and John A. Bensel is appointed engineer in chief.

1898 Greater New York is consolidated, joining the five boroughs together under a single municipal government. This expands the department's authority, and as part of the charter revisions, the department becomes responsible for city-owned ferries and ferry terminals and assumes the title of Department of Docks and Ferries. The Harlem River Speedway is completed.

1900s During the first decade of the twentieth century New York City becomes one of the world's major international ports.

1903 The Williamsburg Bridge opens.

1906 The structure of the Department of Docks is changed from a board of three commissioners to a single commissioner. John Bensel is appointed commissioner of the department, and Charles Staniford is appointed engineer in chief.

1908 The East River subway tunnel links Manhattan and Brooklyn.

1909 The Queensborough and Manhattan Bridges open.

1910 Department of Docks commissioner Calvin Tomkins proposes a new model for waterfront development, which calls for replacing individual piers with larger terminals. The Chelsea Piers are completed.

1913 Dredging begins in Jamaica Bay, Queens, to create a channel from Barren Island to Mill Basin. The department begins increasingly to focus on developing the waterfront in Brooklyn, Queens, and Staten Island.

1916 The Manhattan riverwall, begun under George McClellan in 1871, is largely complete. It consists of 61,962 lineal feet of wall built by the department, 31,940 feet built by other city departments, and 11,925 feet built by private parties.

1917   The northern expansion of Riverside Park begins.

1918   The department transfers the Ferry Bureau to the Department of Plants and Structures, and the responsibility for the care and maintenance of marginal streets given to the borough presidents, reverts back to the Department of Docks.

1919   Charles Staniford retires, and Trougett F. Keller is appointed chief engineer.

1920   The department proposes to develop a terminal facility at Stapleton, Staten Island, and to develop extensively the waterfront in Flushing Bay, Queens.

1921   The bistate agency known as the Port Authority of New York is created by a compact between New Jersey and New York. Initially, it is a planning agency with no administrative powers over physical facilities.

1924   Robert Moses proposes that Jamaica Bay be set aside as a wildlife preserve.

1925   The Port Authority is authorized to plan and construct bridges as well as to take over the construction of the Holland Tunnel.

1927   The Holland Tunnel is completed.

1931   The Regional Plan—a detailed study by the Regional Plan Association of New York proposing a system of land use and transportation improvements for New York City and the surrounding areas in New York State, New Jersey, and Connecticut—is completed. Construction of the West Side Highway (also known as the Miller Highway) is finished. The George Washington Bridge opens.

1935   Work begins on the East River Drive, now called the FDR Drive.

1936   The Triborough Bridge opens.

1937   The Henry Hudson Parkway is completed.

1938   Riverside Park is expanded again. Responsibility for city ferries and ferry terminals is returned to the Department of Docks.

1940   The East River Drive is completed. The Queens-Midtown Tunnel opens, and construction begins on the Brooklyn-Battery Tunnel.

1942   The Department of Docks is renamed the Department of Marine and Aviation.

1946   Jurisdiction over city airports is transferred from the department to the Port Authority.

1950   The Brooklyn-Battery Tunnel opens.

1954   The City declares Jamaica Bay a wildlife refuge.

1960s   During this decade, most of the port's shipping facilities are moved to Port Elizabeth, New Jersey.

1963   The city commissions a comprehensive plan for the Hudson River waterfront from the Battery to West 72nd Street. Known as the "Ebasco" plan, the study is based on the premise that the primary activity of the waterfront will continue to be shipping. Most of the plan will remain unimplemented, although it did establish the basic form of Battery Park City and called for a new convention center from West 38th to West 43rd Streets.

1964   The Verrazano Narrows Bridge opens.

1965   Construction begins on Waterside.

1966   The City Planning Commission proposes the Lower Manhattan Plan, which calls for expanding the entire area with landfill, extending existing streets to the waterfront, and creating parks and plazas. Battery Park City is launched as an urban renewal development.

1967   Philip Johnson proposes a water display to camouflage the rooftop of the planned North River Pollution Control Plant. Construction begins in 1968.

1969   The Department of Marine and Aviation (the former Department of Docks) is renamed the Department of Ports and Terminals.

1970   By this time, the Port Authority is generating and administering most of the pier and terminal construction in New York City.

1972   The Clean Water Act is passed by Congress, which authorizes federal money for the cleanup of American streams, rivers, and lakes.

1973   A section of the West Side Highway collapses under the weight of a dump truck. Construction commences on South Street Seaport.

1974   The federal government proposes to replace the crumbling West Side Highway with a new six-lane roadway. The project involves extensive landfill, parkland, and commercial development of the west side and is officially named Westway. Opponents file their first lawsuit to stop the development. Construction of Waterside is completed.

1976   The landfilling is completed at Battery Park City. The fill came from the construction of the World Trade Towers.

1978   Construction is completed on the North River Pollution Control Plant. Construction commences on the Jacob Javits Convention Center.

1979   Richard Dattner is hired to design a rooftop park atop the North River Pollution Control Plant. Alexander Cooper and Stanton Eckstut develop the master plan for Battery Park City.

1981   The U.S. Army Corps of Engineers issues landfill and dredging permits for Westway. Construction begins at Battery Park City.

1982   Judge Thomas Greisa blocks landfill permits for Westway because the Corps of Engineers failed to assess the fill's impact on the habitats of the striped bass.

1984   Environmental impact hearings are held on Westway.

1985   After years of struggle, the federal government announces that it is abandoning the Westway project. Donald Trump proposes to build a residential waterfront development on the site of the old railway yards between West 59th and West 72nd Streets. Called Television City, this project boasted the tallest skyscraper in the world. Construction is completed on the South Street Seaport.

1986   The Department of Ports and Trades changes its name to the Department of Ports, International Trade, and Commerce.

1990   The North River Pollution Control Plant is fully operational.

1991   The Department of Ports and Trades (the former Department of Docks) is dissolved. Some of its promotional functions are transferred to the Department of Business Services, and its remaining waterfront-related duties are transferred to the Port Authority.

1992   Hudson River Park and Stuyvesant High School at the northern boundary of Battery Park City are completed. The complex now consists of eighteen apartment buildings, four office towers, the Winter Garden shopping and restaurant areas, and park and public spaces including a 1.2-mile riverfront esplanade. The New York City Comprehensive Waterfront Plan is released.

1993   Riverbank State Park, on the roof of the North River Pollution Control Plant, is opened. The Waterfront Zoning Reform, intended to amplify and implement the Comprehensive Waterfront Plan, is approved by the City Council. Hearings are held on the Route 9A project, the much reduced successor of Westway, which proposes to reconstruct the existing West Side Highway. It receives significant support.

1994   A scaled-down version of Trump's proposal for the old west side rail yards, now called Riverside South, receives backing from Hong Kong investors. The plan consists of sixteen buildings on a 21.5-acre riverfront park stretching from West 59th to West 72 Streets. Skidmore, Owings and Merrill is responsible for the master plan, and Philip Johnson is hired to design the first four buildings.

1996   Ground is broken for the construction of Route 9A.

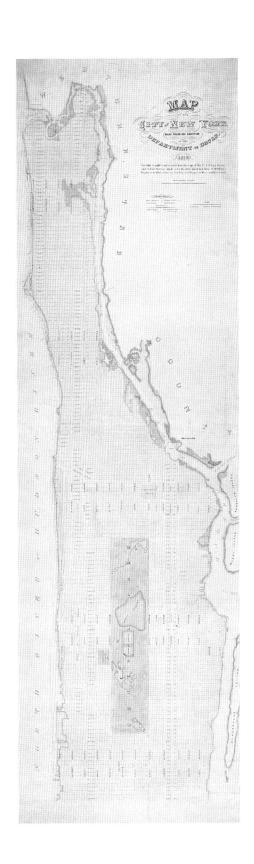

MAP OF THE CITY OF NEW YORK
Plan. Department of Docks. General George McClellan,
engineer in chief. 1872. NYCMA.

GLOSSARY

Anchorage
That portion of a harbor or the place outside a harbor suitable for anchoring vessels.

Appurtenance
An accessory to another and more important thing; any part of a building that is not structurally integral, such as doors, windows, partitions, or ornamentation.

Ashlar
A building stone, squared more or less true on all sides, dressed with thin mortar joints. Used as facing for walls of block, brick, or rubble masonry.

Automatic tide gauge
A self-controlled device that records high and low tides.

Backfill
Soil placed back into an area previously excavated.

Bark
To strip off the tough outer protection layer of a tree.

Baseline
A very carefully surveyed and precisely set line, to which other surveys are referred for coordination and correlation.

Basin
An artificially enclosed area of a river or harbor designed so that the water level remains unaffected by tidal changes.

Bay
Body of water partly enclosed by land but with a wide mouth that gives access to the ocean.

Benchmark
A fixed reference point with known elevation and position from which the elevation and position of other points may be determined. Usually indicated by a notch or mark on a firmly set stone or stake.

Béton
A concrete made by mixing gravel, sand, and hydraulic lime, capable of hardening under water. **Béton en masse** is concrete poured into large-scale forms capable of hardening under water.

Bight
A bend or curve in the shore of a sea or river, or a body of water bounded by such a bend.

Bitumen
A compound of asphalt and tar used in waterproofing and as a protective coating.

Block (or blocking)
Prepared pieces of stone, concrete, or wood used to build up components of a structure.

Block-and-bridge piers
A type of traditional pier construction in which base block structures of stone or wood are bridged with masonry arches or wood framing.

Boom
A wood or metal pole projecting horizontally from a ship or from the mast of a derrick that is used to lift heavy loads.

Boring (or borehole)
A hole drilled into the earth, usually prior to any construction, to obtain samples of the soil for examination. Often, the method of extraction involves working an auger (a screw-shaped tool) through a pipe to yield a core of excavated materials in their original relative positions. In this way information about the strata of the area is collected.

Breakwater
That portion of a foundation used to direct the currents of a river; a barrier that protects a harbor or shore from the impact of tidal waves.

Bulkhead
A retaining structure of timber, reinforced concrete, or steel, used for shore protection and in harborworks.

Bulkhead line
The outermost legal extremity to which solid fill may be extended into water.

Bulkhead wall
The retaining wall along a waterfront, which shores up the embankment in order to stabilize it for the construction of wharves and piers. The term is said to have originated with New York City engineers and has become standard in the profession.

Caisson

A watertight chamber or chest, commonly made of heavy timber, open at the bottom and containing air under sufficient pressure to exclude water, within which workers can excavate. Most often floated above a dredged site with a concrete or masonry pier built on it, causing it to sink. When work is complete the caisson is left to form part of the foundation of a wharf or a bridge.

Canal

A built waterway or artificially improved river used for shipping or transportation.

Cast iron

An iron alloy, usually including carbon and silicon. A large range of building products are made by pouring the molten metal into sand molds and then machining.

Channel

A natural or artificial passage within a stream, river, or other waterway sufficiently deep to support navigation.

Chock

A wedge or block used to prevent movement; also, a metal or wooden fitting through which a rope such as a mooring line, anchor cable, or towline may be run.

Cofferdam

A temporary, watertight enclosure used to facilitate underwater construction. Once constructed, the protected area is pumped dry and building activities can take place within.

Composite pile

A single pile composed of different materials; also a pile made of several members of the same material fastened together end-to-end to form a single pile.

Containerization

A process of handling freight introduced around 1960 that employs forty-foot-long steel containers designed for use on specially adapted ships, trains, and trucks.

Coping

A finishing or protective cap to the uppermost course of a masonry or brick wall, usually sloped in order to repel water.

Creosote

An oily liquid distilled from coal tar, used as a wood preservative and waterproofing material.

Cribwork (or crib)

A large, boxlike receptacle assembled of squared timber beams layered at right angles, often weighted with earth and stones to sink, forming the foundation of a pier or retaining wall.

Cross wall

A structural frame composed of cells that are side by side or in vertical tiers and capable of resisting lateral loads.

Deck bridge

The section of a block-and-bridge pier that spans the blocks and establishes the pier duct.

Derrick

Any of a variety of cranes used for hoisting or moving heavy loads, consisting of a pivoting vertical mast to which a beam (known as a boom) is attached.

Dock

A built inlet or enclosure for receiving vessels. The word is sometimes used for the waterway between two piers, and sometimes as a synonym for pier or wharf. **Wet docks** permit vessels to stay afloat during loading and unloading, commonly utilizing floodgates to control water height. Water can be drained from **dry docks**, permitting repairs to parts of vessels normally submerged; they are also used for shipbuilding.

Dredge

To remove soil from an underwater area; the machine used for this purpose. **Dredge fill** is material obtained in the dredging of the harbor bottom.

Dressed

Describing timber, stone, or brick that has been prepared, shaped, or finished smooth.

Drowned estuary

An estuary where the tidal action of covering and uncovering aquatic life at the water's edge has been eliminated by the creation of steep, defined edges.

Earthwork

The excavation and piling of earth in conjunction with an engineering operation; any construction made of soil or rock.

Embankment

A raised structure, usually of earth, stone, or gravel, built to hold water back or carry a roadway or railroad.

Embayment

A bay or the formation of a bay.

Esplanade

A flat, open space of grass or pavement for walking, riding, or driving, often providing a view. Usually a promenade along a shore.

Estuary

That portion of a river mouth where freshwater meets tidal water.

Exterior line

The outer limit that a pier or bulkhead can extend into the water.

Fender

Any appurtenance that cushions a pier or wharf to lessen shock or prevent chafing from the impact of vessels. Fenders sometimes take the form of chocks or piles.

Form (or formwork)

Temporary boarding, sheeting, or other materials used to give desired shape to cast-in-place concrete. After the concrete hardens, forms are removed.

Galvanize

To coat steel or iron with zinc in order to protect it from rusting.

Gantry

Any of various spanning frameworks used to support a crane, derrick, or other construction equipment.

Girder

A structurally essential beam of steel, reinforced concrete, or timber used to support concentrated loads at isolated points along its length. A girder may be constructed of several members.

Groundsill

The horizontal timber in a framed structure that is on or nearest to the ground.

Groundwater

Water beneath the earth's surface that can pass through strata of soil and stone.

Harbor

A small bay or other stretch of water, situated along and sheltered by the shore and protected from sea swells by narrows or artificial jetties, that provides a safe place for anchorage; to shelter a vessel.

Hardpan

An extremely dense layer of earth that is difficult to excavate; bedrock.

High-water line (or mark)

A line or mark that indicates the highest level typically reached by a specific body of water, often referring to cyclical tides.

Hydraulic cement

A cement capable of hardening under water.

Hydrography

The science of measurement, description, analysis, and mapping of bodies of water.

Kill

A small stream or creek, often a shallow tributary of a river.

Lagging

Frame built to support the sides of an arch, until the keystone is positioned.

Landfill

Solid debris, usually covered by soil and stone, used to extend a landmass into water; an area built of landfill.

Lap joint

The connection of two materials that results by partly covering one material with the other and fastening them together.

Lines and levels
In surveying, a continuous series of measurements establishing the distances between points and the elevations of various features.

Live load
Weight on a structure that is variable and not permanent, such as the weight of people or cargo. As opposed to dead load, the actual and fixed weight of a structure and anything permanently attached to it.

Marginal street
A street situated on or marking an edge or border, as in a street along a shoreline.

Marginal wharves
A structure parallel to or part of the shore, as opposed to a projecting structure, where vessels can dock to load or unload cargo and passengers. Required in narrow rivers or areas of limited space.

Masonry
Stonework or brickwork.

Mooring
Any number of devices used to secure a boat in place; the act of anchoring a boat in place; the place where a vessel can be secured. **Mooring piles** are cylindrical or quadrate members of concrete, steel, or wood driven vertically into the earth and used to secure a boat.

Narrow
A constricted passageway between bodies of water, as between an ocean and a bay.

Pier
A structure built on posts projecting out over the water, used as a landing place for ships or for recreation.

Pierhead
The outermost end of a pier or wharf.

Pierhead line
The outermost extremity to which structures (as opposed to landfill) may legally be extended into the water.

Piershed
A structure placed on top of a river.

Pile
A cylindrical or quadrate member of concrete, steel, or wood, often tapered at the lower end, that is driven vertically into wet or loose earth to establish column foundations for vertical loads or retaining walls.

Pile-and-platform pier
A type of pier construction in which rows of piles are bridged by wood, concrete, or steel framing to construct the pier deck.

Pile cap
A slab or connecting beam that covers the heads of a group of piles and ties them together so they act as a single unit.

Pile driver
A hammering machine that sets piles in place by means of a ram. Also, formerly, the movable block and tongs by which the ram is lifted and let fall.

Pile head
The upper end of a pile.

Port
A city, town, or place where ships load; a harbor with its adjoining settlement of docks, wharves, and transportation and warehouse facilities; a place where ships may take refuge from storms.

Portland cement
The cementitious binder for most structural concrete, made from a pulverized mixture of limestone and clay, able to set and harden under water.

Quay
A wharf, especially one of solid masonry situated along a reinforced bank or shoreline.

Reef
A natural strip or ridge, especially of rocks, sand, coral, or oysters, lying at or near the surface of water.

Relieving platform
A structure of piles and platforms built within a bulkhead or retaining wall to reduce the pressure of lateral loads on the wall itself. Sometimes the platform is constructed to carry part of the bulkhead wall.

Revetment
A facing of stone or cement built to protect an embankment; a retaining wall.

Riparian
Of a riverbank, especially in its legal and proprietary aspects; of a dwelling on a body of water; a person who owns land on the bank of a natural watercourse.

Riprap
A foundation or sustaining wall of stones or chunks of concrete thrown together without order, often to create embankments; material comprised of irregular stones or chunks of concrete.

Riverwall
An embankment built to prevent flooding and shoreline erosion from river waters.

Scow
A flat-bottomed boat with square ends used for transporting freight and as a work platform in harbor construction, usually pulled by a tugboat.

Screw pile
A pile with a screw thread at its lower end for placement by rotation.

Seawall
An embankment built to prevent flooding and shoreline erosion from seawater.

Sheet piles
Thin, broad planks with square edges driven closely together to form a wall. They are typically used to retain soil, and can be interlocked with a tongue-and-groove joint.

Shoal
A shallow area of any body of water; a sandy elevation rising from the bottom of a body of water, such as a sandbar, that makes the water shallow and hazardous to navigate.

Skin resistance
The friction or opposing force that develops between soil and a pressing structure, or between soil and a pile being driven into it.

Slip
The space between two adjacent piers, or in a dock, where vessels moor.

Soundings
An environmental probe for scientific observation, usually measuring the depth of water. **Disk sounding** uses a disk to determine the depth of water. **Rod sounding** uses a rod to determine the character and depth of the bottom.

Spit
A narrow point of land extending into the water, or a narrow shoal that extends from the shore.

Spoil
Earth or rock that is excavated or dredged, sometimes used to create landfill.

Strait
A narrow or restricted passage of water between two larger bodies of water.

Stringpiece
A long, horizontal framing member that lies atop and connects columns or piles in pier-deck construction.

Superstructure
A structure erected on another structure, such as a building erected atop a pier.

Tension rod
A member in a structure or truss that connects opposite parts and prevents horizontal spreading.

Teredo
A small marine borer, also known as shipworm, that tunnels into and devours the wood fiber of piles. Teredos are elongated clams that resemble worms.

Tidal channel
A broad strait of water whose currents are affected by the action of the tides.

Tidal flush
The exchanging of waters in a harbor or estuary due to the ebb and flow of tides.

Tidal prism
The volume differential between low and high tides.

Tidal reservoir
A basin or area of land filled or flooded with water by incoming tides.

Tidal strait
A narrow passage of water joining two bodies of water whose currents are affected by the action of tides.

Transit (or secondary) base lines
An instrument used for laying out angles, distances, and directions in surveying a line projected by the use of a transit.

Truss
A structural framework often arranged in triangles to support a roof, bridge, or similar structure A **howe truss** consists of horizontal upper and lower members, with vertical and diagonal members in between that are designed to take tension and compression respectively. A **king-rod** or **king-post** truss is a triangular frame comprised of a horizontal member (or tie beam) that connects two inclined members joined at their apex; a vertical post (the king post or rod) connects the center of the horizontal member to the apex of the triangle. A **warren truss** has parallel upper and lower horizontal members that are connected by diagonal members that form equilateral triangles.

Waterway
An established navigable route of water, including rivers, channels, and canals.

Wet basin
A type of dock in which the water level is controlled so that the vessels remain afloat for loading and unloading.

Wharf
A general term that applies to all structures where vessels may dock and load or unload cargo and passengers.

Wharfage
The use of a wharf; the fees paid to use a wharf.

Wrought iron
A relatively pure iron valued for its resistance to corrosion and ductility, which can be welded or forged.

Zoning
Regulations that designate land and buildings into types, especially pertaining to their use, and set limits on such use; for example, the height, bulk, and density of buildings and their occupancy, and the relation of a building to its lot and surrounding open space.

BIBLIOGRAPHY

ARTICLES

Bone, Kevin. "Missing the Boat on the Waterfront." *New York Times,* 30 April 1994.

"C. W. Staniford Dies; Consulting Engineer." *New York Times,* 31 October 1948.

"Digging Out the Harlem Canal." *New York Herald,* 19 March 1893.

"The Dock Commissioners." *New York Times,* 2 July 1873.

"The Docks and Wharves." *New York Times,* 12 April 1870.

Dunlap, David W. "Face of Future for Ferry Terminal Is 120 Feet Tall and Has Two Hands." *New York Times,* 6 November 1992.

———. "Jostling for Position on the Riverfront." *New York Times,* 11 July 1993.

———. "Officials Approve Plans To Rebuild West Side Artery." *New York Times,* 2 August 1994.

———. "Queens West Begins With a Park." *New York Times,* 18 September 1994.

Finder, Alan. "Westway, A Road That Was Paid With Mixed Intentions." *New York Times,* 22 September 1985.

Fried, Joseph P. "Catherine of Queens?" *New York Times,* 26 July 1992.

Goldberger, Paul. "Public Space Gets a New Cachet in New York." *New York Times,* 22 May 1988.

Graham, Charles K. "Our Docks and Piers." *New York Times,* 15 October 1874.

"Harbor Models for the Fair." *New York Herald,* 19 March 1893.

"Harlem River Improvement." *New York Herald,* 31 January 1879.

"Harlem's Union of the Waters." *New York Herald,* 18 June 1895.

Howe, Marvine. "Staten Island Ferry Revives a Battle of Boroughs." *New York Times,* 3 April 1994.

"Improved Piers:—Gen. McClellan's Plan." *New York Times,* 30 November 1870.

Johnson, Ken. "Poetry and Public Service." *Art In America,* March 1990.

Lambert, Bruce. "Wanted: Pier with a View." *New York Times,* 4 December 1994.

"Little Old New York." *New York Evening Post,* 15 January 1925.

"Major J. A. Bensel of 125th Engineers Dies." *New York Times,* 20 June 1922.

Martin, Douglas. "Welcome To Donnybrook Park." *New York Times,* 25 March 1996.

McKinley, James C., Jr. "Proposal To Double-Park Area on the Shore." *New York Times,* 12 August 1992.

"More Budget Pain for the City." *New York Times,* 20 April 1996.

"Municipal Topics." *New York Times,* 16 February 1875.

Muschamp, Herbert. "Queens West: Why Not Something Great?" *New York Times,* 22 May 1994.

Nadler, Jerold, and Michael R. Long. "Make Brooklyn a World-Class Seaport." *New York Times,* 13 April 1996.

Natta, Don van, Jr. "Coast Guard Plans to Leave Governors Island." *New York Times,* 17 October 1995.

"The New Engineer in Chief of the Dock Department." *New York Times,* 17 July 1875.

"Our City Wharves." *New York Times,* 2 June 1870.

"Our Wharves and Piers." *New York Times,* 22 April 1870.

Parks Council. "Governors Island New York's Next Great Park?" *Openspace,* winter 1996.

Perez-Pena, Richard. "The Future Home of Yankee Stadium? It's All in the Traffic Patterns." *New York Times,* 14 April 1996.

Peterson, Iver. "Battery Park City: A New Phase Begins." *New York Times,* 19 June 1988.

Powell, Michael. "Adieu Westway Bucks!" *New York Observer,* 25 September 1995.

"Public Wharves." *New York Times,* 16 June 1870.

Ramsey, Lauren. "Battery Park City: Quiet Enclave on the Edge of Manhattan." *New York Observer,* 20 September 1993.

Revkin, Andrew C. "Strides Seen in New York Harbor Cleanup." *New York Times,* 15 June 1995.

Rubenstein, Edwin S. "Cranking The Debt Machine." *City Journal* 2:1 (winter 1992).

Stern, William. "New York Forum." *New York Newsday,* 13 January 1987.

———. "Moscow on the Hudson." *New York Newsday,* 2 April 1993.

REPORTS AND PUBLIC DOCUMENTS

Baiter, Richard. Office of Lower Manhattan Development. Department of City Planning. Battery Park City Authority. *Lower Manhattan Waterfront.* New York, June 1975.

Battery Park City Authority. *Master Development Plan: Battery Park City.* New York, August 1969.

Chelsea Piers Management, Inc. "Chelsea Piers Update." New York, February-June, 1993. Circular.

Ebasco Services; Moran, Proctor, Mueser and Rutledge; and Eggers and Higgins. *The Port of New York Comprehensive Economic Study for Manhattan North River: Development Plan 1962 to 2000.* New York, 28 November 1962.

Federation to Preserve the Greenwich Village Waterfront and Great Port. "Greenwich Village Waterfront News." New York, 1991. Circular.

Hudson River Park Conservancy. "Hudson River Park Conservancy Fact Sheet." New York, n.d. Photocopied circular.

Manhattan Regional Planning Association. *From Plan to Reality.* 3 vols. 1933–42.

Messinger, Ruth W. *Comprehensive Manhattan Waterfront Plan.* New York: Office of the President of the Borough of Manhattan, 1995.

Moses, Robert. *The Expanding New York Waterfront.* New York, August 1964.

New York City Board of Assistant Aldermen. "Act to Reorganize the Local Government of the City of New York." Document no. 35, April 1870. New York: New York Printing Co., 1871.

New York City Community Board 2. "The Special Greenwich Village–Hudson River District Community Board 2, Manhattan 197A Plan." New York, n.d.

New York City Department of City Planning. *New York City Comprehensive Waterfront Plan.* New York, summer 1992.

New York City Department of City Planning. *Plan for the Manhattan Waterfront.* New York, 1993.

New York City Department of City Planning. *Shaping the City's Future.* New York, spring 1993.

New York City Department of Docks. "Annual Reports." New York, 1870–1931.

New York City Department of Docks. *Public Meetings of the Department of Docks to Hear Persons Interested in Improving the River Front.* New York: New York Printing Co., 1870.

New York City Department of Environmental Protection. "North River Water Pollution Control Plant." New York, n.d.

New York–New Jersey Harbor Estuary Program Including the Bight Restoration Plan. "Proposed Comprehensive Conservation and Management Plan." New York, February 1995.

New York State Department of Environmental Conservation. Hudson River Estuary Management Program. "Hudson River Estuary Management Plan, Final Generic Environmental Impact Statement." New York, 28 December 1994.

New York State Department of State. Division of Coastal Resources and Waterfront Revitalization, and Nature Conservancy. *Hudson River Significant Tidal Habitats: A Guide to the Functions, Values, and Protection of the River's Natural Resources.* New York, March 1990.

New York State Department of Transportation. Route 9A "Project Summary." New York, n.d.

New York State Department of Transportation. Route 9A "Reconstruction Project." New York, n.d.

New York State Senate. Harbor Commission. "Report of the Commissioners Relative to the Encroachments and Preservation of the Harbor of New-York." State of New York Document no. 3 in Senate. Albany: C. van Benthuysen, 1856.

New York State Senate. Harbor Commission. "Report of the Commissioners Relative to Encroachments in the Harbor of New York." State of New York Document no. 40 in Senate. Albany: C. van Benthuysen, 1857.

Squires, D. F., and J. S. Barclay. "Nearshore Wildlife Habitats and Populations in the New York–New Jersey Harbor Estuary." New York, November 1990.

U.S. Department of Transportation. Federal Highway Administration. Region One. "West Side Highway Project: Final Environmental Impact Statement." New York, n.d.

Wallace, McHarg, Roberts and Todd; Wittlesey, Conklin and Rossant; and Frank M. Voorhees and Associates. *The Lower Manhattan Plan.* New York, 1966.

West Side Task Force. "Final Report." New York, 8 January 1987.

West Side Waterfront Panel. "A Vision for the Hudson River Waterfront Park." New York, 1 November 1990.

SECONDARY SOURCES

Albion, Robert Greenhalgh, with Jennie Barnes Pope. *The Rise of New York Port 1815–1860.* New York: Charles Scribner's Sons, 1939.

Bonner, William Thompson. *New York: The World's Metropolis.* New York: R. L. Polk & Company, 1924.

Bunker, John G. *Harbor and Haven: An Illustrated History of the Port of New York.* Woodland Hills, California: Windsor Publications, 1979.

Buttenwieser, Ann. *Manhattan Water-Bound: Planning and Developing Manhattan's Waterfront from the Seventeenth Century to the Present.* New York: New York University Press, 1987.

Caro, Robert. *The Power Broker: Robert Moses and the Fall of New York.* New York: Knopf, 1974.

Chellis, Robert D. *Pile Foundations.* New York: McGraw-Hill, 1951.

Forlie, Edward. *The New York City Almanac.* New York: Citadel, 1994.

Greene, Carleton. *Wharves and Piers: Their Design, Construction and Equipment.* New York: McGraw-Hill, 1917.

Griffin, John I. *The Port of New York.* New York: Arco, 1959.

Harbord, J. B. *Glossary of Navigation.* Edinburgh: William Blackwood and Sons, 1863.

Jackson, Kenneth T., ed. *The Encyclopedia of New York City.* New Haven: Yale University Press, 1995.

Johnson, Harry, and Frederick S. Lightfoot. *Maritime New York in Nineteenth-Century Photographs.* New York: Dover, 1980.

Kidder, Frank E., and Thomas Nolan, eds. *The Architects' and Builders' Handbook.* New York: John Wiley & Sons, 1921.

Leonard, John William. *History of the City of New York 1609–1909, from the Earliest Discoveries to the Hudson Fulton Celebration.* New York: Journal of Commerce and Commercial Bulletin, Joseph & Sefton, 1910.

Luke, Myron H. *The Port of New York, 1800–1810: The Foreign Trade and Business Community.* New York: New York University Press, 1953.

Okamoto, Ray, and Regional Plan Association. *Urban Design Manhattan.* New York: Viking, 1969.

Pressentin Wright, Carol von. *Blue Guide, New York.* New York: W. W. Norton, 1991.

Reavill, Gil, and Jean Zimmerman. *Manhattan. Compass American Guides.* New York: Fodor's Travel Publications, 1994.

Rosebrock, Ellen Fletcher. *Walking Around in South Street.* New York: South Street Seaport Museum, 1974.

Stern, Robert A. M., Thomas Mellins, and David Fishman. *New York 1960: Architecture and Urbanism Between the Second World War and the Bicentennial.* New York: Monacelli Press, 1994.

Stiles, Henry R. *A History of the City of Brooklyn.* 3 vols. Albany, New York: J. Munsell, 1870.

Stokes, I. N. Phelps. *The Iconography of Manhattan Island: 1498–1909.* 6 vols. New York: Robert H. Dodd, 1915–1918.

Vitruvius, Marcus. *The Ten Books on Architecture.* Translated by Morris Hicky Morgan. New York: Dover, 1960.

Ward, David, and Olivier Zunz, eds. *The Landscape of Modernity: Essays on New York City, 1900–1940.* New York: Russell Sage Foundation, 1992.

Writers' Program of the Work Projects Administration for the City of New York. *A Maritime History of New York.* Garden City: Doubleday Doran, 1941.